THE
VIOS
VALUES

A Doctor's Journey into
Entrepreneurship

Volume 1

Cover design by: Dr. Ismail Sayeed

Published by: New Swadesh Mudrayon (First publication September 2019)

For information regarding publication permissions or business

Please contact via email

ismail.sayeed82@gmail.com

Manufactured in Bangladesh, for global distribution.

Available in Kindle version and Paperback for International customers

Limited edition printed with permission in Bangladesh for select audiences by: New Swadesh Mudrayon

THE VIOS VALUES

ISBN-13: 9781692035136

ISBN-10: 1692035134

Dr. Mohammad Abu Sayeed Miah

Nurtaj Helal Akbar

Musammat Akikun Nessa

Nusaiba Neela Rahman

Mostaqur Akash Rahman

Saad Abdullah

Abdul Hakim

CONTENTS

PRELUDE

I am sitting in this cafe writing up some notes on this book, if you can call it that (I hope I wrote at least 80,000 words), to be honest I am not entirely sure if I have the mental acuity to actually wrote more than the standard tweet. From this first paragraph you can pretty much guess that I am no literary scholar or even that much of a bibliophile. This is actually my first attempt at a nonfiction work of commercial academia (The chance of convincing someone to pay cash for this amateur construct would be a miracle to say the least, although if you the reader, have paid for this copy then I suppose I have to thank you for putting money in the bank and food on my plate)

Nonetheless I actually hold scholars and academics at high regard. To reach the stage of human endeavour to contemplate and convert thought into a medium to inspire a similar mental exercise in the reader; is by itself a testament to the combined ingenuity of our species. One can almost imagine the situation when a group, maybe even a single person, decided to use the visual dimension to communicate a thought without the need for vocalising, perhaps it is this act that allowed inspiration to break free from the boundaries that limited how far one can throw their voice (even to warn of predators). So you see the written word itself is a feat of human intellect that in my opinion graduated us as a species to the very top of the food chain. Think about it, in order to communicate animals rely on sound, vocalisations and pheromones to signal each other about their immediate thought pattern. I am sure many zoologists can tell about the myriad of similar traits in the animal kingdom. But human beings are the only creatures that have devised a supernatural method to convey brain activity by writing i.e. thoughts, emotions, contemplations, ideas and so on, in a way where the thinker need not be within earshot of another person, needless to say the thinker doesn't even need to be alive during the time the other person reads their words, and yet the very thought patterns that went through their minds can be easily understood and replicated within the mind of the reader (In 2019 one can easily imagine the tragic scenes of any Shakespearean play because the author was so decisive in creating a mental picture of each scene).

This book is not just a vessel of communication or another marketing tool. As I started writing the chapters, I had to trace my memory backwards to many painful moments that deserve to be forgotten in the hidden corners of my mind. Even worse, I had to exercise some deep empathy to understand what kind of value you would appreciate from my life story. It was in these moments that each chapter, or experience allowed me to realign my goals back to the cornerstone of authenticity. It is quite easy to copy another author's works, or hire a ghostwriter to come up with any non-fiction book; but I wanted this to be something more. As you read on you will realise that this book has no theme, it has no storyline which you could identify as some epic fantasy novel. This book is a monument to my own character development, and the effect I had on so many people as I grew, and as I compiled the ViOS Values.

This book is whatever you want it to be. It can be a guideline to identifying bad business and bad business leaders. It can be a map to building your own company someday. It can be a motivational self-help book if you like. I would be deeply honoured, if after all this you would use this book as a mirror, a mirror to gaze towards your own life, and how you lead it.

Read on and rejoice as your life starts to change with every chapter.

INTRODUCTION

My name is Ismail Sayeed (I have intentionally left out the Dr. suffix as I do not want to ingrain my official profession as a stereotype yet). I am the eldest son of the late Dr. Mohammad Abu Sayeed Miah and Dr. Masuda Khatoon. I was born in Dhaka Bangladesh in 1982 under adverse conditions, born prematurely to an impoverished and underweight female Medical student in a country struggling to get on its feet after a bloody independence struggle, in a severely underfinanced and under equipped government hospital - PG Hospital (Now called BSMMU) aptly named since most if not all medical graduates complete their clinical rotation before attaining higher postgraduate certification. So under all these difficult conditions I pulled through, some would say divine intervention, I prefer to add on to it the decisive application of modern technology, at the right time by the right hands, namely my own father (then a pediatric resident) and his mentor - Late Professor F. R. Khan (National Professor of Pediatrics). Those of you not familiar with certain medical terms, allow me to highlight why it is so worrying when a premature infant born in an impoverished setting has such a low probability of survival.

Prematurity denotes the gestational age where a child is born before 37 weeks of the expected date of delivery, this prematurity is more than just about the early birth, it concerns the relative underdevelopment of critical organs of survival most importantly the lungs, immune system, body temperature mechanisms, nutritional processes and pretty much every human system necessary to be called a 'normal baby'. You see without intensive and comprehensive neonatal (relating to newborn children) management by such expert, I the writer of this narration would not exist. All praise to God, and all praise the extreme dedication of my father to introduce cutting edge medical technology into mainstream use.

As you can imagine, I have a high regard of medical professionals with esteemed work ethics. In a time of public perception of corruption, incompetence and sometimes negligence, many physicians are nostalgic to the times when we could really impact on a person's life with our healing touch. Sure technology disruption in healthcare is a buzzword for millennials and others, many of my father's peers would say that a system disruption is required. Anyway I'm jumping ahead to other coming chapters, let's stick to my origin story for now so you can grasp at the process of how I intend to disrupt healthcare from within.

Dr Dad & Dr Mom

As is common in many eastern societies; status is defined by your income, assets, education and maybe to a degree, the vocation that your children acquire. Naturally the white collar breadwinner would insist on similar life goals and paths i.e. my son must be a doctor/lawyer/engineer as he is. So my life settings were pretty much set on default from day one by my medical parents. Not that I have any qualms about it, I do not hold any grudge or feel that I somehow missed out on a life of constant economic hardships, struggles, social angst and other miseries of lower white collar classes - trust me as you read on you will see that I too have experienced hardships that were supposed to be uncommon in the medical career.

So anyway as I graduated high school, not a particularly gifted student mind you, I made it through just like any other expatriate minority in the Arabian peninsula (textbook story thus far). The hunt for affordable and suitable medical colleges was on full swing. Should my parents sell property to send me to the West, should they look for something cheaper in Eastern Europe or (big gulp) should they repatriate me, an overweight out-of-place spoilt brat back into the cesspool that was late 90's Bangladesh? The tension was palpable and the future was uncertain, but as long as I have an MBBS degree from a foreign institution was the de-facto golden ticket. Right? Let's read on.....

So there I was, facing a small viva team from a small medical college starting up (just like a startup) in the middle of the Arabian Desert that was Ajman, the smallest and back then the most impoverished state amongst the United Arab Emirates. For me it was a real adventure, partly due to the extensive brand marketing done by this institution, (I have purposely refrained from mentioning any names or overt reference to certain individuals and institutions due to the issues which I will highlight in the coming chapters.) namely putting into their geographic location as their main selling point i.e. situated in another politically and economically viable Arabian country so that it appeals to expatriate families based in the area. Whether they were qualified, certified, accredited or even had air conditioning was generally irrelevant - as long as their young ones can be within 1hr plane ride away. So on I went to learn the medical curricula knowns as **MBBS** (Medicinae Baccalaureus, Baccalaureus Chirurgiae AKA Bachelor of Medicine & Bachelor of Surgery).

Like any university entrant I was scared stiff about the life ahead, I imagined piles of notes to go through, massive books to read and seeing my parents exhausted from endless and antisocial shifts almost as long as I can remember - is it worth it? I remember coming back to the hotel after my dad and I had dinner, it was the night before the first day of orientation, I told him I was scared I don't think I can make it maybe I should go to some other university and do something else. I could see he was concerned but he still believed in me. Too late to turn around I suppose. Tuition paid, ticket stamped, bags packed - no other way but onwards.

GLOBAL INTERN

Did I mention I was super scared to get a spot in medical school? (So what if I paid to get in, so did everyone else right?) As nerve-wracking as the first few weeks were, I was totally engrossed in the knowledge. The first few formative years were heavily into the theory of human life, the anatomy, physiology, biochemistry and on and on. I may be understating this but honestly the human body is truly a masterpiece; whether it be divine creation, intelligent design. Darwinian evolution, call it what you like but really how well and purposeful each organ and system plays is a sight of wonder. In the American system, students go to Pre-Med to learn ancillary science-based topics to prepare for these subjects too. Both educational systems rely heavily on the theoretical construction of our learnings before diving head first into the real world - real world medicine.

Like any professional discipline, there is seldom any connection between theory and practical applications. This is especially true in medicine. No matter how many episodes of Grey's Anatomy, House MD and other romanticized dramas of the medical world you have seen, reality is much more chaotic. Theoretical knowledge serves as a mental backbone - a sort of ideal scenario which professionals try to mold and shape as per our actual life experiences. Diseases do not always follow 'textbook' rules and expectations of outcome, any experienced physician will tell you this much. Even the most agnostic surgeon secretly prays more than any clergy when operating on complicated cases, remember I told you how wonderful the human body was, well as a side note the human body itself is complicated, fragile, disruptive and well frankly speaking uncooperative at times. (Google idiosyncrasy and nocebo effect).

Lectures melted into each day like the blistering heat of the Arabian peninsula, my mind was filled with every possible pathology and remedy alike. The endless waiting to start our first of many clinical rotations were a constant irritation to all us book-nerds. None of us would listen to the complaints and groans of our seniors (we shared the same hostel) when they returned from their internship-night shifts. Some part of me thought how hard can medicine be? It's all about applying the various treatment modalities highlighted towards the end of each disease chapter, as simple as ABC. I shall wait for you to stop laughing at my naivety so I can explain the horrors of medical internship that threw my book-smarts out the window.

To fast forward the almost cliche clinical rotation horror stories and emotional rollercoaster stories, I will just briefly touch open the various places I have rotated through to give you an idea that I truly am a global citizen and in a small way, a global medical intern (i.e. experience in various international healthcare systems). I spent roughly 4 months at a massive non-profit private medical university campus in South India, a year or so at a poorly designed and poorly managed university hospital/polyclinic (my university bought up a bankrupt strip mall and converted it into a health centre), a year and bit seemingly lost in semi-bankruptcy of my university which couldn't afford to send us to other affiliated hospitals (trust me it happens more often than you think), a crazy but a deeply provocative internship experience in Egypt just a few years prior to the Arab Spring (trust me I saw the red flags of a civil uprising - that I will delve into my next book if this one ends up paying my bills) and after all that running around I was back in my beloved desert and impoverished strip mall polyclinic. Don't let my sarcasm fool you, it is merely a defense mechanism to hide the terrible but necessary memories I have experienced as a resident.

MEDICINE IN THE DESERT

Whatever amount of freshman confidence I had as a newly graduated medical student, was burnt

away on my very first shift as a resident (or also known as a senior house officer).

Phone ringing

Nurse shouting to come to the delivery room

Hurriedly putting on gloves

Bursting through the door

Inhuman maternal screams

Smell of blood, urine & disinfectant in the air

And a limp bag of wet flesh on the resuscitation table......

In the confusion and chaos someone must have uttered the words 'not cried' 'difficult delivery'

'where is the oxygen mask' and other related terms. I was frozen stiff, my neurohormones failing to act.....but it was the NICU nurse that came in did the work. Baby cried, cardio-monitor beeped and pens scribbled the APGAR[1] score in the file.

That's right.

My first neonatal case, and that too not a normal case, a case that required me to get off my ass and upgrade my skills super fast.....because after all, someone else's life depends on me to act right and act quick. The primal difference between internship and residency was now I am singularly responsible for a human life.....that too a newborn life.

I jumped to it. I studied extra hard, I started re-reading the books, which I used to read just to pass the exams but now I needed that knowledge to face the real world problems. Clinical knowledge can be best simplified in two areas - things you need to know to answer questions during the rounds (and appear qualified in front of patients) and things you need to survive every shift. The first is super easy, that kind of book-smarts are part of the classical eastern method of knowledge - mass memorisation of secondary information collected and slightly altered over the decades, just learn the notes and you will get top marks and a cookie. The latter knowledge given by the cruelest teacher - reality, is a more valuable and appreciated method to hard-wire new doctors to accept and cope with the harsh realities of human life.

In the first few weeks (which was during the fasting month of Ramadan) I learned about the gross misinformation of the public about their own health, wrong ways to raise a child, vast differences

---

[1] Apgar is a quick test performed on a baby at 1 and 5 minutes after birth. The 1-minute score determines how well the baby tolerated the birthing

in practicing medicine from what is expected through policies versus what my senior wanted (this was due to their pay structure which I figured out much later) and to just reach a critical point real quick - the fact that by just behaving right with patients and teaching a few valuable health tips, I was seen as a trusted healthcare provider, second only to the head of the pediatric department - the late Dr. Mahmoud Shamseldeen. Ofcourse there are more things I have experienced over the years but I will not discuss those matters yet, that is not the purpose of this literary exercise. I wanted to tell you about my formative years in my medical career that were the key moments to steer me towards healthcare entrepreneurship.

The key takeaway points I wanted to highlight (which I will point to throughout the book); that people seldom ask how many degrees you have or where you bought them, rather they judge your clinical acumen to be a reflection of your own personal character. Let me put it this way, back then (even now) I have a youthful facial appearance so it is obvious I look younger than my age but when you project yourself as a professional it is often assumed you have had years and years of experience when you are able to calm a crying child, administer IV, console a parent of a deceased infant, apply and remove a plaster, circumcise a male baby when half asleep, create a public health service seminar that your senior was supposed to present and many other responsibilities of a resident. You see complaining about one's predicament only gets you heard (barely) but you will never be acknowledged as an intellectual unless you take the initiative to solve an issue without waiting for praise or instructions. This was my first taste of proactive leadership.

Rest assured I have so many stories of my pediatric residency to tell, I think what is most appropriate is if I correlate my current situation to some specific moments that inspire an 'ah-ha!' moment in myself and you the reader. Before delving into them I should probably mention the working conditions and its related issues that often harden that hearts of most private sector physicians and may or may not be the cause for the erosion of the medical career seen around the world.

MONEY

An often unusual and difficult topic when considering healthcare services. How do you reimburse a physician for improving the health of a community? How do you quantify the mental processes needed to judge the next best clinical management for an ailment? An even more difficult question would be - is health a product or a service? To keep things simpler atleast when it comes to billing and human resources, majority of private healthcare is measured by hours and services rendered i.e. number of hours per month and to top it off a generous bonus for additional inpatient admissions, medications, inhouse diagnostic services and who can forget - volume of affiliated prescriptions (Big Pharma-talk). I was nowhere near this contract since I was still a resident, which means a flat salary at the end of the month for fixed hours completed. Basic translation - Overworked and underpaid just like millions of medical comrades around the world. Back then I honestly didn't care, I was contend with my paycheck since I always thought I would get a pay rise next year, my parents can still fund some of my expenses if needed and more importantly after I get that awesome foreign medical residency I was feverishly preparing for - I'd hit those 6-figure incomes that my seniors have told me about.

Reality it seems had other ideas.

I cannot blame my surroundings or point at people for not motivating me or other narratives of a small mind, the reality is that in the end I alone am responsible for almost all outcomes. I wasn't worried about the meager income because I was afraid what extra money would do to me. I was afraid I would not be able to be impartial to the wellbeing of my pediatric patients - a common occurrence is when inferior service is given to non-paying/poor/uninsured patients irrespective of the actual health issue. What this means is that I was given orders to try and admit as many insured cases to the ward for a 'one-night observation', 'prophylactic antibiotics for flu, intensive phototherapy for borderline neonatal jaundice cases, xrays for any newborn with the slightest meconium staining and the list goes on. Why was this done? Am I now promoting extra healthcare? The truth boils down the hospital policy.....sell more sell often. Welcome to privatised healthcare in an impoverished desert town.

I had to get out of there. Fast.

But I didn't.

I wasn't fast at all.

Because I became fat and comfortable with a steady and increasing paycheck. The money was good, I had very little motivation to change my status quo. Whatever little motivation I had to study was just a formality actually, study a little here and there and hope for the best. Typical defeatist/fatalist mentality of a salaried doctor.

Motivation is a complex word to define. You can be pushed to succeed due to adverse circumstances or you can get pulled to success by promises of a rich and fulfilling career. I had neither. In the previous chapter I mentioned that I was compelled to enter medical school due to familial obligations (societal pressures to an extent) that means I had no stake in this career. Motivations, if any, were by and large superficial and featured materialistic gains. No surprise as I grew up in the Middle East during the oil boom of the 80's and now I'm a medical doctor in the Las Vegas of the Middle East, so you can imagine the type of lifestyle I was used to and wanted for later. Can there be passion to succeed when there is no life purpose? I gave you my answer. Study a little, write some exams and hope for the best. Shoot for the moon little man etc etc.

This comfort bubble was badly in need of bursting. There can be no growth in times of superficial excess, trust me I know that all too well. But I was deep in the friendzone of complacency. The sad irony was I that I used to lecture my colleagues about not getting too comfortable and start getting as many foreign degrees in a short time, if there was an avatar for self loathing it would look like me. I am sure many of you would say I had it made anyway, what's the big deal of not going to a foreign country so quickly, there's always next year just relax and help out the community where you are working. The problem with procrastination is that it's like a gateway narcotic - you get addicted to false feelings. One excuse leads to another and then one year bleeds into several and you have nothing to show for it.

The work wasn't all bad actually. I made some amazing friends. I experienced diverse clinical management styles. Saw so many unusual cases (anencephaly, treacher-collins, diaphragmatic hernias, triplet deliveries, meconium aspirations, ondine's curse, hyperkeratosis, chromosomal anomalies and the list goes and if you are not from a medical background I insist you read about them in wikipedia!) that even my late father had never seen such cases in his entire 40-year career. I enjoyed my early career as much as any person with Stockholm Syndrome[2]. Like I mentioned before, I grew complacent and I found ways to delay my own career growth because I was afraid of the unknown. Unknown clinical rotations unknown, health policies, unknown locations, unknown everything. These are known as self-limiting beliefs - a dagger into the heart of self discovery.

I'm afraid it all goes downhill from here.

But before I describe my rock-bottom story, there were some moments when I thought I could change.

Before I conclude this chapter, I think for a nice palate cleanser I say we jump straight to the next chapter and then come back here. I know it sounds strange but in effect that is exactly how my medical career took a sharp left turn, when I finally took some initiative and started completing my postgraduate exams one by one.

---

[2] Stockholm Syndrome - feelings of trust or affection felt in many cases of kidnapping or hostage-taking by a victim towards a captor.

MY AMERICAN HEALTH SYSTEM EXPERIENCE

The USMLE (United States Medical Licensing Exams) are a prerequisite set of exams made up of 3 electronic exams and 1 practical exam that is given by foreign medical students who wish to enter the ECFMG (Educational Commission For Foreign Medical Graduates) board to be considered for various clinical postings/rotations that are available twice a year for resident intakes. It's not a particularly difficult exam, compared to some of the insane national board exams in South Asia, just that there is a lot of consideration into the latest methods in clinical management and their guidelines. There are loads of bootleg Kaplan Institute reading materials and teaching videos available. I finally got around to studying, practicing and finally applying for the exam schedule in Dubai. The exam was gruelling, had to stand in line at the crack of dawn, had to complete hundreds of MCQ's and the worst part was waiting to get the results. 1 week went by. Then another. Then I finally got the email with the PDF of the results.

Not bad.

But not that good either.

America prides itself on attracting the best of the best. And healthcare is no exception. Hopeful candidates must score in the upper 5th percentile to be even *considered* for the residency matching (even to match with a preferred specialty). Sadly and quite expectedly my chances at matching for pediatrics were very slim, and maybe hardly a small chance to match for the lesser desired disciplines like psychiatry or geriatrics (because they are usually low paying jobs, they are given to international medical graduates to fill up their regional quotas). Should I abandon my American residency dream before even applying for the visa? I figured that I made it this far so why should I let my ego and a hyper-capitalist healthcare lobby decide my fate.

The show must go on.

Onwards to the US Embassy in UAE. Papers in hand, appointment slips for even more exams and an uncertain future for a mediocre prospect as I was. Surely the land of opportunity would apply to me as well, fortunes were made in the West so why not give it a go.

As a cosmic joke, my skin colour, religion and context of my Bangladeshi passport proved to be a significant hurdle towards visa approval (amongst other things). 2 months of waiting and all I could hear are my Indian and Arab counterparts celebrating their 'visa victory' while I kept quiet and carried on my regular duties. Was this a sign of future disappointments? I refused to acknowledge this belief, like they say in Hollywood - 'It ain't over till it's over'.

Through various online forums I decided to *clean* my passport - to *whitewash* it and make it more appealing to the American border control departments. Looking back at previous visited countries it appears that me - a single 25-30 year old brown-skinned male from a low income country has only been to other developing countries eg. India, Saudi Arabia, Malaysia and of course Bangladesh. Obviously this poses a high probability of defaulting on my visa requirements therefore I decided to save some money and visit a few European countries as a backpacker or whatever. Atleast a previously stamped and valid Schengen visa would prove how liberal and westernized my world views were etc etc.

My short Euro-trip around Spain, Greece & Netherlands was quite good given the circumstances. The bohemian cultural experiences, managing expenses on the go, learning to cook inexpensive meals, doing my own laundry and also a deep appreciation for the European model of nationally funded health systems. Groundbreaking achievement to provide high quality access to healthcare services to all people - citizen or otherwise (pre-Greece bailout & pre-Brexit ofcourse). The societal impact of such a system was only well appreciated when I had studied Global Health many years later.

So after all this whitewashing and preparing for the next exam portion which was practical clinical skills in a center in Philadelphia, it was time to walk down the corridor, grab the token and stand before her majesty, the clerk in the foreign applicant booth at the US Embassy - again.

Long story short, yes I got it.

My hunch was right.

Visa approved in a few weeks and now onwards to the West. Exam was in February but something in me told me that going to America just to attend an exam and then fly back to complete my duties at a pathetic polyclinic was not worth it. I need to go to America, not as just one of thousands of

exam takers and assorted asylum seekers, but as a true Global nomad (my bohemian backpacker

Euro buddies rubbed off on me), I need to immerse myself in the distinct socio-cultural milieu of as

many states in the United States, if by chance I do get accepted into the residency match and all

that, I need to know what makes an American, an *American*.

I started my journey in New York city. All the Hollywood movies and TV shows came true and

some even beyond expectations.

The lights.

The riches.

The costs.

The scale of healthcare costs (insurance premiums included) were mind-boggling. I heard stories

where one guy had to choose which fingers he could afford to sew back on after an accident, it is

cheaper to fix your car then to fix a broken limb and the vast number of single low income mothers

having to choose whether to continue her medication so she can work or to cut back on heating just

to buy baby formula. I mean for me it was beyond the usual culture shock of Americana, these are

the stories that are the norm in developing countries like Bangladesh, but in the leading economic

goliath of the West people are worried sick about being sick!

Anyway, I can tell you countless patient stories about inability to afford treatment, not being able to find a doctor that would accept their insurance (or lack thereof) and on and on. What about the healthcare providers? Are they responsible for this mess? Where's the Health Industry lobby? Again please excuse my naive ignorance, like I said I learnt the reality *after* studying Global Health and Health economics.

Let me rattle your brain when I tell you that doctors in America are the victims of hyper-capitalist health system (just like here in Bangladesh). I may sound like some socialist wannabe but let me tell you some stories I heard from young doctors who appeared for the USMLE Step 2 CS and Step 3 exams and also my clinical supervisors whom were instrumental in guiding me during my clerkships.

US DOCTORS IN THE FRONTLINE

During our little breaks, I had a chance to chit-chat with pre-med osteopathy students and also pre-match residency medical students; they came from all walks of life - minorities, single parents, white Anglo-Saxon descendants, 2nd generation citizens etc but they all had a unifying characteristic:

Bone crushing student debt.

What can I say when they ask about my background.

(I have a strange hybrid American accent with a distinct South Asian twang)

My whole life was subsidized by both parents who earned their tax-free income from a non-native Middle-eastern country, completed the entire science of Medicine in 5-6 years while they take 9+ years to be eligible and now I'm trying to be a US Board certified physician so I can fulfill the age-old Immigrant American Dream? Heard this before right?

Well yeah actually that is exactly what I told them.

After many years later as I write this book, I feel like I can guess the drive that was pushing us to pursue a career in healthcare for both parties.

We are not that different.

Privately funded medical education (debt or not) means we need a way to breakeven as quickly as possible so we can enjoy retirement content with a *'life well lived'* (whatever that is). If that is not wholly possible then atleast try to pay back in pennies or cultural promises. Imagining how much my parents spent on my education, and also the scale of borrowing that my American counterparts have taken as well, well the total number is enough to make anyone dizzy. Who in their right mind would spend literally millions of whatever currency just to get into healthcare?

To be honest, many would and still do.

Medical career is (or was) perceived as a sure fire way to lead a prosperous life.

The financial security

The material possessions

The prestige

The future?

Let me tell you about my seniors who supervised me during my clerkships.

Apologies in advance as things get quite depressing and I will not be divulging any names out of

professional courtesy.

After completing the exams I had some time on my hand as per my visa. So I decided to incorporate

my US sightseeing tour (my wanderlust was strong as ever) with some voluntary observerships and

clerkships or whatever it was called back then. I rotated through Texas, Los Angeles, then Seattle

and then in Chicago. Amazing experiences of course. I met so many fascinating characters along the

way. So full of hope and admiration for the freedom and '*Manifest Destiny*' mantra of the United

States of America. What I gathered from the handful of acquaintances I had with US doctors

(native or immigrant) was astounding.

I had a hard time finding a happy doctor who is truly in a fulfilling career.

It's true. Beyond the six-figure annual income, I knew quite a few who were about one medical

lawsuit away from being homeless. I couldn't understand it at first. I understand the individual

contextual upbringing from my medical student companions but surely an American board

certified medical doctor would finally 'make it' and it would be smooth sailing from there. As

expected I was unprepared for another culture shock, or rather a future shock. Years after becoming an MD or DO, getting a cushy job at a multispecialty center, partnering up to open your own outpatient center and it can all come crashing down by litigation?

Stricken off the board

Losing licenses

Losing family and fortunes

Physician suicides

This is not fiction my friend, these were real life career horror stories. The following are a few case examples:

I stayed with a close family friend of my parents in Queens, NY. Lovely couple with grown up children, following the ideal American dream of owning a house, nice car, strong career, pillar of the community and........and working at 3 different locations just to make ends meet with no sign or plan for retirement.

I saw the same thing in Dhaka. Compared to the average Bangladeshi doctor these two were earning the equivalent of millions of taka per month, but why are they inches away from bankruptcy? What would drive a renowned physician to make morning rounds at Long Island Hospital, then drive down to Jamaica, NY to cover a shift at a local clinic and then 20 min power nap later headed off to downtown Queens for a few more hours at another clinic? Military background enforcing the strong work ethic? Come on wake up Ismail. Why earn so much and enjoy so little? Their grown up kids have accumulated mountains of debt to get through university (this is unavoidable

in America) and then hunt for the right career path.

I figured this was an isolated case. Surely my old friend 'A' from Medical school who recently

became a naturalized citizen (details of this process is omitted for confidentiality) has a better life

story. Met him down in Texas, looked exactly as I remembered him, small changes such as the

awesome Mustang he drives and the cool apartment he stays in. So I asked him how far he got with

the USMLE or Residency matching etc. His answer did not completely surprise me when he said he

gave it all up, left medicine, now he was busy *hustling*[3] to open an overseas branch for his father's

business. He personally knows board certified US doctors who sleep in their cars, eat canned tuna

for dinner, lost half their wealth in divorces, drive state to state to moonlight at various clinics,

started selling prescription medications and on and on. This guy must be drunk (he was many a

times). I was getting disheartened, maybe California and Chicago would have better career

prospects.

I headed to Los Angeles, California to meet some relatives and friends. Amazing state (Arnold

Schwarzenegger was the governor), totally chilled out just like in the Hollywood movies (I went to

Hollywood as well!). I met some recent Bangladeshi medical immigrants there, few years fresh out

of USMLEs. Young couple who got married in the final year of studies, spent atleast a year or so

just cramming for the residency exams (even had their folks take care of their newborn while they

used to go for Kaplan classes) - as it turned out even though each were triple 99ers[4], due to the high

---

[3] Urban slang for implementing as many schemes and strategies to make some serious cash
[4] Three times getting 99% i.e. upper 5th percentile in their exams

stakes in competing with US medical school graduates for high revenue specialities, there was a long waiting list to get into surgery or gynaecology residencies which they preferred. So what could they do? The husband works in a pharmacy dispensary and the wife helps a local gastroenterologist to compile metadata for a research proposal (his research) - earning a meagre stipend apparently.

Depressing. If you already started a family I understand you have to take whatever scraps/options that are available. And these are very common stories where IMGs (International Medical Graduates) from non-Western countries have to settle for non-preferred residency matches or non-clinical research positions. Not that they are any lesser in anyway, I mean in their own way such jobs are needed to constantly improve the gigantic US Health System. Even down in San Diego, I met a Sudanese former professor who has his own medical marijuana dispensary - where he claims to earn more per month, than he did back in Cairo where he worked for a year! All comes down to the exchange rate I suppose

The sunshine state (California) wasn't giving me much to look forward to. Los Angeles as I figured out is quite a dump actually, definitely not a stable place to raise a functional family. I will probably go more into such details in a different book. But for now the wild American roads were calling to me and I wanted to hide my desperation into backpacking across the breath-taking Pacific North-west.

Eventually I reached Chicago, Illinois. And in good time as apparently my application for a clinical observership (a type of internship) was approved and this was another method IMG's could get hands-on knowledge about the US healthcare system. The arrangement was quite clear cut. Had a 3-month rotation in the pediatrics department of the Norwegian-American Hospital with a seasoned two US board certified pediatricians. Finally some progress I thought to myself. I was also part of a team of IMG's who were also interested in pediatrics. They were a cool bunch - 2 Carribean Medical school graduates and a Venezuelan pediatrician (Associate Professor from a medical university in Caracas who was immigrating due to economic hardships beginning back in 2011). The days were fine, usual cases I had seen millions of times back in the OPD of our hospital, history taking, physical examination, some patient counselling, and learning some conversational Spanish as well!

As I was nearing the end of the observership I got to realise some harsh realities. A US doctor is a cogwheel in the billion dollar medical industry, he/she is stripped of individuality and humanity, work-life is the same thing (one of the doctors is still single until now and also dealing with a medico-legal issue), delayed or denied insurance coverage is a constant hassle for healthcare providers and just like many Bangladeshi physicians - retirement is basically the grave. All thanks to the unrealistic plans of Obamacare.

Slowly it dawned on me that my own personal future would not be anywhere near where my seniors are. The results of all those exams were out and I did not cut it.

They were good.

But not good enough.

As I mentioned in a previous chapter, you need to be in the upper 5th percentile to even have a shot at the Residency Match. Honestly I am not sure what drained my motivation, was it the poor marks, the harsh reality affecting these hard working doctors, the low chance of matching for Pediatrics as a chosen field (at that moment I was even happy to give lab rats a haircut!) or the sudden realisation that I bit off more than I could chew. I came to realise that the reason why I prospered in my dinghy little polyclinic was because my resident team and I had almost no oversight - I mean it as a good thing meaning we were not burdened with so much bureaucracy, we just had to save babies' lives, that is all.

But not here in America - first justify the cost then save the life.

And now I stand before the American Healthcare Goliath, dreams shattered and ego deflated. What should I do, keep at it burn through my parents and mine savings for a sliver of hope for subsequent matches (each application costs a lot of dollars), marry some desi divorcee to atleast claim a Green card/Permanent Resident status or just hang it all up and return to my little clinic and just hit repeat on the VHS tape that is playing my life story.

So I did what I usually do when faced with a mountain of self-deprecating disappointment. I went partying in Las Vegas, mountain climbing in California, got my gun license in Texas and other pathetic attempts at validating my life course with materialism. But before this facade, I did try to squeeze in some professional attempts into getting some kind of career in the American health system.

In Chicago, IL there was an opening at the Norwegian-American Medical center (also known locally as the Chicago Ambulatory Care Center) where I had previously completed a short observership. It was not exactly what I hoped for but like thousands before me, I took whatever opportunity was presented before me in the hopes that it will lead into something better down the line, after a few years or so. The job posting was for a Physician Assistant - basically I would be tasked with taking the initial history taking and some basic health vitals checkup, record it in the patient notes, assist in coding for insurance claims and reimbursements and some miscellaneous clerical obligations, and then present a short version so that the *real* Dr. Pediatric Specialist, MD can dispense the treatments.

How much was the pay?

Can you start a family in the 14th most expensive city in the world?

Is this what my Pediatric career is going to look like?

After few months I could not see myself continuing. Mind you the staff and the doctors were amazing people. I loved the patients, it was fun to practice some Spanish with them (Bengalis and Hispanics are so alike). Mrs Hoi Huin (my landlady) if you are alive and well I missed your Vietnamese cooking and Obama conspiracy theories. But my heart was not it. I used to command an entire NICU, attend deliveries half asleep, calm colicky infants, supervise new interns rotating through our unit, my signature at the end of the duty sheet meant something......and now this?

Time to leave, pronto.

Did not take long for me to visualise the disappointment in my father's eyes and amongst my colleagues back in UAE. I know what you would have been thinking back then, that I should have just stuck with it. Atleast I got a health-related job and maybe in a few years when recruitment policies change I can have a better chance at the fabled American Dream. Who knows I could have become a big deal American Doctor by now.

Honestly I have no answer for you that would fully explain my decision making process. You have probably thought that I am spoilt, not willing to sacrifice personal comforts for the greater good, indecisive in life goals, riding aimlessly through life with no passion. I told my father about my predicament. He always knew when I was trying to hold back tears or rage, but he always had my back. He would never see me in discomfort, but sadly I was unable to give him the satisfaction of my own effort back then.

All those points are correct.

I shamelessly confess that my chronic aloofness was borne out of leading a life without a personal calling.

After much time and dollars spent in touring state to state, I decided to head back to zero. Some of my friends tried to convince me to overstay illegally and just figure out a way to stay in US and work on getting the Green Card and commit to the stereotypical naturalized American citizen with his new life. I have met many doctors who drive cabs, moonlight for Uber/Lyft, run a 7-11, have their own chain souvenir shops along Hollywood Boulevard, work at a Tex-Mex-Bangla restaurant and the list goes on. I am not trying to belittle them, in fact I salute their bravery to stay back and just get by somehow, besides at the end of the day they become (or will become - I will refrain from mentioning names as their naturalization process may or may not involve fraud) bona fide US citizens and can support their families. Perhaps that is one reason why I didn't persevere, I had no dependents.

I was single, young, had no real cash flow problems (bankrolled by the Bank of Ma & Pa like they say in Texas) and a massive inflated ego just because I had letters 'D' and 'R' in front of my name. I thought that if I was a moderately talented Pediatric resident in UAE then that is where I must start from if I was to practice abroad. No job would suit me unless I fully exploited my medical knowledge, I wanted all the personal freedom without the consequences.

I know.

I sound spoilt, but facing that unnecessary hardship made no sense to me.

It was time to close that chapter of my life (and this long chapter too) so I confirmed my flight and headed back 22 hours later to the gleaming sun of UAE.

I tried

I failed

I quit

US Medical career is not for me (one-sided decision from the ECFMG ofcourse)

Let me get back to my comfort zone, zone out and try some other foreign medical career dream......

DEPORTATION/EXILE

I came back defeated and exhausted. I thought about taking a day off to recover from jet lag but I decided against it. Only people who return from a mission (business trip/annual leave/emergency visit etc) deserve to recover, I was just another tourist. As I write this chapter, I feel like a small part of me thinks I went through all that trouble preparing for the USMLE just because a colleague back in Egypt had a similar goal and both of us wanted to be a big shot American doctor[5]. In retrospect I was always a spoilt Bohemian (I saw many in Los Angeles - nowadays they are known as *hipsters*), as long as I had a semi-comfortable albeit complacent existence within a 1 hour flight from my folks I suppose I can just chill out and think of some other way to upgrade my career status. Little did I know that there were tell-tale signs of a major shake-up going on around our hospital.

So next day I sent an email to HR that I will be returning to my duties, called up my colleagues that I will meet them and tell all my tall stories of my American adventure and of course ignore the many elephants in the room. I survived the better part of my life just avoiding conversations that

---

[5]Life takes surprising turns for all of us.

had to do with the future, my future. And my favorite part, explaining to my seniors why I am back to the desert - darker & fatter. So yes I got that conversation out of the way.

Saw some new faces. Many recently graduated specialists from Egypt, India and a few former professors from Iraq as well. Those who could not grasp the Western dream for whatever reason can atleast pay the bills with the Gulf dreams (tax-free income, safety, security etc). I was one of them, it was time to fill up my bank account again so I can save up for another try at the Western dream - maybe a Masters course in the UK or try the medical licensing exam in New Zealand.

Funny thing about plans. They never work out.

Like before, I measured my life-course by the number of night shifts I survived through. I came to notice, though I did not actually complain overtly, that the number of night shifts I was assigned to a week started to increase. The total hours at the end of the month were the same, salary bonuses were predictable here and there, my post-duty off days were slightly increased. It is almost as if I was kept hidden from day time patient traffic and had to deal with the usual night time ER visits, some deliveries and nightly inpatient rounds. Very strange.

The general atmosphere was starting to get really toxic too. Many of use would have the expected quarrels with HR or the canteen, but those days the tension was heavy. Our once upbeat seniors were starting to walk on edge, nurses who used to gossip quietly were now whispering more than usual. And if these subtle hints could be ignored then the next few events would build up to the finale (atleast my finale).

Not sure for how long, but some of my resident buddies used to get annoyed if the salaries were slightly delayed by a few days. Someone had the crazy idea of writing a petition to bring this matter to the hospital director (not me ofcourse) and usually it just gets ignored and that is the end of that. Not this time. Half dozen of my colleagues (whoever signed the petition) was immediately terminated.

Being fired as an expatriate in the Gulf was a literal death sentence.

All notions of a steady income and lifeblood for your family and village drains away.
You have to look for alternative occupation super fast (even in a recession), if you find a job you have to seek permission from your master/*khafeel*/sponsor (yes slavery goes by many names especially if your are brown-skinned), leave the country then apply to re-enter and on and on (these steps are interchangeable depending on many factors)

It was an utter shock to all of us veteran residents who have seen it all over the years. I have only once witnessed such a drastic managerial shakeup. It was halfway through our final year rotations at a major public hospital in Abu Dhabi called Mafraq Hospital (arguably the best in UAE both operationally and financially). All of a sudden all medical staff were to comply with Canadian board certification or similar, till date I have no idea what kind of under-the-table deal led to this, all

I know is that dozens of super-specialized veteran consultants (US/UK/Australian/European-certified) were sacked quite unceremoniously. A government insider tip-off alluded to the massive unemployment of UAE-sponsored local Arab graduates from Canadian medical universities, who were getting frustrated, so they needed to create job postings quickly without building them a separate hospital. Pardon me for this distracting side-story but I just wanted to let you know that even in the medical field no matter how high up you are, there really is no such thing as job security.

Anyway, coming back to our small hospital. Close friends who would never ever dream of speaking up or showing any form of dissent, were immediately suspended. Those who, let us say are known for their corporate brown-nosing got reinstated at lower pay as punishment provided an official written apology was submitted and one of my colleagues who was quite influential in the small local community - plus he was Arab, got his posting back. The rest was no easy story.

Some were just recently graduated from their own country, some barely finished their probation period and others basically dug their own graves a long time ago; signing that document was like carrying your own coffin with you. One of my closest friends was in the latter group. Very cool guy, totally chill, went through each shift or weekend or whatever in die-hard materialistic fashion (just like the author of this book) and basically his posting was non-essential to be honest. HR and Accounts departments deemed him to be a liability (in terms of monthly paychecks) and thus terminated. He was actually glad. I remember him reading the email about his termination and he was cool about. Lit a cigarette in my apartment and just went home to write up a new CV and call some friends to get him an interview at an insurance company (He got the job and he is doing very well).

So now only a handful of the original bunch of pioneer residents of our university hospital were left.

Life went on as usual for the next few weeks. Shifts, salaries, weekends, gossips, filing reports etc etc.

Last week of August, rare morning shift. Taking the quick handover from the previous night residents near one of the wards. Some seniors walking by on the way to the NICU, I said salam but they avoided eye contact and walked away.

Did something happen?

My phone rang, elective Cesarean section in process they need a pediatrician. Nothing major just a little difficulty in extraction and low APGAR score, the baby just needed some oxygen and he was alright. Then I got the call.

"Dr. Ismail, I am calling from the HR department, as per recent memo from

Chairman's office...

We have decided not to renew your employment visa for this year, thank you

for your cooperation"

I have a bad habit of drinking too much coffee and not getting enough sleep before my shifts. There had been times where I thought I got a code red or something and I rush to the resuscitation table and nothing was there. So in my mind I thought I was having a lucid day-time dream/hallucination.

Not renewing my visa?

As in they are firing me?

They can't do that, I am Dr. Ismail Sayeed from the Pediatrics Department.

Just like my friend I didn't protest initially. Maybe from shock and confusion I am not sure. The baby was crying in the background, machine sounds going on, people moving around. I didn't bother to change my blood-soaked scrubs.

As I was heading to the HR office which was a short walk from the main building, one of my pediatric resident colleagues called. Another one texted me. I do not recall the conversation but they were probably consoling me. I went in, I demanded an explanation, I pleaded to speak to the chairman, I wanted to negotiate a reassignment to the hospital insurance support department (where some of the previous suspended doctors were reassigned) and then I left knowing that certain events were carefully put in motion so that the message would be communicated exactly on this day and I would have absolutely no way to charm my way out like I used to. If you read this paragraph closely you would realise that I just went through the entire grief process in just one conversation.

I didn't bother talking with anyone, went back to the OT. Changed out of my. Packed up my things from my locker and just walked back recently blood-soaked scrubs. Went home. Lied down on the floor and called my parents to tell them the news. Voices were breaking, cross-connections going on, my pulse was rising. Maybe today was a good day to have a stroke.

Next few days I tried to appeal the HR decision to whomever would listen but it was no use. As long as the Chairman is out of the country and his army of yes-men (and yes-women) blocked any access to him, my fate was sealed. Nothing wakes you up from an inner slumber like unemployment, and then impending deportation. I asked some of my friends if there was any opening in any other hospital or clinic around UAE, I looked through the vacancies, I even applied for a New Zealand study visa (in case I forgot to mention I recently applied for a medical licensing exam in Auckland - similar to the USMLE[6]). All those attempts went down the drain. The end of my Gulf career and dreams were upon me.

---

[6] My visa was denied as I now had no reason to return after the exam, therefore I am a flight risk

Nowhere to go except return to your home country. No appeal. Penalty for overstaying (which I paid at the airport). Slowly packed my things, transferred my savings to a bank account I had in Dhaka and took a taxi to the airport. The reason why my departure was less dramatic than the first few days of starting medical school was that by coincidence I met with that same friend who was fired and now had a job in a major medical insurance company, he told me the exact same thing we used to tell each other late at night during those days we had night shifts together.

"Dude, we can't live like this......this medical life sucks"

"We should get out of here and go to some other country"

"We're getting too comfortable around here, we need a kick in the head or

something so we can refresh our brains"

Be careful what you ask for, the Universe might just give that exact thing you are praying for. In a small way I am glad I got kicked in the head and slapped by a bucket of bricks. I was finally thrown out of my mind-numbing comfort zone.

Few suitcases and a gym bag. All my material possessions I could carry without paying the airline overweight charges. Stopover in Doha so I can have one last look at pure golden luxury before heading back to a country my parents tried so hard to keep me away from.

"One way ticket to Dhaka. Welcome aboard Mr. Sayeed"

"Have a safe flight."

WALK OF SHAME

So here I was getting out of the airport at around 6am. Thankfully an uncle arranged for transport since I was a total stranger here. I used to barely visit Bangladesh once a year or sometimes after 2 years as a cultural courtesy. I enjoyed my little breaks, not only because I could catch up with my cousins and grandmothers, but I was safely nestled in the assurance that after a week or so I would be back to my lovely air-conditioned civilised Gulf lifestyle. Not this time. Not anymore.

Everyone knew I was coming back. I don't think everyone knew the circumstances of my downfall, it didn't matter really. When you return without riches and that too relatively early in your life then no amount of excuses will save your dignity. I was back and technically homeless. Wonderful.

Just to fast forward the already pathetic turn of events, I will breeze through what my life looked like in the next few months. Trust me there were worse moments before I discovered my calling. The author's journey is never through valleys of roses, one must be dragged through the mud before seeing any hope.

So I was back home. Jumping from one relatives' place to another. Trying to make sense of my predicament looking for any civilised country that would recognise my degrees, documents and damn papers that said I was a good boy and I will behave etc etc. Other Gulf countries were out of the question; due to a wide scale ban on Bangladeshi citizens applying for work visas (probably due to political and managerial corruption that the whole world is sick of), Europe is not going to happen due to strict naturalization and employment criteria (A friend of mine spent years in Norway trying to become a doctor there after internship - he got as far as a home-visit nurse for homebound dependants), UK is open as long as I study and write the MRCP and other board exams and same with Australia. East Asia is just as strict against foreign medical graduates wishing to work there.

Everywhere else not only do you need to know the language plus you need to be a citizen. Doors were closing all around me, the curse of my own existence as a brown-skin national of a stereotypical corrupt Third-world country was hanging from my neck. I was silently cursing every person in my little world - except the main culprit. With dead honesty fate has very little impact on the direction of our lives, the captain is responsible for which way the ship sails so I have only myself to blame. Years wallowing in self-pity and self-depreciation led me here, I tried to follow so many directions, cues and opinions but as often is the case, when there are so many choices sometimes the only thing to do is shut down mentally.

But there was a way to redeem my medical career, family honor and maybe some prestige. Like I mentioned before my exile, I had applied for the New Zealand Medical Board exam, although my visa from the New Zealand consulate in UAE was denied, the exam registration was still valid. So at full speed I was on a mission to get all the subsequent documents to apply for a visit visa; I finally got my new Bangladeshi citizenship papers, Birth certificate notarized, National ID card, Bank account and other miscellaneous supporting documents, and I submitted for review at the offshore New Zealand Embassy visa processing center in India (There was no liaison office in Dhaka). While I waited for a response I started studying for the upcoming exams. For a brief moment I could atleast tell people I was busy studying for a big test to work in a fancy hospital in a beautiful civilised country.

Did you think it was alright from now on?

This book is quite big and is filled with many misfortunes, so hang on.

INCOMPETENCE IS DESTRUCTIVE

The Medical Council of New Zealand has a variety of pathways that a foreign medical graduate can use to get registered be allowed to practise medicine there. One of the prerequisites is to complete the NZREX (comparable to the USMLE exams). Since I had already completed the USMLE and have some certified clinical experience in a Western-standard institution, I could bypass some of the steps and head straight for the Viva and short clinical mock tests, just like the MRCP Part 2 segments that many physicians would know about.

So while my application was being processed, I went through some of my old medical practice books just to go through some of the basics from the other specialities. After all, most of my professional lifetime was dedicated to Pediatrics and Neonatology, I had a lot of ground to cover to pick up on the other subjects, thankfully my USMLE knowledge was still fresh. This is one of the beautiful things about Western standard examinations, most of them are created and assessed by computer algorithms so are incorruptible and since no human intervention is present (*I think*) it is in a simple word - fair. And because it is so well designed, even if one does not go to the USA to practice, atleast the medical curriculum is so adequately curated, your whole clinical practice slowly adapts to the kind of professionalism that is expected in high tier institutions. Have to hand it to them, the Western system is strongly biased towards their own kind, but atleast their systems thinking is very practical.

I had booked my exam hearing for November 2013, and now it is Mid-October and still no word from the New Zealand visa processing center in New Delhi. I was getting very concerned. I got my Schengen Visa and US visa relatively early, why so much of a hassle for the NZ visa? Their call center was pathetic as expected and my emails went unanswered, this was highly irregular. Even in the online expatriate forums such delays were very rare. Literally a few days before I was supposed to fly out I received an email stating that the person who was assigned my documents was on leave for a month, my passport was temporarily misplaced then found and the person assigned to me had just returned a few days prior and will be assessing my application, post-haste. What a load of bull-shit!

I called their hotline again and again. I wanted to know if they 'misplaced' my passport why they hadn't informed that such a delay would occur. Literally a few days left before I had to fly out. The NZREX exam in question was a biannual event and apparently due to the large number of NZ-trained specialists returning from Australia, this will be the last session until they decide to reinstate the exam systems again. Truly was a perfect storm of bureaucratic chaos.

Few days later I received a call from an Indian local line. Apparently the agent wants me to pay an additional processing fee to send the visa application to Singapore or something by tonight and then pay another DHL fee to get the stamped passport back to me. And I have to do this right now. Few days left to buy the Dhaka-Singapore-Auckland plane ticket. I paced up and down, sweating profusely, my mind shattering into a hundred pieces. I knew the stakes and I have seen this type of incompetence countless times.

Whenever a privately outsourced organisation tells their client to hurry and do this and that and pay some additional processing costs etc., something is falling apart. I know this well because I was after all in a private medical institution. I know of so many stories where at the last minute the insurance coverage is revoked, a highly complex case appears and we do not have the capacity to manage and so many more examples of such. Basically I had a feeling that these people messed up big time and probably they are trying to make a rush order, plus who knows how many other applications have piled up on that agent's desk. Talk about substandard management. I had a very important decision to make that night.

I had a very close and intimate female friend I refer to as 'E' whom I met in my US travels, she is very dear to me because of her strong spirit and decisive attitude about life. I managed to get her on Skype and told her about what has happened to me recently and the choices I have to make. She just told me,

"Ismail, why do you keep living someone else's life?"

"Our bodies and minds have enough capacity to make our own dreams

come true - choose whichever road that gives you peace in your heart

"Take deep breaths as if you had nearly drowned and now you are

appreciating life, close your eyes, concentrate on your heartbeat and fall into

the future where you imagine your life would become if you choose either option."

I chose the path of uncertainty, because that is my nature now. Dear '*E*', I hope you are able to get a copy of this book. You know who you are. I wanted to thank you again for that moment, because as you also said life is the sum total of personal moments. And so in that moment I emailed that cheap low-class agency that I wish to cancel my application, I want a full refund of my processing fees and I want a signed report about this gross negligence and misconduct (or else I will press charges with a NZ governing body - India has no oversight anyway but they are afraid of the white man's opinions). A week later I got my passport by courier, 80% refund as per policy and a poor excuse of an apology report[7]. I know I cannot trust them not to lose my passport again - it is the only credible proof of global identity I have. So again I was denied another visa, lost the chance to write the exam that *may* have been my last chance at a Western health system and now back to zero.

Again I called my dad and told them what happened to me.

---

[7] In the report it was made clear that the agent in charge and supervisors were both terminated for misconduct and incompetence. Small victories small justice.

We were both accustomed to my bad luck by now. No big news.

Time to head back to the internet and ask Google; '*What can a washed up loser MBBS doctor do to start a career?*'

By the miracle of technology, I did get some answers.....

BUCKETFULL OF MASTERS DEGREES

Again back to square zero. Dreams based on hype. Dreams based on shiny websites. I spent the next few months in awkward limbo. Christians call it purgatory, I call it Narayanganj, my hometown. I never actually grew anywhere in particular, but I have the mindset to call any place home. Narayanganj was home because of the memories I had here in my brief annual summer visits in my childhood. This is also the place where my father saved up his foreign remittances to build his own nest egg. Back in the 90's it was the tallest apartment, a full 5 stories high. I spent most of my time here as Dhaka was too chaotic. To experience what medical practitioners go through on an average day in Bangladesh, I spent some time with a close doctor friend of the family in his own private chambers.

Given the neighborhood it was nowhere near fancy. The roof was caved in as if the Americans dropped a bomb here. The waiting lounge was a scene from most horror movies and his tools he kept in his clinic, well they are what infection control committees would have nightmares about. The doctor was a nice man, but his office was a disaster. Maybe as a tourist (*probashi*) I was used to a certain way of life or rather a set expectation of what a private care center was supposed to look like, but honestly a paying patient deserves the absolute minimum quality of atmosphere, especially in times of illness. Anyway, let us not get into discussions about postmodern architecture, let us talk about how a well respected healthcare professional conducts his trade on an average day.

After a few weeks most days played out in the usual pattern. As a disclaimer not all private practice doctors have the same lifestyle but the daily burdens certainly overlap. So this doctor friend usually practices a few days of the week in a public hospital in Dhaka, then on those afternoons he has a shared chamber in a clinic. In the evening upon reaching Narayanganj he will sit here in this chamber for a few hours, then sometimes off to the local hospital outpatient department. As a surgeon he may have a few usual cases here and there (abscess drainage, appendectomy, wound monitoring etc). These events can be follow any determinate order depending on presence or absence of booked appointments or expected patients depending on how crowded the waiting rooms are i.e. he may start the day in Narayanganj then go to Dhaka for the whole evening then return at night, it depends. This goes on all day, everyday just chasing after every little bit of taka that can be earned.

No weekends, his children are settled out West, the wife keeps some food in a container at home, socialising means attending a handful of Big Pharma-sponsored lunches/dinners. So is this the career I should be hoping for? By all accounts he has a decent life (according to him), he sent his kids through college, marriage, sent them abroad and he can retire anytime he wants, just chooses to keep working because it is his passion.

You don't need to be a PHD Psychology researcher to identify the many defense mechanisms at play.

As I met more and more Bangladeshi physicians - of many specialities and calibre, the same pattern of this hamster wheel-rat race lifestyle springs up. But nobody complains. Nobody sees that this is why doctors are often more sick than patients. This can't be my future. Maybe it's time to upgrade to beyond clinical medicine, and with good timing, as it appears I am starting to forget many of the doses and diseases.

Through our many discussions and the recommendations from my parents, a foreign masters degree may open up some doors for me. Atleast in some upscale private hospital in Dhaka.

So back to career researching and I came upon an interesting healthcare course in UK:

Masters in Global Health - with emphasis on:

Health Economics

Health Systems

Global Health Policy

Medical Anthropology

Statistics

Social Determinants of Health

Sounded very interesting and it was based at Queen Mary University of London (affiliated with NHS Trust - Royal London Hospital). If you are not that impressed by all this its ok, my impression was sold on the fact that any UK-based degree is a ticket to a sweet life, seeing how our economic status drastically improved after my father completed his higher postgraduate studies in Edinburgh. Another symptom of the superiority/inferiority complex set by Western institutions. Who am I to judge, many of my (and yours) relatives upgraded their lives by using foreign degrees as a currency.

Did some research about some of the topics, really deep knowledge on how healthcare is planned and implemented - seems like a good career opportunity in various NGOs. I had always admired the work of the World Health Organisation, UNICEF, BRAC and many others. I felt a Masters degree from a well-reputed UK institution will make my CV more attractive to the kind of career path I wanted. So I had a Skype session with the course coordinator. Unfortunately there was a small issue, due to the closing dates of the June 2014 intakes and the usually long visa processing times for brown-skinned males from third world countries, it seems I need to deflate my dreams once again.

I was wondering if I should sacrifice atleast a year so I have a better chance at applying for the latter half of the September 2014 sessions. My time is running out, frustrations 24/7 and so many family issues riding on this. Thankfully another opportunity opened up. Not in the UK but in the opposite direction - OZ (Australia). This course was more on my line of study i.e. Master of Medicine (MMed in Pediatrics specifically) taught from the University of Sydney. Best part was that there is an online version. Now you may be thinking about the 'value' or 'merit' of an online course, I mean what can you possibly learn by staring at your computer screen? Will your peers or patients take you seriously if you mention you completed a postgraduate degree from Australia, then they ask from where and you mention it was an online course?

Believe me I thought so too, but as it turns this method was actually gaining some ground in the academic circles. After all the same non-clinical degree that they would mail to you would have the same professional merit if you attended physical classes anyway. Like I mentioned before, in the global education rat race, these degrees are like currency (same as bitcoin if you think about it) their practical value all depends on what the observer thinks. So enough rationalising, diverted the funds which I would have spent for the UK masters course, and enrolled at the University of Sydney (online) course.

Hooray, my life has meaning now.
I can boldly tell people I am a postgrad masters student at a fancy university.

Spent most the upcoming months literally glued to my desk. Just reading through the posted materials, taking online assessments, writing up weekly and monthly assignments which I would forward to my parents to double check (some of the topics went over their heads) and just kept busy completing this strange task. The physical and online isolation became second nature to me, just like it would have been if I was actually there in Sydney University ironically (atleast I saved on flights and accommodation).

So semester 1 was over in a flash, more or less, now was their summer break or whatever. But where do I stand? What am I supposed to do now? I went back to the family friend's private chamber and killed time watching him at his rundown refugee centre-like clinic. I sort of felt more sorry for him than for myself, many times I saw him doze off from exhaustion at this desk. God knows which clinic or hospital he just finished a shift before coming here. After almost 5 months since we last met; I noticed that the endless worrying magnified his wrinkles and quite ironically, worsened his diabetes. Somewhere in my thoughts I was trying to piece together the reason why the more degrees and dollars a doctor earns - the closer he gets to his grave. Very strange phenomenon. (Must be a weird Asian thing I suppose)

My parents used to come down from Kuwait every few months just to check up on me. These were rare moments when I could talk to my father about all my daily little trials and tribulations. Both of visited many of his old medical school friends who were either permanently settled in Dhaka or have returned from abroad, some were in top consultancy positions at high end private institutions, others were not so lucky but still somehow were making a living. He tried his level best to secure some kind of hope for my dead-end career (with or without a foreign degree). We repeated this act countless times, many kept saying I should just sit in a corner and learn german to get into Germany, or study for PLAB and keep trying. The same repeated answers were mentally exhausting. Years later I realised the joke behind this moment and why I was further demotivated - I was hoping to hear about a golden opportunity from amateur physicians (compared to me father) who themselves tried and failed the very steps they were recommending. Would you take career advice from someone who wears sandals and smells of cigarette smoke in his private practice? I think I made my point clear.

After many of my father's visit to Bangladesh I asked his opinion about this crazy idea I had. I asked him instead of chasing the next big thing i.e. PhD in some obscure topic with an unknown career value (I met a Polish friend who completed his PhD in something related to healthcare and is now working in a McDonalds), how about I pursue that UK degree while I wait for my eligibility for the next MMed online semester. My logic at that time was that if I had 2 high calibre Western degrees then it would multiply my chances at getting a strong job opportunity, either in my very own private practice or even as a side gig as a visiting lecturer. See how the Western academic industry inflates the hopes of desperate professionals? Do you not know of family members or associates who willingly go into debt to just taste that foreign success story? I sure did.

Without any hesitation, I got my paperwork and documents ready, consulted with a professional UK education consultancy based in Dhaka and on I went. The process went on quite smoothly unlike my experience with whatever organisation that sabotaged my NZ dreams. Waited a few weeks for the processing and fees to get cleared. Meantime I reached out to some of my old medical school buddies who had settled in the UK. Most are doing quite well by my standards, cleared their PLABs, MRCPs and various other qualifications and are working in their own district clinics and some LOCUM[8] work as well. Money seemed to be quite good from their many shiny Facebook posts.

---

[8] A Locum doctor is a physician who works in the place of the regular physician when that physician is absent, or when a hospital or practice is short staffed. These professionals are still governed by their respective regulatory bodies, despite the transient or freelance nature of their positions.

Finally reached an advanced Western civilisation and reached my friend *E's* place in East London - the irony is that many of you might know about East London is that it is basically a slightly cleaner version of a Bengali slum. I had a few weeks to find a decent place and get some quick tourism out of the way so I can concentrate on the upcoming masters coursework.

I thoroughly enjoyed the classes of Global Health. I learned so many topics that upturned my beliefs about people, culture, economics, politics and ofcourse Health.

How do governments plan, pay, produce healthcare services for the people

Why are health costs increasing

Why do some people mistrust Western-style clinical management

What do international trade tariffs have to do with public health

What is Big Pharma and Intellectual Property

Value of innovation in healthcare

and....

What is *Health*?

I loved staying back in the library, I used to read so many articles every day after classes. I was amazed by the impact that the UK's National Health Service (NHS) has done for its people. And perhaps more importantly I came to terms with my own medical career since now I knew why certain doctors prescribed that way, or insisted on admissions, why I am forced to jump through exam hoops and basically what is my role as a physician in a health system[9].

The university year was ending, my masters thesis was submitted for assessment and now I had to think hard about my opportunities in the UK with this potential MSc degree. I did the same thing like in America, I investigated the personal and career livelihoods of many UK doctors especially amongst my friends who have settled there.

In conclusion things were way better as a doctor here in the UK than anywhere else. Reimbursements were quite good especially if you did some locums or had your own community clinic, life was expensive but affordable as a white collar worker, career advancements were possible - even in the same field that you studied from our country of origin and above all else a generous state-run pension plan.

So I found my niche right?

Why am I wasting your time with the previous chapters?

I could have just skipped all that.

As luck would have it, there was a dark cloud on the horizon. It's name was *'BREXIT'*. From my understanding Brexit was just the result of rising EU administrative costs that UK was not willing to pay and so a trade issue was at the centre of it. On the ground it affected other areas as well -

---

[9] Majority of public health achievements occur outside a hospital and is actually done best by people without a medical degree!

especially healthcare providers' salaries, immigration, NHS procurement, hospital budgets and a whole lot of other things. In short there was mass movement of UK doctors to USA, Canada and Australia (also NZ). Let me tell you something, if a white guy leaves UK for better livelihood somewhere else - you should probably pay attention.

Now what?

Another one way trip back to Dhaka?

This has to be some cosmic joke on me.......why am I being punished this way?

These questions were going through my mind 35,000 ft in the air across Europe, then Iran, India and then you know where. The questions followed me out of the terminal, into our home and as soon as I woke from my jetlagged nap.

How do you restart a career after returning from abroad? Twice?

REDEFINING YOUR CAREER GOALS

- a cautionary tale

So here I am again. A recently returned non-resident postgraduate professional back on the job-hunt. I did the usual routine of updating my CV, getting hard copy of some degrees here and there, made some calls and just waited. Thankfully about a year ago a few recruitment startups named Bdjobs and Bikroy was launched, according to my cousins it was a good way to look for jobs and opportunities.

Signed up. Made a profile. Uploaded pdf scans and cover letters. Searched as many health related openings as possible. Applied to a dozen or so hospitals, clinics and NGOs per day. Weeks went by and no response. My thinking that health jobs are always in demand - especially foreign degree holders would get calls left and right - was slowly falling apart. Really frustrating time for me.

Thankfully, a family friend who works at a high-end hospital in Dhaka referred me to their director, as a personal favour to my father. Comparatively it was a really nice upscale institution. They were decked out with the latest medical interventions, in house pharmacy, fully staffed outpatient department with top tier foreign trained consultants and fairly strong branding. A dream job by all accounts.

I met the director and gave a viva. He was really impressed and invited me for a type of observership/internship in the pediatrics department to start me off. I accepted just so I can get an idea of the inner corporate culture plus I had to go back to London for my convocation. Finally some good news sails. All I had to do was just go through the motions, learn the ropes, make the right connections and (although not the way I planned my life to turn out) I could be posted in the NICU and make some good changes, a place to practice the skills I had acquired over the years.

It felt empowering to wake up, dress up and prepare for the day ahead. Especially as a healthcare provider - even as clinical observer for now. The day started like in most tertiary level hospitals; morning rounds through NICU to check on progress, issues, changes in management plan and counsel new parents, then pediatric ward rounds and finally to the doctor's chambers in the outpatient department. As the first few days went by, I could not help but notice the vast deficiencies in quality of care. I am not talking about between Chicago and Dhaka - that is beyond comparison. I am talking about between Chennai and Dhaka, or even Ajman (my previous hospital) and Dhaka. Honestly it is quite amazing how quickly Bangladeshis accept low standards as a fixed definition of how their lives should be. As an outsider I am both disgusted and saddened to see how quickly Bangladeshi doctors accept their ignorance as part of some personal culture.

Let us start from the NICU - by far the most critical and high tension environment in any hospital. You are constantly dealing with the most vulnerable population (sick newborns) in their most vulnerable moments of their lives. Expert care is absolutely essential. 24/7.

I was horrified to see such lapses in quality, skills and basic knowledge. Not a single senior staff was certified for advanced neonatal care. As a *'observer'* I actually taught the senior resident how to calibrate and alter the ventilators. And of course there was no notion of standard practice policies. There were UK/US/European guidelines, all you had to do was choose, educate and implement. Nothing was done. I think most of the books were unopened. Seems most residents are just killing time and eating up their salaries. Many were studying for foreign postgraduate degrees. If your English is as substandard as your practical clinical skills - well, you are better off buying lottery tickets.

I saw critical mistakes in intubation/extubation, unclear antibiotic prescriptions, unclear management of neonatal jaundice and probably the most horrifying - a newborn died because the on-duty resident was unreachable for whatever reason and the nurses had no one to shout orders to them. (I really miss the brilliant Keralite and Filipino nurses in Middle east - one could run an entire NICU). Amateurish counselling methods just worsened the ideal for the poor parents, as a non-employee I had to sit in the corner and pity them.

They deserve better. The baby deserved better.

But these are not uncommon errors. It happens to the best of medical teams and in the best hospitals even. Just a fact of life actually. What is really terrifying is the total lack of oversight, there is no system or best practice discussion even by senior staff to atleast decrease these errors. Merely swept under the rugs. Typical *bengali* response is that it was '*God's will*' blah blah. I have heard this heresy before, and also this culture of culpable murder of little children. It used to occur in my hospital back in UAE.

There is a popular notion called the 'Pareto Principle' or as I like to call it the 20:80 rule. This simple concept states that 80% of an outcome can be related to 20% of an action or inaction. Meaning that 80% of an occurrence or outcome can be related to 20% of a completed task/omitted task/decision/system. A real world example can be like the butterfly effect - let us say you ignore the recommended oil change, after some time this leads to bigger faults in other systems such as the air conditioning, fuel spark plug, overall fuel efficiency, exhaust blockage and many other magnifying defects until your car breaks down in the middle of nowhere (real life personal example). So what does it mean for a healthcare system?

As part of a quality improvement policy and overall safety standards movement, before any surgery the head OT nurse or anaesthetist would go through a simple checklist such as reading out the team member names, tools, oxygen tank pressures and of course the important detail - patient name and procedure (many healthy organs have been mistakenly cut since dawn of medicine!). A simple checklist is a step towards a safe clean uneventful quick standard procedure, even if the cost is the surgeon's ego and their precious time. This is one of millions of tasks that is implemented, followed like a religion and if any deviation occurs, a type of court martial occurs i.e. medical audit which may lead to malpractice/negligence/assault case, in all JCI-accredited[10] and similar internationally recognised organisations. Except here.

Pareto principle in substandard healthcare services i.e. 80% of all errors, poor bedside manners, improper recruitment policies, deficiencies of billing transparencies and a long list of similar patient grievances - can in practicality be related to just 20% ignorance of basic training and human resources management (as an example). It all sounds too complex and yet also too simple to explain the shameful and pathetic state of the Bangladesh Health System. This thinking can be applied to high performing hospitals and teams as well; it has been shown that by creating a system that teaches and enforces a handful of safety protocols (20% effort) they can minimise harm and maximise positive health outcomes and patient satisfaction (80% output). Clearly there is a strong economic gain for all parties to upgrade themselves, so it stands to reason that widespread medical incompetence is due to resistance to change by the ignorant few. Sad reality check.

As a recent Global Health graduate, I could not ignore what I am seeing. The potential was there to make some significant improvements to quality care, atleast to the pediatric unit (I have no idea about the state of the other departments, but I am sure they may have their own issues). I approached my unit supervisor and I spoke to her about giving me the task of drafting some improvement designs for her unit, and even giving a presentation to the NICU staff as well - a sort of awareness program. She wholeheartedly agreed and off I went. A renewed commitment came

---

[10] Joint Commission International - Non-profit US organisation that surveys hospitals to assess their safety and clinical quality standards. Being certified raises the status of an international hospital to be on the same level as their Western counterparts - which also means they can raise their prices since high end patients will be more comfortable to avail their services. Win-Win?

over me, as I have learned not to wait for external motivation, one must find a passion and invest in it.

As it turns out there was an entire course library on quality assurance, safety standardisation, skills development and in line with my degrees - designing surveys to assess patient satisfaction. Less than a month before heading back to the UK for my convocation, I had a lot of data to gather and practice recommendations to make. I spent most of the evening reading through peer-reviewed journals, NICE guidelines, JCI protocols and even some articles from the Medical Council of India (since our cultures were similar and there is a superiority complex that most bengalis aspire to anyway).

The best method was to walk the path of the patient i.e. the newborn who was just delivered and to follow a handful of babies to whichever direction they took such in normal deliveries which way does the nurse take to go to the delivery suite, the mother's room, phototherapy room if needed[11] or in worst case scenarios to see the path of a sick newborn on its way to the NICU for further management. Same methods with some of the admitted pediatrics cases as well. I do not want to dwell on the negative, rather I phrased my findings as systemic challenges which through some small tweaks in training recommendations (eg. Neonatal resuscitation refresher courses) and maybe overall layout of some of the units could in fact improve overall outcomes (20:80 rule). I summarised my findings and ideas in a simple powerpoint presentation for the NICU staff and colleagues.

---

[11] Phototherapy - Cost-effective and safe treatment for elevated jaundice status in some babies.

The response was a mixture of lukewarm to very interested as was expected. To be honest they were not the primary audience to discuss such practices. Decision-makers stay on the upper floors and their business suits cost as much as 10 lab coats. Like any corporate bureaucracy, to get *that* type of audience it is not *what* you know but who you know that gets you through their doors. Since I was a mere observer and outsider, such plans were irrelevant in the bigger picture, besides I was more eager to return to London for the ceremony. My ego was thirsting for the overpriced black gown and the overhyped piece of rolled paper I would get. Just a few more days left in the unit and I can prepare my luggage and get in touch with my university colleagues to see how far they went in their careers after 3 months of completing the Global Health course.

CHASING DEGREES : CHASING RENT

Watching the clouds go by, skipping through the in-flight channels and planning to visit all my favorite London spots to visit in the upcoming short 2 weeks (especially the Queen Elizabeth Olympic swimming pool). It had been a rough past 2-3 months since completing the Global Health course. Could not match with a suitable job, still have half a masters left over from before (Semester 2 of MMed course from the University of Sydney) and restarting a career in a Third World country. I hope my former classmates could uplift my spirits.

We had a small get together in the lunchroom of our small campus building. Most of them flew all the way to London for the event. After all the greetings and reminiscing we had a heart-to-heart talk about the real world. The local GPs (UK General practitioners) went back to their clinics after the year off they took for the course, a few applied for a job placement in their country's health ministries, oddjobs, internships, externships and a handful were considering a PhD to get into a future tenureship in a university back in their country. None of the non-EU international students even took the chance to apply to something in the UK. It was indeed a crowded market filled with PhD-certified baristas, cleaners, food delivery people and others.

Our Health Systems professor tried to motivate us to keep trying, it has only been 2 months since graduating, way too early to say where your skills will take you. Thinking back to his background I did not find much comfort. After completing his army conscription in his country he completed his medical degree, then he joined Medecins Sans Frontieres to help in the Cyprus conflict, then worked locums throughout the UK due to the emerging economic crisis back in his European homeland, completed his Masters and PhD and then took one many teaching jobs before landing at Queen Mary University of London. He is in his mid-50's, single and does not look well off.

I remember my old buddy 'A' from Texas joking about academics - they have all that knowledge but no way to change reality or their bank accounts. After all that time it dawned on me about this obsession with academia, sure people look at you with intellectual admiration (having the letters Dr. and MSc beside your name is quite cool) but I wonder if bankers, landlords and debt-collectors give that much respect.

We had a nice group selfie. Atleast we can cherish this memory and use it to inspire us to carry on. Just like that British saying;

Keep calm & Carry on

Ok mate.

I will keep calm and carry on and on.

Return flight to Dhaka. Economy class. Confirmed.

CAREER IN THE NON-PROFIT SECTOR

Back in Dhaka I was back on the job hunt. This time atleast with a CV upgrade. Foreign degree and

foreign work experience. Time to upgrade my chances to get a dream job, earn some cash, do some

good and get my life back on some kind of track. So I rewrote my CV and cover letter, uploaded it

back on those online job portals and ofcourse emailed directly to the HR department of some of

the top hospitals - with special interest in the hospital my cousin's son was already in (by the way he

got better and got discharged during the time I was in the UK).

Weeks went by but no response. Even the kind hospital director could not give me any response

either, since it was an HR recruitment issue and he had no direct say in it.

Feeling of self-doubt was creeping in.

A glimmer of hope did shine through at last. A distant cousin of mine who has extensive experience in all the major international NGOs that work here, gave me a call to guide me in a potential career in health-based NGOs in Dhaka. She gave a good word to her previous boss who was the country director of a renowned NGO. Got myself an appointment and took all the hard copies of degrees and articles and whatnot. The viva went pretty good I thought, neither of us were sure what role I would play though. I mean like MSF as a physician I would be posted on the frontlines of poverty and areas of deficient healthcare, but as it was my first entry job as an NGO physician the path was not as clear as public sector health careers. In the moment I suggested a type of internship (again) so I can get an idea of this sector and the work culture.

I got in.

I got the spot.

After so long my life would finally change. FInally a door opens for me, and best part their country headquarters was 1min walk from my place. Literally just cross the street and its there in an apartment building. How cool! I can go back and forth during lunch break, no traffic jams and no need to wake up so early.

The first few days were a little slow and boring as the team was busy preparing for their end of year audit reports for their foreign donors. Slowly I got a chance to talk with most of them during the breaks. Many came out from the public sector, went to the London School of Hygiene and

Tropical Medicine (LSHTM), did various stints in many domestic NGOs and then the top tier International NGOs before joining here. Some were from non-medical backgrounds but their unique work experience was well utilised here such as anthropology, communications, gender empowerment, development strategies and others. It was a tight knit group of highly skilled highly motivated individuals unified by core values and vision of the organisation.

NGOs or Non-Profits as I understood over the weeks, are somewhere between the highly functional specific goal-oriented drive of the corporate sector (including a strong interest in organisational branding) and the public health sector where they identify and implement evidence-based health programs to deal with their target population. The difference being the financial angle. Obviously private health organisations are obsessed with for-profit fee-for-service activities (I know this all too well) and the public sector, which although are rooted in free services for entire populations, are publicly funded or supported by foreign aid. NGOs derive their sustainable economy by utilising the vast reserves of foreign donor nations and organisations (and sometimes philanthropic individuals) to pay for all the activities and processes that have a clearly defined and measurable public good e.g. healthcare services for marginalised populations.

It was truly enlightening to be associated in some way with a health NGO. I often romanticized the life of an NGO doctor - just like in the commercials and movies. The rugged visionary braving danger to help the sick. Very catchy. I knew it would be some time before I am qualified to go with them in their field trips. So most days were spent correcting reports, double-checking audits, reading about their previous mission statements and also designing case studies for potential surveys that they might consider in the future. Sure it was a bit tedious, but I too was motivated by the greater good.

After some rapport was established, I managed to get some practical information about where all this is heading, the organisation and the people in it (especially my role). Non-medical related personnel mostly did the administrative work such as in brand communications, accounts, HR and maintaining liaisons with partner organisations. The former physicians who are in charge of the main operations of capacity building of field personnel, units, divisions and even large hospitals; had the most responsibilities and also the best remunerations. Somewhat higher than private physicians and definitely higher than public salaries, with some fringe benefits as well (allowances). Like I said it was a relatively cushy job; regular hours, high fixed salary, respect, camaraderie, had unifying values, mostly indoor report writing and many opportunities at professional skills development - in foreign countries, in first class hotels. So far nothing new, I knew about the difficult but also trendy lifestyles of NGO doctors.

In the past, the bulk of any public service was taken up by NGOs. It is a common global phenomenon (I studied about it in Global Health ofcourse) in any impoverished setting. But a global paradigm shift was occurring. The need and public perception of NGOs (even health NGOs) was under some scrutiny. The true identity of foreign donors, their true intentions for such valiant work (religious reasons?) and the inadequate financial transparency of the dollar papertrail; were a significant threat to their sustainability. Plus with economic downturn the willingness to be so caring for poor Bangladeshis and other similar demographics becomes a lower priority when they have their own fiscal issues to deal with. What this means to the staff is that at any time their entire network would collapse if they could not justify the expenses in providing impactful and cost-effective health interventions. A memo could mean that they have to liquidate all assets and entire teams would be unemployed.

But that is a doomsday scenario, and it mostly affects local *low quality/effective* NGOs (they have an over-reliance on emotional branding of their values without proof of financial effectiveness, therefore donors are hesitant to support them). For the foreseeable future, a career in the NGO-sector is quite promising, and lucrative. Regarding career development, there is no real such thing as promotions in most NGO organisations; the exact reason is not known but according to some articles I read, due to the flattened organisational pyramid (public and private organisations have a steep pyramid shaped design of their organisations and jobs with specific roles and pay structures, but in NGOs as everyone does everything, such roles and positions are not that well defined) the only way to upgrade your career (and paycheck) is to move to another NGO which may have a vacancy due to the resignation of that person who is also looking for an upgrade.

I came to realise that I may be too old in this race and also I may have missed out on prerequisite field experiences that may have helped me (eg. voluntary work, rotary activities, UN internships etc), so the only way to move up is to move out. Meaning as soon as my internship is over I should apply for a position in another NGO. Not a big deal, as I felt more confident that atleast I got my foot in the door. Plus the country director was gracious enough to write me a letter of recommendation and a handful of personal emails of his known associates in the NGO sector.

The internships came to an end; I learned how to write reports, make abridged copywriting, understand the logistic shaping of their capacity building projects, importance of local partnerships and the impact of strictly translating an organisation's values into daily operations i.e. tell your beneficiaries exactly what you stand for and provide *only* that and nothing more. OK, cool. Interesting viewpoint I suppose. Most of my romanticized beliefs about non-profit work was swiftly cancelled out. It really is difficult but in a different way, sure they are doing great work for the community, but from law of economics - they intentionally work at a loss eg. from my occasional peeks at their regular monitoring and evaluation frameworks (M&E) it is obvious that a lot of dollars is spent to help a handful of people for a specific time depending if their budget allows it. If there is a shortfall from projections no big deal a report is given to ask donors to increase their worthy contributions, but if targets are met and there is some money left over (being a non-profit this part is a no-no) it would seem their targets are incorrect and maybe donors should not give much money next quarter, that is why most International NGOs have the latest SUV transports, fancy city center headquarters, have meetings in fairly nice hotel ballrooms and other perks. Whatever no judgements, given the intense workload even I can justify some luxuries.

So what does it mean for me? Where do I join?

The thought of remote jungle work sort of disgusts me (since I am after all a spoilt city boy) but if these fringe benefits are included then why not. After my time with them got over I started on the job hunt again, with emails, letters, online posts again and again. I managed to get 2 interviews, both highly reputed and well paying healthcare job vacancies - but due to my poor grasp of the Bengali language I was not suitable. I guess even getting the call and sitting for the written part is a plus point but the sum total is still zero income. So frustrating.

After many months of the same trivial existence - wake up late, sign in to bdjobs, apply, upload, email, hope, then silence, sleep then repeat, I received a call. The programs director from my internship gig asked if I was free for a consultancy opening. I have no idea what that means but I said yes and yes and I will definitely meet him at their office for a formal interview. I felt so relieved.

Went for the meeting, fairly basic set-up. I had to design and implement a sort of feasibility study for one of their capacity building projects in a medical hospital north of Dhaka. I was grateful and honored (deep down I knew it was because I had the lowest consultant fee bid and they were having budget cuts) and ready for the mission. Due to confidentiality clauses I cannot give much information except I really enjoyed it. Had the chance to feel important and valued by an International organisation and a local healthcare facility. At long last I had that feeling that my skills, reports and recommendations could potentially impact on the lives of so many poor impoverished families. Hooray!

The whole project was merely paperwork really. Make and take surveys, ask questions, go through hospital records, make observations, compile my opinions, make even more reports, submit, make corrections, re-submit...and get a fat paycheck. Two weeks, 1 project, some paperwork and cold hard cash.

I felt proud, family felt proud. I thought I could really get used to that lifestyle. Plus the nametag on my fancy new business card sounds cool - Pediatric Healthcare Research Consultant.

But I needed more projects and more referrals. Being a *consultant*, though very empowering; the financial payback is difficult as you have to constantly look for other projects to get another hefty paycheck. No project no pay. Simple. I soon learnt about this unstable lifestyle from associates I met. It can be quite unsettling to be unemployed for long periods before the next project bid comes along. There are thousands ofcourse but the HR process of matching consultants to projects is extremely poor, even for the UN databases. Could this inefficiency be the reason for the poor cost-effective design of their humanitarian work? Controversial topic indeed.

I applied to many domestic and international projects which were about to start or have finished their implementations. Basically the idea behind these reports is that it is a sort of explanation for why this NGO deserves money handouts for the next fiscal year. In a way to legitimise their existence. And the staff salaries. Personally I do not care about such politics, since I am in the same pool I need to constantly compete anyway. I did manage to get 2 more relatively high-paying projects from the same NGO, but it was interspersed with many months of unemployment. If I was to make a prediction, I would say this is definitely not a long term sustainable mode of living, bouts of anxiety hoping and looking for a project bid then short levels of high stress workload to produce high quality deadline reports.

The conclusion to this chapter is best exemplified by the lifestyles of my seniors - sure the NGO salary is a definite upgrade to their past government sector jobs, but I do not see them in that much of a luxurious lifestyle. Absolutely some good work is coming from their brilliant daily efforts, but at these costs I am hesitant to think that those unknown donors would remain generous all the time. I remember hearing whispers and jokes about opening their own non-profit venture or emigrating abroad. After careful insight I presumed the main issue is their own (and mine also) financial confidence that is having the comfort to execute your own concept of a sustainable healthcare model and not to worry about when the funds would run out.

Very confusing and frustrating revelation as you can imagine, what is left I began to wonder. I tried my hand in the private health sector, then public, non-profit, domestic and abroad. So what can a professional do to get some stability and financial independence in such harsh economic times?

THE ACCIDENTAL ENTREPRENEUR[12]

I had just finished an NGO project and my parents had come down to Dhaka on their annual visit. There was some kind of alumni ceremony hosted by a close friend of my father's friend - as he was a reputed retired army personnel he shall be named '*G*'. So '*G*' invited us to this little gathering of medical graduate alumni from a medical university based outside Dhaka. Apparently the host organised the whole event while he was enroute to Bangladesh from USA, I did not know much about him then, only that he was a US-based medical doctor who graduated from this university and he is announcing a prosperous healthcare business involving Bangladeshi doctors from various specialities. Needless to say I was very much intrigued, given my unstable employability status of course.

The event started off fairly usual, round of thanks to their teachers, prayers for the recently departed, some amateur singing by gifted alumni and so on. Then the main guy came up. For all intents and purposes he shall be referred to as '*N*'. He was a very loud and expressive person. Had the typical *Banglish* accent (mixture of bengali and American accent) and claims of world-changing

---

[12] Now and again I will highlight specific moments that were clear red flags.

opportunities in America. Nothing out of the extraordinary. Then came his pitch, with slides even. In short he is busy creating a global alumni association to help healthcare professionals who wish to practice and settle abroad - a type of craigslist for doctors of bangladesh. Impressive initiative or so I thought, definitely not the sort of grand scale project that most nerdy professionals (including the type of doctors I met so far) would have the confidence to do, and the boisterous persona that he displayed on stage, real showmanship appearance. I was intrigued beyond words, for sure I wanted to be a part of this movement.

Red Flag #1 - Overly confident and showoff presentation is an overcompensation

for some level of incompetence

Managed to get his local mobile number for a later call. Even 'G' was swept up in the whole show. On the drive back home I heard that both these guys are trying to gather established and influential medical professionals into a type of investment forum or shareholder group for an upcoming major project. What it was is not known or rather only this so-called 'inner member committee' would be allowed to discuss. Both my father and I thought long and hard about this concept, since neither of us knew anything about business or whatever this was supposed to be, there was a great deal of skepticism. 'N' was not on any major online health forum and neither did he have any extensive social media presence, even his existing company website was not that clear about what it does. I figured no big deal not everything online truly represents what the actual process occurs on the ground - being from the non-profit sector I know this all too well. Even my father was unsure as to what to make of him. Our hesitancy was based on several red flags, but like any any red flags to the inexperienced or blindly trusting - they are often ignored.

Anyway a few days went by and I got a call from 'N'. Just basic introduction from both sides, what can I bring to the table, my experiences and wishes for the future etc etc. Naturally, I had a lot of questions about what exactly is this all about, is it going to be like an NGO or something or is it like a collection of doctor directors who will pool their resources to start a hospital. 'N' just said that it is going to be something new and unique - and information is not for everyone, whether you are in or your are out. Typical American Hard Sell - I get it.

Red Flag #2 - The visionary is too paranoid to share even the

basics of his idea/vision unless you pay upfront

Both my father and I were still skeptical. It was a sort of defense mechanism whenever someone promises the moon and gives you rocks, but like I said, I was in a moment of personal professional crisis and my father wanted me to have some form of stability so I can move on with my life. Even 'G' jumped in to give personal guarantee about 'N' character and shared ethics. After much thought we both thought let us see how far it goes, the investment cost was surprisingly low but since a large pool of shareholders was needed it was somewhat affordable for us. Since a fortune was spent on my entire life career development, this shares cost was frighteningly negligible. So we got our cheque books out.

Red Flag #3 - Too good to be true at such a low cost is very concerning

There were a few group messenger meetings where we introduced ourselves, what were our backgrounds, where is our home district blah blah blah. 'N' and 'G' took the center stage to rile up support for being part of the entrepreneurship movement. They had a lot emotionally charged narratives as to how we as professionals should not rely on the public sector or any megacorporation to give meaning to our lives - agreed, and by being an entrepreneur you can take charge of your life and provide realistic values to your community - agreed, and best part whatever healthcare project we do as doctors it will surely be so innovative that a big cash prize is waiting for all our hard work - I had no idea about business but as long as a US doctor and a high ranking former army personnel is backing this up then sure why not.

Red Flag #4 - Beware of economic promises based on emotional

taglines by amateurs

Next few days were some more pep talk and talks about the state of the Bangladesh health system especially regarding the healthcare career of young doctors and healthcare professionals (like pharmacists) and all their trials and hardships they face. The actual business part came in small stages, such as the discussion of what it means to start a business here in Bangladesh, of course most of it went above my head, not only just the terms that were used but also my Bangla was not so good back then so I could not really participate even if I wanted to. No big deal, I figured I would just 'wing it', like learn the steps along the way like on-the-job training.

Red Flag #5 - Do not feel overwhelmed by professional jargon.

Make the effort to understand business basics before spending

a single taka

When everyone was more or less on board, each of us received a word document pertaining to a Non-Disclosure Agreement (NDA) which basically was to keep all professional discussions confidential from outsiders unless they steal our grand designs. No sweat sounds like a smart decision. Then came another file regarding a type of disclaimer which stated that whatever resources (financial or otherwise) utilised as investment would not only be non-refundable but also 'N' would not be personally accountable for the very very tiny chance the project does not make us all extremely rich. Little extreme but since I have experienced all this disclaimer talk in America it was not uncommon. Signed and scanned copy of these documents were mandatory before any further talk about a potential business venture could be possible, 'N' and 'G' insisted. We agreed, signed, scanned and uploaded.

So far so good and professional. The next couple of online messenger meetings was about discussing proposals for a healthcare project. Nobody spoke up. Again it was asked and nobody suggested anything concrete like opening a clinic or pharmacy or anything. Later I proposed an idea I had been considering - basically like a Corporate Coaching service to help professionals deal with work stress management and instituting a type of health insurance pool for such customers. 'N' sort of liked it and said we will consider it as he had an even grander plan. But first we have to discuss the overall mission, vision and objectives of this healthcare company.

In the minutes of meeting 'N' and 'G' asked us all to complete a homework, each of us should write a few lines under those three headings i.e. what do we want to do and what are our core values to follow. A lot of time was spent discussing amongst ourselves, nothing specific was brought forward since in all honesty none of us knew what these things meant. From my NGO experience I just changed around a few words from some NGO organisation website and posted it in the group chat. Some moments later 'N' posted a long word document with those headings and the points to incorporate. They was a long list of non-specific, some grandiose, some unclear objectives in the mission statement, vision statement and the objectives were little confusing. Maybe since I was a non-business person I would not understand - 'G' mentioned that it is best to remain vague so that when the company is formulated we can adapt and alter our projects as we like without being so specific. In some way it made sense and we just moved on with it.

We had a few more of these messenger meetings, some were just pep talk by 'N', others were just casual chitchat - days went by and finally we started to be serious. Another document was shared highlighting the shares distribution of the company, as per this memorandum we would all get equal shares so that no one person can claim to be superior and we would all be equally responsible for the success of whatever we wanted to create. We would each invest a fixed amount and claim equal ownership of a potential million dollar healthcare company. Impressed and onboard without question.

Afterwards 'N' wrote up a complicated set of documents which I later understood to be referred to as the articles of association and the company memorandum, incorporating the shares distribution and the mission, vision, objectives clauses. We had long discussions about the wording and the definitions since we were mostly from the health sector such literature was somewhat hard to grasp. It took another week of group chats until we decided to move on to the discussion of the actual project. As per 'N' and 'G' it was not the right time as we have legally create an enterprise before we have the professional discussion about any money-making venture. As amateur entrepreneurs we all figured that makes a lot of sense, first make the hospital before treating patients (as we understood).

Red flag #7 - Wasting valuable time and resources to first

creating a pseudo-business before even considering the what

and the how is a dangerous mistake.

We have been having a lot of online meetings and now there was talk of meeting in person, since in human interactions, a lot of subtle communication concepts can be missed without seeing your business partners in real life. There were understandably some logistic issues namely many of the interested parties live outside Dhaka and some live outside Bangladesh such as 'N'. A compromise was met, one of us already has a small startup-like health venture so he had graciously invited us to use his office space for any necessary meetings. Initially we had a few such meetings where some of the local-based doctors came in person and we had one of our mobile phones connected to the messenger group chat so atleast others could join in online.

Except there were some serious issues with this telecommunication strategy (which magnified over the coming months), firstly due to the hectic work schedules and time zone differences it was often difficult to harmonize these meetings so as many people could be available either offline or online, and possibly the most unusual and annoying was that one of the seniors was not tech-savvy at all, meaning he had no idea how to use any smartphone device and was actively against learning this vital social skills. You may say that due to age maybe that person was hesitant to keep up with trends and whatnot, but reality was my father and others were much older to him and more knowledgeable about app-based communication so clearly there was some kind of psychological

factor involved with this behaviour, initially it was played off as personality quirks and so we

relayed any minutes of meetings via phone call update when required.

Red Flag #8 - Business evolves faster than society. If you are

unable or unwilling to keep up with trends in technology or policy,

the market will not value your existence.

Documents ready, cheques collected for the starting capital[13]. Other personal information was

needed such as passport copies and photocopies of National ID's for the company registration

process. This action took an unusually long time since poor coordination of individual members,

inability to understand how to email a scanned copy, poor quality scans and in some cases expired

NID's which had to be rectified. In this context an interesting delay had also occurred, it seems as

per local law, government service holders e.g. public sector doctors were not allowed to initiate or

be part of any private sector enterprise. In these cases their relatives were assigned as proxies to

represent them as per shares. There were ofcourse last minute bailouts of interested people and

some additions as well, all in all 16 potential investors agreed to join in (me included)[14]. Obviously

segregating and coordinating whos proxy represents who was another source of confusion.

---

[13] Exact amount will not be discussed but I can say it is a very low amount compared to what other businesses collect - this point will be discussed later

[14] Many ventures have started with dozens of people with various responsibilities. Many want to actively participate in return for equity and some would invest money for shares and just observe and then collect dividends when profits appear. Sadly this concept was not made clear and as you read on you will realise an important factor in business failure.

Red flag #9 - If someone cannot be represent themselves in the

public eye as a member of a venture - this person may not be

motivated nor experienced to initiate certain activities that

require 100% ownership of responsibilities in a company i.e.

if they do not have a tangible stake in something, there is no

motivation to participate actively.

After much back and forth on collecting the required information from everyone we finally

compiled all the necessary paperwork to apply for registration. As is common in many sectors in

Bangladesh, epidemic corruption is a significant barrier to ease of starting business. As soon as

certain parties realise that influential people are part of a venture i.e. doctors, retired army

personnel, corporate executives and so on, there is a strong demand for bribery to get the necessary

approvals. Avoiding this corruption is not easy until systemic digitalisation is implemented, what

could have been done was to hire an experienced corporate lawyer who can bypass all this

inefficiency but the opportunity costs would be almost the same - albeit the process would be

completed much faster. For some reason 'N' and 'G' decided against it and insisted that 'G' and

other doctors would go themselves and apply for trade license registration themselves.

Sadly this took many months to get ourselves registered and on track. We lost atleast 4-5 months just waiting for the trade license, registration copy, VAT clearance, company TIN and for some reason, which I just remembered, we spent weeks trying to think of a name, logo, slogan and other corporate formalities. And what did we decide on you may ask, a generic name that was probably derived from an existing company and an amateur looking logo (I found out much later that one of the doctors simply downloaded the logo of a hospital from Google and just inserted a dot and some color change here and there). Months went by and still I could not tell people what am I actually doing.

Red Flag #10 - Not putting the right effort in creating a memorable

name or even a simple but original logo can be a sign of amateur effort

into being a truly original brand.

Almost half a year later, we were finally a fully registered business entity. Next we had to assign roles and responsibilities. Unlike 99% of other business arrangements, which one would assume would have positions filled out by appropriately skilled individuals - 'N' and 'G' simply promoted themselves as Chairman and Managing Director, and assigned the rest 14 into other positions such as 3 financial officers, public relations, media, human resources, science officer, international executive representative (for those based overseas), some other roles I had no idea existed and myself as company secretary. The rationale for this division was not clear since none of us knew anything about what each role was about. I would assume that 'N' simply came up with this arrangement just on a whim without any actual expert consideration.

Generic definitions and expectations were handed out to each of these posts (probably from Wikipedia). Naturally many of us raised the issue about how the 'value' of each person's contribution would be remunerated since we all had equal shares i.e. why should 'N' be the chairman and why not another senior doctor in the team who has some concept of business strategy. The argument was that since it is the first venture, 'N' will start us off and in the next few projects we will circulate our roles accordingly. Being so naive many agreed and others simply stayed quiet[15].

Red Flag #11 - Never start a venture without knowing atleast what each

person in the team is supposed to do. Many chefs spoil the broth, therefore

a large group of amateurs cannot be suited for the tough roads ahead.

Initially everyone must do everything to make a positive outcome, as mentioned by 'N' and 'G'. Their unusual comraderie became quite apparent, it was quite obvious that they have regular conversations with each other before the general meeting with the rest of us. Nothing really out of

---

[15] It was apparent to those that remained silent or disinterested on day one, that they have already lost that investment since the goals were unclear and the team was made up of amateurs. Since most were quite well off from their regular jobs, there was no real incentive to recuperate the investment. It was seen as just a hobby.

the ordinary but this excessive need for privileged communication was a source of concern. Nonetheless we were already moving forward; papers done, names registered, company account opened and capital deposited. Now we have to talk about the actual purpose of going through all these obstacles.

'N' asked us in one of our group chats if anyone had a business proposal that they would like to spearhead. He wanted a detailed business plan that we could all work on to generate the kind of revenue that would allow all of us to retire very soon (according to N of course). Some may have mentioned opening a clinic, pharmacy dispensary or some medical school, but seeing the amount raised as capital such plans would never be feasible. Questions were raised as why the initial minimum investment was so low, what kind of business could ever be launched with such a relatively low amount. Even I was thinking that many businesses spend years collecting millions of dollars in funding just to get off the ground, and yet here we are with no business idea and not even an office.

Out of mental desperation I submitted a plan I had during my unemployment days, basically a type of stress management coaching consultancy. I figured it does not need a large investment, almost no overhead and it just needs people with the right connections to get clients. 'N' mentioned that the idea was fine but he had a better one. However now was not the right time to discuss his plan, we needed staff and office headquarters, since it was not professional to hold meetings in mobile phones and someone else's office lunchroom.

Red Flag #12 - Without knowing what exactly is your business idea

(customer, need, skills, resources, budgeting etc) you should not:

(a) form a company first

(b) blindly make a team just to raise money

(c) waste time thinking about having an office to sit

(d) make wild guesses on what kind of money is needed for an

imaginary project

We got divided into two teams, one was tasked with finding a suitable office space (why this early with no resources is beyond my imagination till date) and the other team was in charge of recruitment. According to 'N' and 'G' we needed an office manager and few marketing executives. What office will the manager manage and what exactly will they execute in the market was not clear, apparently they were needed to form the foundation of the company while we figure out the secret project details amongst ourselves.

Red Flag #13 - Do not hire a single salaried person unless their

exact purpose is defined as per skills needed to execute.

Every startup company must begin their operations with the

skills and resources at hand.

Out of eagerness I volunteered to use my own home as a staging ground for this recruitment drive. Living room as a waiting room and the dining room for the interview session. 'N' was very good at handing out vague orders, but he would never be clear on what is needed, especially in this extremely important stage - recruitment of company staff. I asked him what should be mentioned on the job description, expected responsibilities and salary structure. He had no idea, stating the excuse that since he is a non-resident US-Bangladeshi citizen he is unaware of the job market per se, therefore he *tasked* me with looking through previous job posts in online portals and just copy-paste them into our own job opening post. Being the eager little entrepreneur I jumped to this opportunity, searching through Bikroy.com and some Facebook job pages I made my own vacancy posts and set up the recruitment process.

Red Flag #14 - If someone is not clear on the basics of business

strategy, he/she will have no idea what kind of person is needed to

execute it. Simply recirculating the same job requirements that

never get filled by quality applicants will be your company's downfall.

An important stage I had almost forgotten to mention was our online presence. Companies must have a digital blueprint to showcase their uniqueness to the public eye. A company website and social media presence is the hallmark in effective marketing. Unfortunately this step was poorly executed from the beginning. There was a budget for the future office rent and staff salaries but apparently there was no way we can hire a professional web designer to make our website - therefore I had to do it. The absurdity of this task was beyond me, it was one thing that I among others have zero business experience, and now to learn coding and programming or whatever it was called to design a functional website. Where and how would I begin was mind boggling. I knew for a fact that 'N' was not a practicing physician in the US, he spent most of time working from home (that his wife owns) and he knew some basic concepts of IT anyway, so logically he should have created the website to begin with instead of asking a novice like me to create something out of nothing.

Red Flag #15 - Although taking a chance at learning new skills is

important, some essential tasks should not be left for

amateur experimentation. If a founder claims to have certain skills

but is unwilling to execute - this raises serious doubts about their

claims at their leadership

Arguing with 'N' was pointless as his true nature became apparent to everyone by now[16]. There

was a time when I even mentioned that if we had to take on so many responsibilities such as

company secretary (whatever that was), then we should atleast take some crash courses on things

like sales, negotiation, project management and so, using some of the capital funds as a skills

investment. 'N' was against it, his reasoning was that on-the-job experience was better and that

since he has 17+ years experience as a successful American entrepreneur, he would mentor us and

future staff individually. The sheer absurdity and pathetic lies still boils my blood as I type these

words.

---

[16] As you may have noticed there are more than a dozen red flags even before beginning the business, you may wonder if we were all naive sheep or just indifferent to our eventual failure. I can only speak on my own behalf and proclaim that the gross incompetence of 'N' and 'G' was crystal clear from long time ago, I remained steadfast to see it to the bitter end for the sole reason of learning about the practicality of business. I often surmised that learning about all these red flags was more cost-effective than joining an expensive MBA course. I was correct.

Red Flag#16 - Beware of people who are not interested in investing

in skills development for themselves or in others. Learning skills is

more important than raising funds.

Anyway just to avoid his annoying demeanor I started watching some youtube videos about web

design. It honestly was an uphill battle, the IT jargon was as complicated as medical jargon to a non-

medical person. I voiced my frustration to him stating that the time needed to even get an idea

about where to start would take many months, and honestly it was a waste of my time. Finally he

mentioned an online website builder named Wix where you could use their pre designed templates

to type in your content and just drag-drop pictures to customise. I had a look at it and it was an

amazing tool. No technical hassles, just use it like you would use powerpoint.

In a short time I filled out a fairly basic template with company name, mission statement, some

vague about us introduction, put our names into the meet the team page (only the proxies

ofcourse) and some fancy stock images. I paid for the basic membership to remove any ads and gave

it out for feedback. Days went by and nobody bothered to purchase the domain to host the

template, nobody volunteered to buy it stating that they do not have a credit card or that they are

afraid of online purchases etc. Finally one person did buy the *.com* domain name and we published

our primitive website onto it.

Red Flag #17 - Do not waste to learn a skill just to save a few dollars,

shop around for someone to do that small task for you in a short time

while you complete a more important function. Being so

cheap and uncoordinated in the early stage will affect your momentum

Still no word from any of the other members, nobody gave their feedback or any suggestions as to

how the website should look like. It became painfully apparent that the vast majority were, for a

lack of a better term, dinosaurs. Grossfully inept with technology, business behaviour, team

building or even common communication courtesy. I noticed certain mannerisms in

communication between certain people. Doctors who were from the public sector kept quiet most

of the time during the group chat sessions, occasionally spewing out some inane comment that had

nothing to do with the tasks at hand. Those with experience in the private sector or atleast had their

own private practice on the other hand were obsessed with how quickly they can recuperate their

investments and what is the project going to be and who will runt where is the office and on and

on, basically they were inpatient. I remember one conversation by one of the doctors who he his

own side gig (and we used his office for some meetings - he will me mentioned as "A"), he asked

why should anyone in their right mind give up a single minute from his private clinic to work on

this insane business proposition. (Clearly this guy has issues).

To which "*N*" replied, "*Name me a fruit that you can enjoy without caring for the tree, the soil needs to be watered frequently, and the low hanging fruits are not always the best ones, you have to be joking to make sacrifices to enjoy the true blessings that come later.*" One of those rare moments of wisdom I heard from him. But "*A*" was not the only dissenter, many others voiced their concerns. I was concerned in secret, but I had to persist to see it to the end, even though we have not even begun.

Red Flag #18 - In any team there will always be a naysayer. But a whole

group that questions your direction - that shows poor communication of

values and vision

After long last I completed the rough draft of the website, even paid for the voting from my own credit card that I had. It was very primitive, just generic content here and there. Did not really explain who or what we do - (just like "*N*") but atleast one part was out of h way, and atleast I learned a new skill. "*N*" wanted to rewrite the content to show visitors that we are an established company for many years, with existing clients and quite strangely - that we had a global presence with field offices in almost all continents (he told me to insert the names of some of is contacts who were based in those countries and refer to them as field office). I protested on the basis that it did not make sense and it looks suspicious, he strongly insisted and sai that since I was a novice I would not know that all new companies bend the truth a little just to look authentic. I complied reluctantly. Now I realised why his own so-called biotechnology firm website looks so amateurish and with zero social presence.

Red Flag #19 - He who claims authenticity seldom has any to begin with.

Our next crucial phase was the recruiting. We needed to look for office managers and marketing executives. Like I mentioned before, some basic job post description was posted in some Facebook groups. Within few days a barrage of applicants emailed us their CVs. Regarding the job requirements, understably a new business does not have enough capital to hire top tier applicants, however placing the bar so low that extremely fresh graduates from every single discipline (bpharm, mba, bba) and every university (some from outside Dhaka) bombarded the company email. Still we have no idea why will be their exact function. I was dreading the fact that we may hire totally incompetent dropouts just because they would be a cheap hire and worse dismiss a dedicated but forward thinking fresher. Why do we need staff so early in the business was a hotly debated topic. "N" refused to answer properly and "G" became his little lapdog. Oh well atleast I will get some amateur human resources experience.

Red Flag 20 - Hiring unnecessarily with no clear objectives to their

functions, and with no specific job requirements. This is sabotage.

I volunteered to use my apartment for the interview process. With so many applicants, and the reluctance of 11/15 "*directors*" to do any of the work it became an exhausting effort. Slowly we started contacting some who were filtered out by some non specific criteria based on the usual CV writings written by thousands of incompetent and unskilled youth (I came to realise the short supply of jobs is only one half of the coin, the immense number of pathetic low level graduates was the main cause of the poor international ranking of Bangladesh skill force). A cousin of mine who heard that *my company* was hiring an office manager, wanted to submit his application. I said sure he can send his CV by email and the group tasked with recruitment can assess him, obviously I could not sway the decision to him as that would be unfair. Those who have arranged to have a family member to work at their establishment will know that I was in for a colossal mistake.

Red Flag 20 - Amateur hiring personnel with no clear guidelines will end

up hiring amateur applicants. The blind leading the blind......

HBS INTERNATIONAL

OR, THE MANY WAYS TO KILL A COMPANY

Bad Leadership

Even today I am amazed that 16 people took almost a week to decide on the name of this venture.

Somebody said this, somebody said that. That sounded too hard. That name was already taken. But

finally the name was decided - HBS International was selected (or did "N" choose it for himself, I

am not sure, since he named himself Chairman of the Board). No slogan yet but a logo was hastily

put together by one of the doctors, ashamed to say that it was actually bootlegged from the logo of

an Indian hospital. Well what else can you expect from low level amateurs.

Job application deadlines were approaching. About a dozen profiles were selected arbitrarily i.e.

There was no clear guidelines on what qualities are we looking for, applicants were chosen based on

how desperate they seemed from their CV. I know not a very professional way to start a so-called

million dollar health company. As you guessed by now that this is what happens when a bunch of

people with zero business acumen are led by an eccentric (but naturally this was all apparent after a

few months in).

Lazy & Unmotivated CoFounders

The chosen profiles were divided into batches and forwarded to the doctors so that they can call each person individually for a kind of telephone interview. Needless to say there was already a great deal of resistance by the doctors - a) unwilling to do this task b) did not want to spare any time from their busy schedules c) paranoia about faint a bunch of kids d) there was no guideline on what is the job actually and how to gauge persons worth by a phone conversation. "*N*" as completely useless and clueless, even he did not give any framework to use, just told us to have a conversation and judge their conversation skills so to see if they have enough phone etiquette (whatever that was) and then finalise them for a physical interview at my place. It was total chaos. Only a handful of these lazy directors took the initiative (I kept wondering about that. What kind of doctors these people were, if this was their usual behaviour) But somehow a few dozen were chosen and scheduled to arrive over 2 days.

Unstable Entrepreneur Mindset

I have had some private chats with "*N*" about his approach and unusual work behaviour I raised many suggestions and criticisms by he was definitely not the type who wants to hear anyones point of view. Clearly this guy has some serious underlying mental issues. I am not a psychiatrist by training, but basics taught in medical school is enough to tell you the tell tale signs of narcissistic personality disorder. As I am not a writer by profession it is difficult for me to use the right words to describe what "*N*" looks like as a person, but why I can tell you is that he definitely does not carry himself as if he is a successful character in any way. Obviously he is rude, callous, disrespectful to seniors, arrogant, emotionally unstable and a host of other descriptions which is interestingly the character traits of may first time entrepreneurs. This was worrying to me, how can a long time entrepreneur who claims to have a global presence not know how to talk to people nor lead a team (even a remote team that is based in a messy third world city and he is calmly clicking away at his home office while his wife works)?

Red Flag #21 - A leader who cannot control his ego cannot control the destiny

of his team or company.

It was too late to turn back, I assumed. The investment cheque was already collected and deposited into the company bank account, company registration process was almost complete, job applicants were on their way, the other team who were looking for an office space found one and my social circle were finally pleased that I found a career path. It was times like these that I had a hard time to decide if I as having a panic attack or it was the thrill of entrepreneurship that propelled me forward. In all honesty it was just the simple fact that I was already exhausted and just wanted to start this damned project, whatever it was.

Time to start the interview.

Wrong team

Tables were set, living room furniture reorganised and email invites were sent out. Long day ahead indeed. Some of the applicants came early and sat around while only 4 founding directors bothered to show up. There was no script, there as no leading questions we could use because after all none of us had any idea what we are hiring these kids for. In haste we wrote down some weird questions related to the usual uninspired HR banter like what are your career goals, why do you want to work here, what is the expected salary, and in between we assessed their English vocabulary skills.

It was an absolute nightmare, I am not disparaging the majority of applicants - after all they were products of a pathetic and decomposing Bangladesh education system. The real losers were us actually, it seemed to me that we were just wasting each other's time pretending to be a big shot corporate leaders (who were using my dinner table as a board room because the office procurement team still were dragging their feet). "*N*" as on phone while his own personal proxy "*G*" was congratulating everyone on a job well done and busy typing up the minutes of meetings. Perhaps because the vast majority were public *servants* - an obsession with antique organisational behaviour was their only value i.e. The blind acceptance of an authority figure, somehow most (including myself) were just going along as we did not know any better.

Out of maybe 15 or so applicants we chose 2 people - a young kid named '*GS*' as a marketing executive and 'S' was chosen as an office manager, later on joined by a few more employees . All of us patted ourselves on the back and had our usual idiotic group chats and juvenile pep talks (with emojis).

Wrong Office

Few days later I received the coordinates for the new office space. It was in a commercial building called Nahar Plaza in Hatirpool. If you are a Dhaka resident I am sure you are well aware of this neighbourhood. In simple terms for my international readers, it is a commercialised cesspool. The lowest dregs of the knock-off wholesaler businessmen of Chinese products, especially sanitaryware, have their offices in this area. Narrow congested roads, tightly packed alleyways, beggars everywhere and the building itself is a joke.

Broken windows, overwhelming smell of cigarettes and urine, 1 out of 2 elevators work (sometimes and it only stops at a few floors), every shops sells low end garbage, the shop patrons are obviously from low socioeconomic and educational classes, poor lighting, no air conditioning (have to install your on ceiling fan), the garage was like a set from a horror movie (one of the directors claims that there is story about a woman's murder by the building owner and that the body is cemented into the walls - not surprising) and with no real surpass - our office space was an absolute pigsty. Even 'S' nearly vomited when he entered into the office through the rusted and padlocked metal doors.

What kind of low class low standard doctor would ever choose this scene as a place to start a healthcare business? Apparently the many low class low standard public servant trash that wants to make millions by spending peanuts. As you can see I have a lot of tension with many of these so called entrepreneur doctors in the board, you have to excuse me if I find it difficult to assess the credibility of a doctor who wears cheap sandals, smells of cigarettes, wears the uniform of a government office peon and can barely use simple professional courtesy. Many times I talked with my father about these issues, he insisted I just pack up and leave this mess, it was already doomed to failure by these amateurs. In my arrogance and ego I stayed and persisted. A sixth sense told me that I will learn a lot from this adverse experience.

The office space was a mess; no furniture, no lighting fixtures (torn out by the previous tenant out of rage or pettiness), small broken window for ventilation, both bathrooms in bad shape and I am sure there were other faults on top of that permeating smell of cigarettes and urine from the hallway. Definitely a lot of work to be done. 'S' was already contemplating to quit even though it was his first hour at 'work'. I took pictures and showed it to the directors messenger group. We needed an immediate plan on office maintenance and supplies. We had to sit down and discuss a cost-effective budget to make our premises livable.

Now you may ask why I did not take the initiative to look for a suitable office space from my end, truth is ofcourse I had. I combed through various online vacancies, I did find quite a few office leases in established neighborhoods with complimentary wifi and other amenities, the monthly charges were quite reasonable and some even negotiable if we shared with another company. But as usual it was shut down by 'N', supposedly it would not fit into the budget and we couldn't afford it from our raised capital. Over the next few months it became apparent that the amount we spent on rent, repairs, cleaning, office furniture, supplies, wifi and ofcourse the lost productivity while trying to work in such hot sweaty weather and from the daily load shedding; we could have easily afforded a more respectable and quality commercial space at ⅔ the amount we spent per month. So what was the rationale for choosing hatripool as the ideal location - as per '*N*' it was closest to Dhanmondi which has the highest concentration of medical and healthcare related institutions. I suppose he thinks the success of a venture relies on how physically close you are to your supposed clients. Very strange thinking indeed.

We tried our best to decrease the expected overhead costs of setting up this office, when I said '*we*' I actually meant to say me, as in '*I*' tried to figure out ways to get the necessary supplies to get on track as quickly and affordably as possible. I loaned my brother's PC to use as the office PC, donated a few chairs, a serving table, a small bookcase, lamp and other miscellaneous items[17].

Given the difficult circumstances, I kept telling myself that this was just a staging ground. Many top corporations started from much worse. But in retrospect, we spent way too much for such low quality standards. The stereotype of the low standard Bengali was much too apparent, even after all this hard work to set up a semi-decent office environment, the mere mention of the address was enough to disgust anyone.

---

[17] Other directors were too cheap to even consider. One made a big deal about him bringing some cheap plastic chairs all the way from his house.

Red Flag #22 - Setting up an office space unnecessarily bleeds into your savings very quickly. Most corporate offices are just for show, a young company should never be obsessed with having a corporate presence without even getting a foot into the market.

Wrong Human Resource Management

Slowly the office environment was taking shape, although there was no real difference between us and our neighboring offices who sell toilet commodes, cheap chinese tiles, discount Hajj tickets and who-knows-what-else. Both 'S' and 'GS' had to report for duty at the usual corporate timings at 6 days a week. 'N' assigned mundane tasks to them such as fixing the logo, making a slogan, designing brochures and posters. Imagine hours spent everyday playing around with online design softwares and pretending to be little children who play with crayons. What is the theme, what is our message, who are these brochures for, what is the content and so on. No answer and no direction from 'N' as usual. *"Just make a bunch of designs, write whatever that other healthcare companies write in their brochures and we'll just change and adapt them later"*, he said. This frustrating cycle of mind-numbing stupidity went on for almost a month, with no assistance or feedback from the other directors either. I was counting the days that we wasted on this idiocy, not only because it was a total waste of my skills, but also the fact that these two staff salaries are actually partly paid for by my shares investment - which is spent on them designing pretty little posters.

Red Flag #23 - You do not need salaried staff to waste time designing

mundane items for a company that does not exist nor does it even have a

goal. Many of these tasks can be outsourced to a freelancer communities;

who can do the same job at a much lower cost so that you can concentrate

on the business at hand.

WRONG HUMAN RESOURCE MANAGEMENT

They say people are the real untapped goldmine in any venture. I would say people management is

the true test of a leaders skills. Whatever that is written in the CVs is mostly lies, whatever reason

there is for hiring someone is often based on emotions instead of logic. In our case I could not argue

that we started off totally in the wrong direction, and worse already incurring expenses (office rent,

supplies, salaries) and quite frustrating to say, still no headway on the what of the company's

existence. 'N' really know how to put on a show, because all this while i was more a glory game

instead of a professional venture. There was no policy on human resource management, discipline,

staff motivation and penalty. I honestly lost count how many times "S" and "GS" used to have

verbal fights right in front of me, number of late days, frequent absenteeism and just in general a

total lack of work ethics. I know many of you will say something like they are just incompetent,

they are the product bad upbringing and substandard education and so on. Those may be true to a small extent, going back to the 80/20 rule, the reality is that HBS did not the kind of organisational structure to maintain nor enforce a strong work environment, occasionally things fell in order when 'G' used to come in with a commanding tone (due to his military background) but no one else took the initiative to maintain order - especially me since I inadvertently became too friendly with the staff (plus the familial connection) just makes it difficult to be objective. Staff behaviour was frequently brought up in the group chats but swept aside as being the "growing pains" of any new company.

Red Flag 24 - Never hire from your social circle, and do not treat your staff as family. When things turn sour, you will have to choose between an awkward confrontation or the eventual end of the company

WRONG USE OF COMPANY TIME

Time is more important than money. The day a single dollar or taka starts to bleed out of your own funds (office rent, subscriptions, salaries) you will never see it again, unless of course it is part of a larger more precise revenue-generating action. Ofcourse life and business is never that well constructed. However the essential rule of entrepreneurship (which we have violated) is to only officially begin your enterprise when a cash flow possibility is in your immediate future. In simple terms, there is a time to have your own office, to buy the corporate chair, the bossman table, 2-3 salaried staff to say 'Good morning. Sir' and all that bullshit, we began too soon and spent all that precious accountable weeks on the mundane. Most days were spent playing around with online design programs whilst waiting for company registration papers to get ready. The directors in charge of running behind the papers were too cheap to bribe the right officials to get the work done, in trying to save corruption money, we bled out from our funds by the second.

Red Flag #25 - TIme is like a river. Do not waste time trying to save pennies by not spending the big dollars. Bribe who you have to spend on quality hire on tasks you do not have time to learn and count the hours like you count the dollars slipping out of your own savings.

WRONG HIRING STRATEGY

As I talked about earlier, we had no clear vision or even had any idea about the project at hand ('*N*' was very paranoid about anyone trying to steal his precious billion dollar dream) there was no way to decide what kind of help was needed to implement the venture. What kind of person is needed to execute a task, measure its efficacy, handle financial gateways, customer relations, organisation of duties and many subtle but essential components of any professional project, and who exactly is well suited for these duties is crucial in the hiring process. There was no strategy whatsoever, as Bangladesh has a monumental graduate unemployment situation, we incorrectly assumed that anyone with such and such GPA, recommendations, notable university experience would be ideal to train up and execute our business strategy. Nothing can be more farther from reality.

The seeds of insubordination was coming out. Frequent lateness, absenteeism, toxic work environment, demotivated workforce and ofcourse demotivated me. As the other directors were lazy and uncooperative, 'G' and I would be the only ones who tried to maintain a regular presence to ensure some kind of professionalism. A separate messenger group was made to incorporate the staff - sadly this was just for show as many a time there was online absenteeism. A critical moment occurred where one of the staff displayed a very immature and unprovoked outburst whilst most of us were engaged in one of our group messenger sessions. Needless to say the termination was swift and without mercy.

Red Flag #26 - The people you hire reflect the standards you have for yourself. It is easy to blame the workers, but the majority of their behaviour is a reflection of the environment you have created for them. An institution without structure will automatically produce anarchy in your workers.

WRONG GROUP OF FOUNDERS

Many months later it became apparent the kind of people 'N' has attracted into this circus called HBS. Perhaps I should have mentioned this section much earlier but I wanted you to get a mental picture of the kind of circle that is involved in this already doomed venture. I have already mentioned more than 2 dozen red flags, you are probably wondering who would be so naive to continue given the situation (still we have not discussed the actual goal of HBS). The 16 of us were mostly from the medical background from various specialties, one is a retired army personnel, 2 were in a multinational corporation outside Dhaka and then we have the ringleader 'N' - nobody really knows what he does or what is his credibility as a so-called 17-year successful American physician entrepreneur. A third of us were either based outside Dhaka or even outside Bangladesh (like 'N'), most were fairly established middle to upper middle class professionals, some had families and property to maintain. Our main unifying trait was greed. No other explanation actually.

We were bought in by 'N' about the wonderful opportunity for financial prosperity from his regular speeches, supported ofcourse by his very close comrade 'G'. It was obvious that the only reason 'G' was so intimately involved in a healthcare objective even though he was not from this background, was that 'N' needed a spokesperson with an established/assumed reputation he could manipulate. As I type these chapters I often wish I was scammed out by a global pyramid scheme, it is somewhat redeemable in my circle to say I was robbed due to my naivety, but as is apparent I and others were just forced to paddle a sinking boat by an unstable high-school boy who was frustrated by his 'house-husband' role[18].

---

[18] In any society, a man who cannot provide and has to take pocket money from his wife is at the lowest levels of existence. Naturally there is an obsession with shiny subjective labels that have no weight or meaning behind them eg. Chairman of HBS.

Until now, I still have no idea why he would create a business team by people who have no clue about business structure whatsoever. Is it possible that someone with some experience would call out his inexperience and undermine his fragile ego?

Red Flag #27 - Organising a homogenous collection of business amateurs will only create an army of pupils who will agree with everything without question nor have any motivation for innovation. Complex tasks require the right mix of skill sets to lead each other to an effective outcome - sales, design, strategy, marketing, negotiation, resourcefulness and tact are just a few of the many roles needed.

THE WRONG PROJECT

AKA TRADE FAIR TO END ALL TRADE FAIRS

After a bunch of staff was hired after that incident, the logical thing would be to be cautious about the next hire, atleast to be more picky when choosing. That was not the case. According to '*N*' he will be unveiling the project (finally) within days and he needs an army of marketing people, to spread the word about all the amazing things HBS will do and can do with his guidance. We hired some people based on their desperation to get a job rather than any measurable skill sets that would define their supposed marketing ability[19]. Possible out of haste but nobody was in the mood to argue as it is obvious that any disagreement, criticism or alternative suggestion with '*N*' was immediately shut down - like a toddler would.

A large document was shared with us, highlighting the blueprint for a health expo; a once-in-a-lifetime golden opportunity to showcase the various health sector opportunities and institutions that are available in Bangladesh and the upcoming healthcare innovations from around the globe.

---

[19] The term marketing is often confused with sales. Both terms are completely different activities requiring completely different abilities and at times, opposite mindsets to execute properly. In Bangladesh there is a very low threshold on what a marketing personnel can do rather than should do.

Such a grand scheme would literally put us on the map (supposedly) and we would get offers left and right to help foreign investors to carry out various high end healthcare projects since we have so many health-related professionals in the mix. It would be a grand undertaking; not only involving top tier consultants and hospitals, but also Big Pharma giants, NGO's, health industry experts and so much more. So much more indeed.

What was the business angle we all asked. Quite simply 'N' said that we each stand to make literally millions (no specific currency was mentioned). He had done some kind of market research and said that most industry experts are very eager to participate and attend such trade fairs, if we created the right environment for influential people to move things forward, we could all reap the rewards of this innovative entrepreneurial endeavour[20]. Interesting proposition we all assumed.

A blueprint was laid out. We need to make a separate website, mailing lists, flyers, posters, guests lists and start hunting for appropriate venues to hold this global healthcare event. At long last an objective came out from all these delays, slowly people were trying to get involved somehow. Tasks and duties were laid out. A lot of work needed to be done.

---

[20] If you read the paragraph again you will notice that the question remained unanswered. There was no business angle.

RED FLAG ALPHA[21] - A plan with no tangible evidence of a need or a specific benefit needs to be further researched for relevance, or it should be totally scrapped. If a project has no real business model, it does not belong in business.

WRONG OUTSOURCING PROCESS

The HBS website had it own domain (bought by me ofcourse) so it was suggested to save the content that was there about the company, and replace it with the typical introduction and registration template that most top level exposition had. Interested participants could find it on Google, read the main attractions of the health expo and then sign up on the registration page. Most have the entire process in a single webpage. 'N' wanted a completely separate website for the event and a separate one for the company - citing that these were separate entities each requiring different marketing strategies. I insisted we hire a professional web developer to make the right design template, make it look more professionally appearing as it took so long for me to make the ultra basic HBS website, a functional event website will take me a longer period.

So again we sat down and held a job circular to hire a local freelance web developer. Many came with their CV's and proposals, it had not occurred to me that a wide range of fees were charged based on so many criteria. Naturally none of us tech savvy enough to understand such prerequisites, 'N' was supposed to be more knowledgeable about IT (since he works out of his US

---

[21] This is the essential red flag for any business. No clear business model - no evidence of sustainability. It will never be a profitable venture, rather it will just be an expensive hobby.

home office and supposedly has two tech staff based somewhere), he simply mentioned that freelancers cannot be entrusted with such an important topic and he wanted a developer to be on a sort of payroll so that here would be a stronger contractual agreement. As far as I knew this would not be effective as anyone hired as a consultant will delay the project delivery deadline as long as possible to maintain a regular income (as a consultant I knew this) and giving a salary is not a strong incentive for quality work - ofcourse 'N' would not hear any criticism of his supreme plan.

We hired a web developer who took a lot of convincing to work on this website, he initially asked for a large amount (realising that we were mostly middle-class professionals) and a product delivery of a few weeks at most. Somehow or the other he agreed to be on a retainer, work on the website, do some digital marketing, bring in some ads on the website and handle other tech support responsibilities. He did not agree based on the meagre payment, rather it was because he sensed that I was the only person having enough sense to realise the outdated mannerisms of the other directors - maybe he had pity on me in this troubling time.

The work went on very slowly, many times it was difficult to get him on the phone. There were many mistakes and issues with the website design, which he took many days to fix (even though he said he was an expert) and the only way to make any logical progress was if I invited to stay over at my place while I physically supervised the coding and construction of each page throughout the night. It was during these times that I realised what a freelancer actually does, and why there is often a large discrepancy in quality outputs on various projects. A freelancer is like a *ronin* (a samurai without a sensei-master) there is great freedom in hours worked and earnings especially on the global market. There is another freedom involved; there is freedom to remain in a constant state of financial turmoil unless you have continuous high income projects lined up from multiple clients from all timezones.

This explains why he took so long to edit any minor details in the website, and why it was shaping up to be quite amateurish (even by my standards). The reality was that he had multiple simultaneous projects worth 10 times more than the meagre salary we offered him, so by economic terms he spent more time and personal effort on those tasks - and our agreement was just a low level side hustle. Stands to reason why a few days later we were contacted by a legal representative of a local professional photographer for copyright infringement of a photo he inserted from Google images, and even more embarrassingly - our unsecured website was spammed by a pornographic website!

As Company Secretary I did what I always did, just clean up the mess of the overwhelming HBS failures (more like a secretary it seems). Website was scrapped and I had to relearn some of the IT skills in creating event-based web designs. Thankfully there were some ready made template available, they were not cheap but under the circumstances it had to do.

Red Flag #28 - Never bring an experienced freelancer to do high quality

salaried work for very low pay. You get what you pay for, cheap product

output for cheap income.

WRONG PLATFORM

In a way the value of a successful event depends on the scale of the audience. And if you want a

high caliber audience you obviously need a high value venue. We spent a few weeks back and forth

between various high end hotels and community centers to use as the official venue space for our

event. They were shockingly expensive as they were lavish. For most medical or healthcare-based

events, such venues were frequently hired by experienced event management firms sponsored by

major pharmaceutical corporations. This would hardly be possible for a tiny group of amateur

physician entrepreneurs.

We finalised our venue choice down to 4 top tier locations - frequented by politicians, ambassadors

and other high value persons. We went through each one, assessed their facilities, location, previous

experiences with conferences but since we ourselves had no predetermined budget, there was no

way we could decide how big we wanted our event to be. Some were fully booked during the

winter seasons for various conferences and weddings, others were perfect except for a crucial detail.

If a government sponsored was to take place, the venue had to be vacated without notice and without refund. This was a very worrying development.

We had to make a crucial decision to postpone for the year after when demand and prices would go down, or to make a risky choice for an expensive choice. In our excitement we foolheartedly chose to go ahead with our winter event at a very lavish location[22]. We had to invest a very large portion of the raised capital just to make a reservation. And so we did.

This venue hire was chosen, in spite of nearly exhausting our capital, so that it would be a strong motivating force to make sure we make this event successful, and profitable. In reality we had committed the cardinal rule for first time entrepreneurs - we bit off more than we could chew.

Red Flag #29- If this is your first business venture, start small start cheap so you can afford it when things go bad. And do not obsess about over the top displays of marketing when you have no ounce of market credibility.

---

[22] For the sake of professional courtesy, various organisations and locations will remain anonymous.

PRIMITIVE MARKETING METHODOLOGY

- Unskilled marketing team

Placing a new venture into the market - local or global, requires intensive brand creation, marketing resources and overall branding strategy. All very high end ambitions. There is an old saying that *'if you build it - people will come'*. It is a complete myth. Even if you build a gigantic stadium, mall, zoo, hospital or whatever just the visual presence has no meaning unless there is an overlying 'value' to your customer (no matter how intangible, subjective or unmeasurable). I can guarantee that in my intense experience with HBS - I can tell you the many ways <u>NOT</u> to do marketing in 2017 and onwards.

First of many mistakes we had committed was the wrong hire as I highlighted previously. Marketing is in reality not something that can be certified unless that person can individually carry out an act (such as in design, merchandise production, content creation) and then measure the direct engagement response from a population. Due to the vague definitions of this *art*, there are many fake experts. Vast majority of marketing executives and departments lack any gram of imagination or intuitive initiative. Marketing strategy that we followed as per the primitive and outdated standards of '*N*' and many of the senior directors - was based on trends set in 1970's apparently.

We wasted almost 4-5 months and thousands of dollars on mediocre poster designs, amateur brochure outlines, TV ad tickers[23], low quality TV interviews featuring 'N' only, a poorly made radio broadcast and the online digital marketing approach was by far the worst. In all this outdated approach one would wonder who would go ahead with such an expensive waste of poor marketing styles. If you had seen some of the finalised poster designs you would realise that the main decision-makers have no design sense, no concept of branding trends and in my own assessment, most of the shareholders/directors were from the public sector which is without surprise have no standard quality to maintain in many cases (grammatical errors, poor choice of colors, generic stock images).

I can only imagine the financial catastrophe if we had listened to 'N' when he wanted to rent a few billboards in Dhaka, the sheer absurdity given our rapidly decreasing bank account. It was clear to everyone that by far the biggest barrier between 'N' and the rest of the team was the total disconnect in values and culture. Such outlandish marketing methods are possible in the US, maybe due to the large economic market there is room for negotiation and price ranges - but here in Dhaka such strategies are not cost-effective. Or in my opinion it was the output of low self esteem, narcissistic personality disorder and just need to show off like many pretend entrepreneurs[24].

---

[23] Tk12,000 on 2.3 seconds of display time for a small strip of advertisement text to appear during a news broadcast for an obscure TV channel!
[24] Wantrepreneurs

Red Flag #30 - If you do not know what exactly you are selling, you will never figure who should see your posters, flyers, banners and others. Spending thousands of dollars to decorate the skyline is an act of madness (from a practical marketing position)

PRIMITIVE MARKETING METHODOLOGY

- Poor social media approach

Beyond the poorly thought out process above, our digital marketing strategy was planned out by people who barely know how to use Google. We created social media profiles for the company - but as we had no tangible product or services, there was no scope for original content - as far as we knew back then. Our Facebook activities were isolated to reposting some health related topics from other sites and posts. We had to beg people to Like our page as there was no content to attract people there anyway. Ofcourse hiring even a semi-professional Digital Marketing person was never considered, 'N' simply insisted that everyone just keep sharing whatever was re-posted into the amateurish FB page, in the hopes that someone's distant FB connection will be intrigued enough to be an investor or something vague.

There was no agreed upon marketing budget either, even one of the senior directors who atleast knew something about media activities had frequent arguments with the group. Without a financial projection or any type of cost analysis, we were simply executing all types of outdated advertising methods with no tangible proof that anyone of interest was even looking at them. Return of investment was close to zero and there was no way that any of us was measuring our bleeding bank accounts. As the 'N' was cheap and stubborn, 'G' and other seniors had no idea what was marketing and I had no clue about SEO, Adwords, AdSense etc, there was no way the broader public could know or even understand what HBS was about. The staff that we had was in no form or shape related to marketing as I told you before, therefore they knew even less about Social Media marketing. The sad part is that our venture was turning out to be the same kind of low-class chaotic grocery store - no order, no audit, no budget, no oversight.

> **Red Flag #31 - Poor business process stems from poor budgeting. It is all about the margins first, then about impact. You cannot measure ROI if there is no expert-oriented method to devise a budget as a measure of your marketing strategy.**

PRIMITIVE MARKETING METHODOLOGY

- Obsession with outdated practices

In business, and in life, there really is no right or wrong way to do things. The only way to measure the value of an action is by its return. As amateurs we can use our inexperience and faults as a valuable learning tool. If a strategy does not yield the expected results the idea is to learn, adapt and try something else, in design methodology this concept can be summarised as PDSA (Plan Do Study Act) in a continuous cycle until you get what you wanted. So what did HBS do wrong.

True that none of us know the rules of entrepreneurship; we did not raise enough capital, our mission strategy was not clear and the long list of issues I have told you so far; but one would assume that a team of high level professionals would know the basics of learning from mistakes. After all, a successful medical career is based on learning the mistakes of wrong doses and interventions!

Our poor methodology is based on these failings. We had no path to educating ourselves. We were led by an unstable and inflexible amateur. Our understandings were based on outdated trends of a previous generation. An unmotivated and unimaginative staff that had no real stake in the venture, except the regular paycheck and the overwhelming deficiency of a growth mindset.

Sending boring emails to people who do not open emails, or know how to use it. Scripted sales calls with no value proposition behind them. Zero attention to digital marketing as a viable tool instead of a sideshow application. Most of us knew these were not working, atleast not here in Dhaka. 'N' and 'G' who had pretty much hijacked the group kept holding on to this status quo as if their lives depended on it. Without much surprise we failed to convert anyone to join us in any shape or form.

Perhaps the most expensive marketing mistake we made so far was to rely on a mass marketing poster campaign i.e. blanket the city in thousands of event posters. The design was mediocre, too many texts, cartoonish font, unclear who we actually wanted to see the posters and the biggest obstacle is there is now way to measure their effectivity of attendance until the actual event day. We spent thousands of taka, many days to print them, hire people to stick them on various locations and then the next day to see *every* single poster get ripped out[25].

So much for million dollar ideas.

---

[25] Vagrants use them as bedsheet covers and unsolicited postering in low class areas get torn out by miscreants if they are not bribed prior to placing them.

Red Flag #32 - Beware of a single team member, especially the founder, who has a rigid-fixed mindset. The market does not care about your beliefs or feelings. Either you evolve or you become erased.

EVERYTHING COMES DOWN TO SALES

(and who is selling)

Events are a powerful tool for highlighting the value and potential influence of an organiser or organisation. The ability to gather people under the banner of a common interest, and make an impact on them is a very profitable marketing venture. Big Pharma corporations invest heavily in arranging conferences with top tier professionals, in lavish settings, so as to have a strong industry presence. HBS wanted to bank on this idea as well. The marketing process is very difficult without the endorsement of an influential third party; namely sponsorship by major corporations, therefore the overall business outline relies on utilising the raised capital from sponsorships to create enough of a '*buzz*'. Reaching out to these corporations and convincing them the value of their investment with us was the central goal of the sales strategy.

Over the course of several months after we finally started our project, and while we faced all those obstacles (website fails, staff fails, leadership fails etc), an extensive mailing list and guest list was compiled from phone books and web searches. The idea was to reach out to them and bring them on as exclusive sponsors for our event. In return for an opportunity to showcase their brand image to a large gathering of healthcare-related audience members.

The sponsorship agenda was divided into tiers (bronze, gold, platinum) each with various 'benefits' (such as scale and channel of advertising available) and their corresponding prices[26]. Nobody in the

[26] The many obstacles that a company (whether it be products or services) faces during its birth, is how the market places a value on it. At the end of the day it all comes down to an acceptable price that the target market is willing to pay.

team had any clear idea about how much we should raise from sponsorship in the long run, obviously the massive venue hire has to be covered, but without a budget there was no way to judge how much money to raise and the scale of decorations and event management required, which in Catch-22 fashion goes back to costs. Based on rudimentary assumptions we placed a massive price tag on each of the sponsorship tiers - in the hopes that only large established corporations would be able to afford it. With the pathetic marketing strategy, using our absurd branding, you have rightly guessed that nobody in their right mind took our offering seriously. We had downgraded the prices almost every two weeks just to atleast sound affordable to even local based healthcare industries (even those importing hospital supplies). Almost everyday that I came to the office to supervise the 'marketing executives', the same cycle of rejection took place day in and day out:

1. Read the mailing list
2. Find a number and email
3. Email our event proposition (which was too long and boring)
4. Call the number
5. If someone picks up they give a memorised sales pitch (crafted by N)
6. If call lasts longer than 10s they gave more information
7. Call hanged up
8. Email them again - also fax[27] if possible
9. Call back after 2 weeks (in case they change their minds)
10. Repeat.....

Weeks of frustrations from these 'cold calls and cold emails' were occasionally improved by 'hot leads' like they say in marketing, the ratio was 500:1 conversion. Sometimes curious professionals

---

[27] Yes - when you have such an out-of-touch amateur leadership this is the kind of 1970's business trend you would follow.......

would inquire a little more about our event strategy, guest lists, venue and other things before circling back on the sponsorship pricing tiers. As expected, without a solid pre-existing brand (I am sure they saw the absence of a credible online presence) it was difficult to translate the value of our efforts into a price tag.

From another point of view, the human aspect of the sales strategy is the main ingredient. There is a popular American saying about the skills of a successful salesman, where he could quite literally 'sell snow to an eskimo'. These skills are sometimes inherited, some trained and some acquired through years of personal mindset development. If you could recall the first of many conversations I had with 'N' about investing some of the HBS capital on business skills development - and how it was passed over, well now the most essential skill set is severely deficient in us (not only in the staff we hired but also in the active directors who are actually doing anything about this project).

Following up on these hot leads required some of the staff members to physically go to their offices for a short introduction and motivation of key persons there. There were a few days where even I approached some of them to lend some professional credibility to these meetings. In reality none of us displayed the kind of 'sales persona' to really convince them to agree to our project. The staff were not only very young but obviously had no background in sales,I was in a much worse standing. Many a time I had gone to these meetings in poor attire (such as a simple shirt and low priced shoes), somewhat unkempt and quite frankly my Bangla was terrible due to the absence of local interactions for many years.

The cumulative output was zero in all these interactions. No impact. No sales. No sponsors. The deadline for the event was coming dangerously close, hardly 2-3 months - and worse the venue offices were inquiring about when we would complete the next round of payments as agreed upon. Tensions were, there were many who were prepared to not only bail out but also put a class action lawsuit on 'N' for his poor management techniques. 'G' was trying his best to stir up nationalistic pride. Ofcourse I was completely demoralised by now.

In flashbacks to the many days I spent coming to the office to cover the shifts of lazy directors who did not make an effort, the amount of money spent on web development, petrol costs going back and forth and naturally the personal sacrificed time for this absurd venture; I reiterated that since all other costs were non-refundable, I refused to back down. Mailing lists and guest lists were forwarded. It was the point of no return, therefore I wanted to continue onwards with the event in whatever fashion - even under ridicule or impending financial ruin. I remember I told 'N' that everyone else can give up and hide, I would run the whole event myself and turn it into some kind of discussion panel or something. My egotistic rant has officially exposed someone else's even bigger more unstable ego - 'N'. It seems he had found the passion to continue as our diligent leader and resumed command of this sinking ship. I had correctly foreseen an embarrassingly public display of juvenile ego.

Red Flag #33 - Inability to sell is a marker of doom. What you sell is not as important as the ability to sell. If a business has no model to systematically create the demand for something, identify the right customer, at the right time, with the right team and of course at the right prices.....

the end is guaranteed.

UNCLEAR VISION = UNCLEAR THEME

To be brutally honest, till date I still have no idea what we wanted to do back then. I still have no idea what HBS was all about. So many lofty dreams and inflated egos, there is no way I can explain to you what was the idea or innovation we desperately wanted to create. You can ignore the business angle, as there are many inventors who atleast tried to introduce their brainchild to the wider world, but we as a group of professionals led by '*N*' were blindly sailing in the storm.

We could not decide on the actual theme of the medical expo. Was it about medical careers, some new medical device, healthcare policy, some new disease management or what? 'N' said yes. Yes to all of this. It would be a grand medical AND healthcare event that will cover everything and will feature everyone. This was absolute rubbish.

No wonder we could not be united as a team. No wonder the staff had no idea how to respond to customer queries. No wonder we could not target our marketing strategy to the right audience. Another failing was the speaker segment. If there was no agreed upon event theme, I had no guidance on what type of speaker should I invite, and what the speech will be about.

Through various connections I did reach out to several notable medical experts, based in Dhaka and abroad, to come down to our event for a speaker session. As a recent graduate of Global Health, I atleast mentioned that the speaker could touch upon health related trends. Believe me they were just as confused, but like any career professional, a stage is a stage. Any type of public event exposure increases their social value. Even if we could not reimburse them, atleast we assured them of a large enough crowd.

Red Flag #34 - If nobody except the 'founder' knows what it is all about then that is a primary failure in communication skills.

REMOTE CONTROL DOES NOT GUARANTEE REMOTE WORK

As I had mentioned, the shareholders or directors were scattered around.'N' was in USA - handing out orders and whatnot via messenger, my father was in Kuwait, another doctor is based in Saudi Arabia, a few were based around Bangladesh (Rangpur, Sylhet, CHittagong), the rest were in and around Dhaka city. The irony was that those physically present in DHaka, or were even in close proximity to HBS office - were the least bit bothered to give a hand to our operations.

Both 'N' and 'G' tried to rile up some support for our corporate cause, spewing out pseudo-motivation speeches to atleast show up and supervise the staff - beside me. The constant and daily commute from Gulshan to Hatirpool was taking its toll on me, physically (massive weight gain) and ofcourse the financial toll on petrol. I had taken out a sum from the capital funds which was earmarked for miscellaneous expenses - naturally as I was not working and had no personal income, plus I was incurring most of the daily expenses on futile and ,quite honestly, tedious managerial legwork - I saw it fit that I should at least me reimbursed for this 'sacrifice'. Those two were deeply resistant to that, citing the usual motivational BS and need for personal sacrifices and so on.

In that moment I realised what I had really gotten myself into. I had bought shares to buy myself a peon's job, quite literally. Instead of the assumed Company Secretary, I was in reality the *company's secretary*. And that too unpaid.

I saw it was time for a break. I took 2 weeks off and silenced my phone and the messenger alerts. These old guys need to know their place.

After a few missed calls I managed to negotiate a small stipend payment to cover my petrol costs atleast. And placed invoices for all overlying costs I had incurred into the company accounts.

Red Flag #35 - Do not join a startup on sweat equity - when all they do is make you sweat without pay. Know your worth, before *wantrepreneurs* realise they got themselves a peon who paid to get work.

AVOIDING CORPORATE FRAUD

Being part of an upcoming business is a wake up call to so many realities and choices that are 100%

dependant on your own moral compass. Some start a business out of desperation or boredom. And

some start it to get rich quick. Honestly there is nothing wrong with these beliefs. Each to his own

as they say in America. But one thing I learned during my USA tour; is that the psychotic pursuit to

give false promises for that quick cash is a sure way to land you in hot water.

We had been sending hundreds of cold emails to various people and organisations to promote HBS

and to interest them as a potential participant in our project, and nobody replied as usual. One

evening I was going through the company email and came upon a strange message. Apparently it

was a request from a non-profit organisation that is building a rural primary care and emergency

ambulance system, using specially made motorcycles and other equipment. I assumed there was a

miscommunication or some confusion, probably someone had visited our strange company

website and thought that HBS was some kind of healthcare logistics and medical equipment

supplier. Honest mistake, it happens, no big deal. I replied that we are unable to fulfill that large order as that infrastructure is not in our capacity at the moment and other details. And of course to keep in contact for future associations.

The next day 'G' came down to the office as any other routine visit to see the progress (or lack) of the marketing team. We had a side conversation about that email that came yesterday. I responded that it was obviously a mistake and that there was no way we can procure and transport thousands of motorcycles, bandages, oxygen tanks and other medical equipment. From his blank expression I sensed underneath he must have had a sinister conversation with 'N' that this naive wannabe entrepreneur (me) just foiled their change at a multimillion dollar deal - because of a simple apology email. I conveyed very clearly that this person wrongly assumed that we can fulfill that order in such short notice and of that conditions, where there was not a single proof of any logistic capacity to do so. 'G' said that 'N' promised that NGO that we can provide these items easily since we have so many doctors in our shareholder team that they would all come together and use their networks to make that deal come true. I laughed so hard on his face. We barely have an office bathroom and 'N' thinks we can outfit a million dollar international NGO deal? This topic was never spoken of again, but a week later 'N' did ask for privileged access to the email - which I had since I set up the mailbox with my own credit card. I told him that to reimburse me the dollars I had already spent and to give his (or his wife's) credit information to transfer ownership. He replied no need.

I have no idea what game these old dinosaurs wanted to play. Since both were beyond middle aged with no job, I slowly realised how the allure of quick cash was to them. Like I mentioned, everyone can have the desire to defraud any faceless organisation - but not using the reputation of

hardworking doctors. I have to be careful around these fake entrepreneurs.

RED FLAG ALPHA - Never ever give total access to company accounts, databases and public communication channels to a single person.

(Especially if they have antisocial tendencies.)

WRONG TEAM MOTIVATION APPROACH

Everyone was demoralised. Many stopped attending the online group meetings. Accusations of incompetence were expressed to us, the 3-4 active directors by people who were obsessed with trying to recuperate the meagre investment they had made, but the bulk of the anger was towards 'N' and 'G'. Failure and ruin was imminent. Not a single entity in the whole of Dhaka was interested in our venture. As amateurs we blamed the entire Bengali population for being too illiterate to understand the wonderful value and importance of HBS. This was just the outcry of desperation, of course nobody wanted to confess their inadequacies.

All of a sudden a post was made by 'N' saying that he is flying in all the way from the USA to have an emergency group meeting with us. Hurriedly we booked a separate corner in a fly and maggot infested restaurant in the same building of our office (no idea why 'G' would choose this disgusting dump) and I made a few slides on the computer. 'G' was more excited than all of us combined, he was in complete military mode to make sure this meeting goes in tip top fashion, with the right images, with the right words in each slide and various over the top arrangements.

I wish there were enough words in my vocabulary to describe this sham meeting. It was an absolute waste of time. There were some directors who flew in from outside Dhaka to attend - possible just as a get together if nothing else. Many, including myself, got food poisoning from the overpriced filth that they served (I paid for it as the company cheque for the month was denied due to incorrect spellings). 'N' clearly displayed the traits of a narcissistic child - with 'G' as his personal aide (or enabler).

Sure there was some pep talk here and there. The sleeping directors were reminded of the project details and goals just to keep everyone on the same page - except when the really important questions were raised, namely the business model. 'N' responded like a high school loser who is caught cheating or something. He would not allow anyone to comment on the financial futility of it all. Most just ignored his ramblings and just left after the fiasco. I wish I had left too, but my amateur entrepreneur ego held on for that slight chance of success.

Red Flag #35 - Shallow charm, quick to anger when confronted, superficial courtesy, selfish obsession, lack of teamwork skills - are all traits of a psychopath.

ATLAST SOME GOOD NEWS!

So far you have been reading all the negative outputs, negative experiences and negative outlook of entrepreneurship. At this moment I can atleast tell you about the brief moments of a silver lining after all this hardship. The only person who has actually executed the *'hustle'* mode of a typical entrepreneur was '*G*'. Despite his personality quirks, patriotic zeal, rigid adherence to conformity and strange brotherly attachment to '*N*' (in spite of his incompetence as a leader); he had really sweated to gather and follow up with each and every top level lead. Though his diligence we actually managed to get a dozen companies to sponsor us, a few were *pro bono*[28] just to use their brand name, but the other half actually deposited the cheques to our company accounts. We were finally in the green, atlast there was enough capital to pay the next installment for the venue hire, we could negotiate the fees for the event management company and start production for banners, posters, crests and other miscellaneous merchandise.

I had given the recent turn of events, some inner thoughts in those brief moments of rest that I had. I came to realise why so many managing directors of almost every major Bangladeshi corporation

---

[28] free

(even private hospitals) had a military background. Where they fell short on business persona or tact, their hard wired discipline was the real company asset. Through their commanding presence, entire teams would fall in line (I have seen this amongst our small staff too). And ofcourse everyone automatically respects a retired army personnel, this brotherhood carries on into civilian life as well. So it stands to reason that the only reason why we managed to get partnership/sponsorship deals with this small group of companies; had absolutely nothing to do with our branding strategy - it was all on *'brand-G'*. *'N'* knew this and was able to motivate or manipulate his school friend so he can ride on his credibility.

You can call it sneaky, unethical or whatever. In business it is always about the bottom line, the endgame, the margins. As an outsider, sometimes you need to ride on the coat-tails of an established and credible character so others will even look at you. Think of it as authenticity by association. I am sure you know plenty of your social circle who act this way. And you already have an impression about this type of character. As necessary as it is to get things going, people are not stupid. Reality exposes all faults and your shallow reputation will decrease even more when your incompetence shows through, and the public image of your puppet gets ruined as well.

Even after all this, I do not have any ill will towards *'G'*. He truly is an honorable man. He was a close friend of my dear father. And in a way I do sincerely respect him for his efforts and personal sacrifices he made for HBS. As he was retiring from service when we were introduced to 'N', I understand that the sudden change to the chaos of civilian life caused him to accept the partnership from any source.

The drowning man will grab onto any help......just like I did.

Red Flag #36 - Beware the allure of authenticity by association.

POWER CORRUPTS EVERYTHING

We were counting the days before we finally unveiled our event. Time was slipping away. The pressure was reaching boiling point for the few that actually gave a damn and were trying their level best to see it through. 'N' decided to come down to Dhaka early to set up a press release for the event. Perhaps to increase the marketing angle and get more publicity for HBS and whatever future lies ahead. At breakneck speed we jumped around to get the big hall at the Dhaka Press club, arrange snacks and bribes for the journalistic scum that are usually scavenging around.

'N' came down and just took over the whole operations and went full 180 degrees on all last minute designs. Rewrote the opening ceremony scripts, cancelled the brief rehearsal we planned at the venue and just took my car to go around for his own whims. Supposedly he went to a few local TV channels to give a quick introduction interview (they were pathetic) and for the strangest reason he had an appointment with the Embassy of Myanmar(?). This was during the height of the Rohingya massacres and public outcry - and here is an unemployed American-Bangladeshi *want*repreneur (pretend entrepreneur) walking into the Myanmar Embassy to talk business with HBS? Madness or not I was just too busy dealing with the event management company to spare a thought.

Next day we arranged the setup for the press release, 2 days left for the event (and unveiling of HBS to the public). A large crowd of local journalists gathered (lots of free food and spare change floating around) and it was time to give the opening speech. 'G' started off with the high praise high patriotic speeches to warm up the crowd and get the photo clicks. Surprisingly 4 of the other silent directors who in the entire 6-7 months of the project planning period, only came a few times, dressed up to sit in front of all those cameras[29]. Now it was time for the Chairman, Founder and CEO of HBS (and apparently his other US company as well), 'N' took the spotlight and took our breath away at the same time.

There was never a time that I really wished for a riot or a fire alarm to go off, then the entire time 'N' had his mouth open for the press release. The look of confusion on the journalists' faces was so heartbreaking, there was no way anyone could understand what on earth a bunch of doctors and a retired army personnel was doing or was trying to do with this event. There was no mention of a product release or any sort of health-related service that would be given in the event. One of the journalists thought we were opening a hospital or something. I am not sure of any digital or print copy that may exist of this press meeting, but you can clearly see my face is down and eyes closed, from exhaustion and embarrassment.

When an unstable personality is pushed to a corner and his fragile ego/vision is questioned (as it happened when a well-known female journalists confronted N), the mind reaches into the

---

[29] Now you know the losers I had to be around

emotional memory banks to come up with a response. It did not work. Honestly I cannot repeat the garbage that was spewed out of his mouth - I may have repressed that memory as it happens with any trauma. I do remember quickly writing down on a piece of paper to give to 'G' to immediately tell 'N' to shut up and change the subject.

The press release was thankfully over, I wasted no time to leave immediately to avoid further loss of the little reputation I had, and there was a mountain of work left as we still did not finalise the design, print the merchandise or even finish the script for the emcee. I let those two handle the scavenger journalists. I was at breaking point with all this rubbish behaviour.

Red Flag #37 - Press releases have no measurable ROI. They are a poor attempt at expensive branding, it only inflates the ego. And if you are going to do a press release, invest in a PR session beforehand.

CHAOS BEFORE THE STORM

Less than 1 day left before our event. Phones ringing every minute to confirm venue, stall designs, catering orders, speaker timeslots, speech topic edits the list goes on. Staff were on their hustle mode as well, even our small volunteer group was on the go. 4 senior directors came down to give whatever support they could, for a brief moment we actually thought we could pull it off. Engines were on full speed, the wheels were turning. HBS was trending online too.

And then the founder of HBS exposed his tiny fragile ego to everyone in full view.

I was in the other room fixing up the speaker timeslots as per request of the speakers, which 'N' kept changing so that he can have more stage time for his own facetime. The 5 of them went to the small room we had in the side as a meeting room. I did not hear what went on but his voice was very high and sounded like an animal. The directors left disgusted. This was not a good sign.

He burst in, told everyone to stop what they were doing and to look at him. In a bounding voice he proclaimed himself the visionary founder of a million dollar American biotech firm[30] and now HBS. All must follow his orders no matter what, from here on out all decisions must go through him. Fine.

What font do we use?

What colour filter for the stage lights?

How wide should the banners be?

Catering by whom?

How many brochures to print?

What merchandise do we give the speakers?

What if a speaker cancels, how to fill the deadtime?

The videographer wants more money....

7 Shareholders want to quit now after his outburst, maybe 1 will sue him......

He started to sweat more than us. Ofcourse we had no air conditioning, but this was because of his first taste of real founder responsibility. Anyone can claim a title, but the ability to delegate to an effective and responsible team, clear precise directions, is the true measure of a founder's value. 'N' was a complete zero - it was painfully obvious (painful for him).

---

[30] Arroyo Research, Inc. - Google maps shows it as a residential building - maybe his bedroom

Less than 10 hours left before the venue hall opens. One group went to an all night print shop to print out a set of brochures, posters, crests, pins and other miscellaneous merchandise (we forwarded whatever design template was available without waiting for anyone). Another group (me included) went off to the venue to oversee stall preparations. No sleep no water for 2 days straight.

'*N*' took '*G*'s car to head back to his hotel so he could rest for *his big day.*
'*G*' was abandoned back at the office, he called me to drop him at his home as he did not know how to use the Uber app.

Wonderful world of entrepreneurship.

Red Flag #38 - Pressure turns stone to dust, or coal to diamond. Entrepreneurial teams have to wear multiple hats at different times. Titles mean nothing in the real world, if someone cannot deliver outputs under tension, then that person is wearing the wrong hat.

THE WORST MEDICAL CONFERENCE IN THE WORLD

(AKA HEALTHCARE, PHARMACEUTICALS & BIOTECH TRADE FAIR 2017)

I wore my brand new suit.

Arranged the banners across the venue building, across the walkway, across the stage

Set up the posters, registration desk, presentation computer, flowers, gifts etc.

Gave a pep talk to the emcee, volunteers, staff and others

Slowly some audience members starting coming in. The online registration showed about 80 attendees but I was hoping 5 times more would come down atleast. Many of the representatives of the sponsor companies complained about giving them the wrong stall dimensions, spelling mistakes and giving them the wrong stall locations as per layout designs. I was jumping around left and right to fix up all these issues. Eminent speakers came down, especially government officials and national professors (all mentors of my parents). The game is on.

Opening ceremony started. Emcee did her best given the fact that there was no pre-event rehearsal (as per 'N') and at the last minute the script was changed again (by 'N') - it was full of praise and glory for the great and wonderful physician entrepreneur 'N' and his revolutionary vision to change the entire country, and soon the world. 'G' went on stage and gave quite a brilliant speech (he was a great orator) and I multi-tasked at the computer table arranging the slides and other tasks. In a glimpse I saw the emcee returning to her seat beside me. She was trying to hold back her tears and was visibly shaking. I asked what happened. Was it because I was a little rushed and could not speak earlier. She said no. After the first few speeches her father came and took her outside. From one of the volunteers who introduced her to us, I later found out that 'N' had verbally abused for not reading the script correctly and had insulted her offstage. The entire audience saw her leave, crying.

Not a good start.

First few speeches went on fairly well. I had no idea at the time what was going on in the other room, where we had the stalls. I do not recall the names of all the companies that signed up; there were 3 hospitals, 2 local health non-profit organisations, a complementary medicine institution, 4 empty stalls (the sponsors did not bother to show up) and smack in the middle was HBS and 'N's company. I managed to peak in while there was a short intermission, gift-giving ceremony or one of the directors volunteered to cover the presentation booth while I looked around.

The venue was amazing, decoration was not bad given the rush job; but the scattered number of visitors was really disappointing. The worst part is that in this moment I realised how pathetic and misguided our marketing strategy was. We spent a large amount of money in all the wrong directions and wrong channels. It did not appear that even a single doctor had bothered to come down. Not only was there no certification program like a workshop (which I had suggested but got rejected) this 2-day event was in the middle of the week[31], so it figueres that no influential white-collar professional would waste time and petrol to come to an obscure event when there was no lunch, certificate or anything of value. I mostly saw the volunteer crowd loitering around, that was coerced to come down and pretend to be part of the audience crowd.

While walking around I tried to understand the actual reason why 'N' would even think up such a grand idea all the way from his little study room at his wife's house somewhere in America. I tried to dig deep into the emotional pathways that would convince an old unemployed social outcast to set up an overseas team of inexperienced almost retiring Bangladeshi physicians and others to start this strange venture. Never mind the business model (or the lack of one), but the simple logic escaped my imagination. Until I saw him on stage while we he was giving his own introduction speech.

It was all a sad little scam. The whole time he had a mic in his hand, all the noise he made was about his so-called entrepreneur success, his own company, his own invention (I was too tired to focus on it) hs own vision of Bangladesh health system. It was as if he was running a political campaign or something. A few of the directors were discussing amongst themselves, about whether or not this whole scam that they were dragged into, was some kind of publicity stunt on his behalf.

---

[31] The directors all assumed that most doctors leave the city to do some charity work or other obligations on weekends, so having this medical event on a weekday would be the right move. The basis for this assumption is unknown. Genius move indeed.

I may have forgotten most of the details, as a mental coping mechanism, but I do not exaggerate when I tell you that the whole project was one big joke. It was all a giant scam. When he was not on stage, apparently he organised a side meeting with some representatives of the US embassy and that it was all paid for from HBS accounts. 'G' had authorised it. If it was a business collaboration, then why was the Company Secretary (me) not there to take notes? It was all a farce to promote himself and his imaginary company back in America.

THE CLOWN ENJOYS THE STAGE

Ego is such a powerful force of destruction. It is nature's forest fire. Self-fulfilling desires have no

function to preserve the social structure of any living thing in its path. When a man has no original

goal in life, or maybe has failed countless times making the same mistakes, in a pathetic attempt to

fulfill that *photocopied-goal* at the expense of others' reputation; you get the little mental recording

that tells you that no matter what happens you are still the boss. Everyone else is wrong or

incompetent. No matter what, you are and will always be the Chairman of whatever company

name is created that year, in your honour. Because you are the boss. There is no money, trust,

product, team, customer etc. but it is alright, because your ego keeps telling you that you will

always be Chairman '*N*'.

Whatever script that the poor emcee failed to express in the opening speech, '*N*' made sure

everybody keeps hearing how he has 17+ years experience as a successful entrepreneur, has created

countless number of successful companies, is a personal friend of many influential dignitaries and

that we are the privileged few that has the honour to view his world-changing idea at an electronic health mainframe something that will connect every single person in Bangladesh to his wonderful concept that he and his beloved research facility - ARI Inc. has planned out.

Even after ignoring his grammatical errors even though he is a US-citizen, the amateur powerpoint presentation, lack of any explanatory details on his own company stall in the next room, cheap looking suit he was wearing, almost drunken demeanor towards some of the other speakers (who took a leap of faith to attend when we begged them), after all that show-and-tell, it all came into focus.

Every single red flag I had mentioned[32] and every single interaction with 'N' and his little buddy 'G', confirmed his diagnosis of narcissistic personality disorder. Year 2017 was all about finding a way to promote his own personal brand and whatever his US company was about. It was indeed all a scam. He was not interested in values, business ethics, product development, services quality or anything related to healthcare in any shape or form. The whole show was to get his photo taken with some of the chief guests, talk about some unrealistic or unproven rural project (which was just a simple PDF diagram on a pendrive) and just chase after imaginary investors who may be in the audience. Any chance he got, he would grab the microphone and waste time just to divert the attention to him and his obscure project, he would be openly disrespectful to the speakers in plain view of the audience. The most strangest and funniest moment occured when a speaker was talking about a new disease management, while seated on the stage panel, 'N' took out a selfie stick and take a photo with the chief guest! The entire crowd was laughing and taking pictures of this clown![33]

---

[32] Actually there are a dozen more red flags before this moment. I did not want to spoil the overall theme of this book by mentioning every single judgement error on my part. There are a lot more failure stories coming up!

[33] The event had no real theme or structure, but atleast some moments of entertainment occurred!

Only 4 other directors came to visit. Not a single mention of their contribution or atleast recognition was given by '*N*'. They were absolutely disgusted by his behaviour. Halfway through the event, '*N*' and '*G*' disappeared backstage to have a company sponsored fancy business lunch with some American embassy representatives - leaving the entire stage empty and without order for the next set of speakers (since he had the time slot schedule and the microphone). I had to jump on stage and fumble through the speaker list and try to move things along pathetically. Another of the directors helped with slides, another director handled the volunteers in giving out plaques, crests, pins and other cheap memorabilia to the speakers.

It was an absolute joke.

The worst part is that it was a two day event, so more humiliation and chaos to follow. Honestly I do not have the vocabulary strength to describe anymore sad pathetic moments that we faced in these two days. I have already painted the mental picture of this disaster - just imagine the most amazing conference you may have attended in the past, and just imagine the exact opposite:

That would be '*Healthcare, Pharmaceuticals & Biotech Trade Fair 2017*'.

We all knew that it was all for nothing. We raised and spent all that money on a clown show. There was absolutely no way we could recover from these two days of public shame. Sometimes I still have flashbacks of all the people who laughed at me and the disappointed look by the top consultants who had come to the event. One of the sponsors threatened to sue us for fraud because of such a low audience turnout, we had to refund them their heavily discounted stall price. Towards the last hour many speakers who had arrived out of curiosity were visibly disgusted - by seeing such a large hall with empty seats.

Obviously there was no closing ceremony. Obviously I was exhausted from not sleeping for 3 days, enduring public shame and coming to grips about another gigantic failure event in my life. I think I stayed till the end just to watch the ending fight that was sure to happen against 'N'.

He did not care, as long as the spotlight was on his face and the microphone was still on. There was a small crowd of angry sponsors who wanted to talk to 'N'. He just pretended to have a career talk with the remaining volunteers - so 'G' could use his diplomatic negotiation skills to calm them down. He was just as rude to the young audience as well. Many had questions as to why they submitted their resumes when there was clearly no job recruitment going on at the event, and how his so-called job placement system which he made into his company mainframe would connect them to a job site *'anywhere in the world'*.

The lights switched off, the curtains were drawn and 'N' made a hasty escape (he had brought his carryon luggage with him[34]). I honestly did not care. I was so tired and hungry. The damage was done and HBS is over.

No point crucifying a clown.

---

[34] Seems he anticipated the failure as well. And the need to escape before the anger swells up.

MILLION DOLLARS WORTH OF EXPERIENCE

People often ask me about my formal education, I tell them I *received* my academic knowledge through a massive number of books, articles and lectures - but I got *taught* the harsh realities of life by my hardened exposure in the dirty streets and sweaty waiting rooms, of all the leads I tried to gather during my time at HBS.

In the previous chapters I have told you the perfect formula for self destruction and guaranteed startup failure. I have faced the kind of struggle that would break down a grown man into a crying child. But you cannot build an empire on tears.

I had switched off my phone, turned the air-conditioning on full blast and got a solid 10 hours sleep after so long. The difference between resting and recovering is all down to what you do next. If rest is a way to charge your batteries so you can repeat the same mistakes on a new day - you are better off asleep (atleast failing in your dreams will not cost you a fortune). I was recovering from a painful but necessary learning opportunity.

The small mind will ask how much money I had lost in the HBS circus. The even smaller mind would ask why did I not see those earlier red flags and saved myself the mass public humiliation. The mind of another entrepreneur would wonder how many million dollar experiences I had gained through this setback. I had learned a lot indeed. I learned a vast library of what *NOT* to do when starting any venture, I had learned the value of adaptation, opening your mindset to *present* trends, I had learned about resilience - the key trait of any entrepreneur.

By some coincidence of blind digital marketing, it seems one of those digital posters I had posted on those various Facebook health groups related, was seen by 'S', an Indian healthcare entrepreneur based in Saudi Arabia. The night before our event (just after 'N' had his temper tantrum), we had a short Whatsapp introduction, 'S' had asked if there was any method HBS could help him transfer a stroke patient (a Bangladeshi citizen in Riyadh) to any high end private hospital in Dhaka as soon as possible. It seems that the insurance company he works with, wishes to repatriate the patient back to Bangladesh to decrease premium costs. In a way it was a type of inbound medical transfer, or medical repatriation. A completely new concept as far as I knew.

We started talking business. What was the exact work that needed to be done, the responsibilities, the remuneration. It seemed like a worthy cause. The poor patient wanted to return home to recover from his neurological disability. As there was no policy or process for this type of work, 'S' wanted to collaborate with a Dhaka-based organisation to facilitate the patient transfer from the airport to any high end Dhaka hospital, as soon as possible.

I did not waste time in counting my losses, or getting ready to sue 'N' and 'G' like most of the directors, who did nothing to help us anyway. The first lesson I truly understood for the first time in my adult life, was to accept circumstances instead of passing on blame - there is no end to that path, only more self-destruction. I saw to it that over the next few days submitting all receipts for various expenses I took on for HBS matters (office supplies, few months of wifi rent, some HBS catering and others), and ofcourse I took back every single item I *donated* for initial HBS operations including my PC, some furniture, stationary equipment and miscellaneous cutlery. I did not wait for those time-wasting messenger group chats to decide what to do. The snake has bitten its own tongue, and I will not be its tail any longer.

For someone who is always online in messenger, always sending progress messages and whatnot; 'N' was suddenly so silent. We all wanted an explanation for this joke of a project, his abnormal unprofessional behavior (not only to the audience but especially to eminent medical experts), what happened with those American guests (if HBS paid for the expensive lunch meeting - we want explicit details - he remained silent) and when will we disband HBS.
No reply.

Even 'G' had nothing to day, his best buddy had left him to the wolves as they say in Europe. It was clear he was reading our messages, he even blocked many on Facebook, but he refused to answer. 'G' tried to calm us down, telling us to be brave, we still have a bright future with HBS - all propaganda of course. We created side messenger groups to discuss what we will do with HBS, what about remaining funds and dues, how to dissolve any assets and what to do about '*N*' (if he

had any sense he would realise he can never set foot in Bangladesh).

Even a secret meeting back at the office of one of the directors, it seemed fitting that HBS would be

finished from where it all started, without notifying those two ofcourse. There was total consensus

that it is time to pack up. Either a full report of what was discussed with the Americans - using our

money, or there would be a class action suit.

To be honest, it was cheaper to just admit failure in our first business venture and just move on

with our lives. At their age, I understand how a wounded ego would seek a fiery vengeance.

Each to their own, I have better things planned.

Growth Mindset Tip #1[35] - Stop obsessing over every failure. Learn

about the paths that took you to that end-point, and set about a

new path with this powerful knowledge.

---

[35] After facing so many red flags, I shall educate you on the tips to achieve a positive growth mindset to keep you on the right path

TAKING ACTION AFTER A LOSS

After I retrieved my property from HBS office, in that disgusting building and that disgusting neighborhood, I started contemplating about other future-proof ventures I can start on my own. I contacted 'S' about that medical facilitation concept. And somehow I got in contact with a representative of a major Chinese electronics manufacturer; who is reaching out for a global distributor for one of their innovative neonatal monitoring medical devices.

So many ideas, so many ways to get back on track.

We had a long discussion about that stroke patient, how the Dubai insurance company would oversee payments. He shared with me a partnership agreement, it was quite complicated for me back then, so I asked one of the directors who were more civilized than the others. She suggested to talk with some experienced corporate lawyers that she knew. We had good feedback, the commercial angle seemed quite profitable. I signed up and was eager to put the memory and bad aftertaste of HBS behind me.

This was a pivotal decision I took, not just to move on, but to recover on a deep psychological level. If for whatever reason I decided to curl up into a ball and just hide in the shadows; that would show true defeat. To fail is to actively find methods of not fulfilling a specific goal - such is the process of all of life's goals, whether or be taking your first baby steps to driving. Defeat is the end. Full stop. True defeat is when you do not get up after a beating, after a deep personal humiliation, to give in to the ridicule of the masses. I can fail, but I will not be defeated.

So before taking any step to this new international business venture, I did what I had learned over the years. Research. I went through whatever content that was available about "S", his company and the possible market size of global medical tourism. So far quite impressive branding, market presence and massive economic potential, respectively. A total 180 degree alternative to where I was hardly 1 week ago.

Growth Mindset Tip 2 - Give up and move on, or Grow up and move on. Whatever you do it is entirely up to you, but do it fast. Time is the real deciding factor, it will rust your dreams if you do not make a decision fast.

'N' - THE ANTI-ENTREPRENEUR

I know what is on your mind. I know the burning question since you were reading the last chapter.

Who is this 'N'?

Who is this amateur?

Who is that loser?

The real question is - what will you do if I reveal the full name of 'N'? So what if you do your own little detective work and find out that he had tried this same mistake with a dozen or so Bangladeshi medical doctor communities around many states in the USA? What will you do with the knowledge that he has failed multiple times and never learned from his mistakes, and ruined the reputations of many other eminent medical professionals, his own alumni classmates disown and ridicule him, his children live with him as the so-called father-figure when he never had a job or social standing. What will you do? You may say that in the chance that you decide to become an entrepreneur and a mysterious US-Bangladeshi doctor approaches you with a business proposition, you will be warned.

I desperately want to tell the world about this clown character, I know this coward needs to be behind jail for his fraud. The truth is there is something far worse than the idiocy of '*N*'. There is someone much worse than what '*N*' has done.

Anyone can be '*N*'

As far as you know, I might be '*N*'.

Any of the other shareholders could be "*N*"

The persona of '*N*' is the main thing that I was trying to warn you about. The Anti-Entrepreneur - a person so consumed by their own ego, greed and ignorance that everything turns to garbage. The core beliefs of a growth-mindset is humility and curiosity - the realisation that nobody knows everything and it is a privilege (actually duty) to try to educate oneself on constant daily improvements. The anti-entrepreneur believes in self-promotion above all else, he is unwilling to hear criticism, has no imagination whatsoever. He will steal others ideas to gain some quick cash in unethical and unprofessional methods. The true definition of immaturity and corruption.

Many of you know of these wannabe-businessmen who copy-paste existing ideas and try to market it as their own. With no surprise they fail spectacularly. That is why you see a dozen pizza restaurants in the same building, many boutique stores in the same street and Facebook ads for the same product from various ecommerce sites. These were most likely ego-centered businesses, atleast

for the next few months when lack of business shuts them down, so another of the same can

probably pop up.

So you see, 'N' can be anyone. Even you.

'N' is a symbol of caution for people in general. A person who only lives to chase coins instead of

providing value for others is destined to fail.

Growth Mindset Tip 3 - Ego is the Anti-Entrepreneur. Best way to shut it down is to practice humility. Walk in the footsteps of those who have made mistakes and have taken personal responsibility for them.

GLOBAL HEALTHCARE FACILITATOR

I started going around to some hospitals by myself, pretending to be a family member of the stroke patient who "S" was trying to send back to Bangladesh to continue his treatments. Initially I started approaching some of the ER residents to get an idea of the process of admission and approximate costs.

Needless to say, I did not get very far, not only was it all chaotic, the pricing was too generic to write a report about and also in reality I had no idea what I was doing (or supposed to do). I mean even if I did manage to get a hospital to accept a Bangladeshi patient into their ICU, how would I actually organise an ambulance with trained staff to escort him from the airplane all the way to the ER? Just imagining the lengthy paperwork was giving me a headache. ICU costs here were astronomical, just getting the reimbursements from the UAE-based insurance company to pay up was the next obstacle. I was way over my head with this. I needed some professional help.

I called up Mrs "S" who was the wife of one of the former HBS shareholders - she was very helpful in the days of HBS marketing and was keen to start a business of her own. We sat down and I told her about this medical facilitation project. Even she was much interested in its prospects. She advised me to consult with a corporate lawyer to make sure I was doing the right thing.

I met three lawyers at a coffee shop and had a short discussion of the concept. Being corporate lawyers they too assessed the revenue angle. Double-digit commission per patient transfer was a highly lucrative offer. And the best part is that two of them had connections with the board members of some of the top hospitals. Always an excellent asset to have, friends in the right places.

Over the next few days the three of us sat down and plied through the MOU that "S" wanted me to sign. There were some edits to be made. Most important part was about the remuneration to the various parties. First the hospital gets a lump sum depending on the healthcare package for treating the patient for the set period covered by the insurance, then the facilitator (me) and then the remaining portion back to "S" for referring the patient. This was all a gigantic financial confusion.

We visited the marketing and international patients department of two major hospitals in Dhaka, had a little discussion about this facilitation process. Unfortunately the idea was not well received. There was a major question regarding legal and financial responsibility for the actual patient care. Complex medical cases are extremely unpredictable, not only in its prognosis but actually the incurred costs. Who would pick up the bill if there was any delay in insurance reimbursements or worse case scenario - expensive management is required.

The revenue model seems to have a lot of holes, for a country with almost zero medical insurance presence, international medical facilitation process has a lot of resistance from corporate healthcare institutions. From my experience in NICU care, I know firsthand that a single patient can incur a large hospital bill in a short period of time, and often the parents of sick newborns are the ones most likely to default on those payments. Understandably million dollar hospitals in Dhaka have the same concerns too.

Besides the complicated revenue process, a senior marketing executive raised the issue about the requirement for a valid trade license - even if it is for a sole proprietor venture. I suppose that would be the logical step to take before approaching any prospect. It is one thing to work out of a home office or even just a mobile phone. But business is business, and business needs a trade license. Good thing I know a pair of corporate lawyers to help me out.

The lawyers went through the MOU again to make it more suitable to the present situation, most notably the fact that sending a single coin outside the borders of Bangladesh is an absolute no-no. This means that there will not be an easy way for "S" to receive his cut of the facilitation commission, a massive tax will be levied on that transaction as the Bangladesh Bank relies heavily on inbound currency for its stability (eg. Remittances). Simply put money can flow in but cannot flow out. A very primitive but necessary fiscal policy in the bigger global picture.

The plan was good. The idea was sound. The money would be huge. But before all that I need to incorporate it into an actual organisation.

Growth Mindset Tip #4 - Take advice from a strong and experienced legal team. You may be an army of one, but protect yourself *from yourself* with good legal counsel.

HYBRID HEALTH SYSTEMS

A name defines a legacy. A name defines power. A strong name to stick into the decision making process of a client's mind can make a lot of difference in a sale. And for this reason I was tearing out my hair trying to come up with an appropriate name.

I needed a name that speaks professionalism, honesty, empathy, a global touch and simple enough to pronounce. Or atleast with simple abbreviation which a client would remember well. And a more important note was the value of a unique web domain which I could purchase on an affordable budget. As I had learned from HBS, buying a domain is a lot like a digital real estate market, there are people who speculate the potential value of a company name, buy up the rights for the domain address and sit on it until a prospective new company wishes to acquire it. Going through godaddy.com and other domain sites, I had personally seen simple 3-4 vowel names with ".com", ".net" or whatever, with a price tag of a new Mercedes!

I agree that one of the hardest tasks of a founder is to think up a good name for the company. I played around with the usual generic medical tourism or medical services related names. I went through atleast 3 pages of Google and Yahoo searches for some inspiration. Most were generic as those you find in any alleyway inside a cheap mall, while others were somewhat vague. Later on I decided that it is bst to remain a little vague so that there is a kind of organisational freedom to try out different branding techniques, business models or even other projects outside of medical facilitation and usual focal tourism.

I finished my choices to Global Medi Services Ltd, International Health Process Ltd and Hybrid Health Systems Ltd. My lawyers advised me that I should choose three names with ranking preferences so assess if there was any our company with the same name (highly unlikely). I submitted these names and waited for their next steps.

Part two of this difficult stage comes the logo design. I had mentioned before that the HBS logo was basically the cheap knockoff of the logo of a well known hospital, with the letters HBS copy-pasted on it. Obviously I will not stoop down to that level of pettiness. There are a bunch of online freelancer communities who can provide various graphic design support. Many choices were available depending on individual skill sets, ratings, recommendations and of course design fees ($5-$500+). Again I played around with the letters, drew simple monochromatic shapes and fonts, an important point to keep in mind is how will the logo look at different sizes depending on where you would use it. I remembered the time I worked for that NGO a few years go, there as a chapter I was reading regarding international corporate branding, they had detailed schematics on the dimensions of every single font, the colour palettes and which areas of a letter, brochure or even a social media post that their logo was to be used in. I went through atleast a dozen different drafts before I just gave up and went to sleep.

I am not sure if it was the fever I had that night, but I woke up in a cold sweat and immediately reached out for a pen and paper. I started drawing the helipad sign which you see on top of major hospitals, and two open brackets on either side, with some minor edits I finally created the symbol that I saw in my dream. Agreed it seems like a Hollywood cliche that such innovation would come from such

a dramatic source, but yes, that is exactly what happened.

After I got cleaned up, I sat down and started some amateur designing on some online software I had used for the HBS poster designs. Along with the detailed design process to trademark the logo of course. It was not that cool or flashy, but it got the job done.

My lawyers had informed me that the name *"Hybrid Health Systems Ltd"* has been approved and now I had to provide the other necessary details to complete the company registration and incorporation. This part meant that I had to make up my own official company memorandum, articles of association and of course the shares distribution - a limited company must have a minimum of 2 shareholders, of any scale, so I enlisted my father to be a 1% shareholder just to fulfill this requirement. I could sense the feeling of pride in his voice, he too could understand my new found enthusiasm to start my own path to something fulfilling, and hopefully impactful too.

Learning from the errors of HBS was quite straightforward, all I had to do was the exact opposite. Nonetheless there were some strategies which did make some sense, such as the basics in branding. Social media presence, business cards, company SIM, brochures and maybe miscellaneous merchandise. I got another SIM, designed my very own set of business cards (*Founder & CEO of HHS* sounded quite cool), ordered some coffee mugs, notepads, badges and started working on the website too.

After all that mess last year, atleast I can say that I learned a little bit about web design to not rely on others. Domain was quite cheap (only $2 per year), the website creator software *Wix.com* had an affordable yearly plan with your own customisable mailbox (*info@hybridhealthsystems.com*), I could easily design the business website using their own templates, play around with colours, images, fonts and content.

The digital marketing process was still confusing. Opening an official social media page was the easy part, now the main issue was to get people to follow it and post content that would make people believe in the new HHS brand. I boosted a few posts then designed some ads and paid a small fee just to get some idea on the feedback. There were the usual LIKES and a few responded to page invites to follow the HHS page, but going through some of the profiles of these leads was really frustrating. From their profiles it was so obvious that they were no way near my target demographic, and yet they just pressed the LIKE button as a knee-jerk reflex.

Of course the first step in self branding is to reach out to family and friends, not that they would tell you honest feedback, so as to not hurt your inflated ego, but atleast you can start off on their social circles to expand outwards.

The next and crucial step was the physical location of HHS. Definitely I will not choose an office location as disturbing as HBS was. From a logistic and personal status point of view, I thought it would be necessary to find a suitable location near my home. There is no point in finding a cheap office space when the price of fuel is increasing day by day. It makes more sense to find a decent place in a decent area to atleast give some comfort when working and ali when entertaining future customers.

From my regular readings about entrepreneurship, starting a small business and other related literature, I came upon the concept of a shared office space or co-working space. Basically it is a large commercial plot that is shared by a relatively large number of professionals to use for their own enterprise functions, complete with office supplies, printing materials and most importantly various sized meeting rooms. All that for a highly affordable membership fee, based on number of hours used and/or monthly packages. You would not believe how happy I was to hear that such a concept has become so common here in Dhaka.`place was available and becoming more and more popular here in Dhaka[36], and Chittagong.

---

[36] Just type 'coworking space' in Google Maps, and you will see atleast a dozen options scattered around Dhaka.

I visited a few that were within a short driving distance from my home, some were somewhat beyond my budget and others did not convey the 'serious','professional' and 'pro-business' environment that I needed. By luck I had found a wonderful little place in Banani. Designed literally from the ground up and A-to-Z by two entrepreneurial architects who created the coworking space as a multidimensional business ecosystem - for their own architectural firm as well. The membership structure was very affordable and flexible for pre-startup entrepreneurs like myself. Without a second though I immediately signed up and set myself up there. It was very hip and professional at the same time, mostly young freelancers, some NGOs, a few marketing consultants and other tech-related startups based their operations there. The environment was 150 times better than the prison cell from HBS, there was air conditioning, refreshments, kitchenette, housekeeping, fast wifi and probably the most important asset - the proximity to highly skilled professionals who are more than happy to help you with any issue (plus their espresso bar was an added bonus!).

All that for a tiny starting budget was just too good to be true. As I had learned from before, high overhead costs to just 'run a business' can be the nail that punctures your capital budget if not managed properly. Ofcourse as I imagined myself getting bigger and maybe hiring some people I would have to look for a larger space, but the initial processes in starting are always the most expensive i.e. staff salaries and office costs. The initial stages had to be done by myself; in terms of branding, strategy, marketing and ofcourse gathering the first few sales opportunities, therefore I will avoid the unnecessary hiring of support staff (the coworking space had basic secretarial support) and office rent is now so low that it would be an almost minor investment to the potential revenue return that I predicted. After all, whatever clients I would get, I could just tell them to come down for a quick consult in one of the fancy meeting rooms (with wall-to-wall glass windows overlooking Banani commercial district) and the busy neighboring 'co-workers' can inflate the perception of HHS!

So far so good.......

Now I have to find a better smarter way to tell my future customers about myself and HHS....

Growth Mindset Tip #5 - Always imagine an alternative to every decision. The 3rd or 4th option can sometimes save you thousands of dollars of initial costs, if properly researched. Be open to new trends in business circles such as automation, coworking spaces, outsourcing etc.

LAUNCHING HYBRID HEALTH SYSTEMS (HHS)

One day while I was busy designing one of the brochures for medical tourism services, I received a call from a major events company, they are a global brand in professional corporate events for B2B and also public access events. The marketing executive on the phone inquired about my interest to participate in the upcoming MediTex Expo happening in early May. Apparently only a handful of stalls were available at discounted rates. I thought for a while about this opportunity,

I have personally attended various medical expos in the past, and was considering it as a unique way to showcase HHS to the wider public, maybe even form a partnership with any other healthcare-related organisations I meet there. I asked to meet with him at their office to get an idea of the floor layout and negotiate stall costs.

After going through their program, although the available stall locations are not ideal from a foot-traffic point of view, I had to alter my initial idea for the stall design. It is not enough to simply design a pretty-looking stall where there is no customer interest/engagement, there has to be a way to specifically target and influence the crowd to come *towards* you in a strategic method. I remember watching a YouTube video about *"gamification"* and *"event activation"*, from my understanding I realised that I had to make my corporate presence *fun*.

I planned a type of carnival where casual visitors can be converted into *leads* i.e. potential customers after some *nurturing* and *value-addition*[37]. This process is extremely difficult due to two views, either the sales initiator is not able to express the value of the proposition (medical travel using HHS) or the lead is not open to this suggestion. This resistance is a natural response due to the hyper-consumerist lifestyle that we live in, everyone and everything wants us to make a purchase or transaction[38]. So it is the primary goal of the initiator to bring down this defensive mental blockade, one of many methods to do this is to make the lead-generating process like a participatory activity - this is known as *event activation*. In simple terms what I planned to do was to make a carnival type set up where people can spin a wheel (on my laptop) and each place the arrow ends it would grant them a merchandise; like a branded mug, a simple poster, a pen and for the younger crowd, I made a pair of cardboard frames with an outline of a typical Facebook or Instagram post with the center cut out so they can post a 'cool' picture to their social media (and promote the HHS brand too). All this was possible as long as the stall visitor provides their contact details and likes the HHS Facebook page.

---

[37] It is vital to get accustomed to using business language as quickly as possible - not just for sounding professional, but rather to communicate well for B2B engagement.
[38] We are exposed to hundreds of overt and *covert* ads in every shape and form, every second of our lives, so naturally we have responded negatively to any such sales activity as a defence mechanism.

I designed all the merchandise, the posters, promoted the fresh Facebook page of HHS and the stall designs. It was an exciting time for me. Fresh blood coursed through my brain, this was the true feelings of entrepreneurship - the surge of neurohormones and emotions flashing through at lightning speeds. A lot of work was to be done, less than a month left before this highly publicised medical expo.

Growth Mindset Tip #6 - Don't be afraid to try out innovative business strategies. Don't obsess about what others may think, this is your time to literally bring your dreams come into reality. The only way your marketing strategies will be judged is by the Market - the customer feedback will determine how your strategies worked out. The most important thing is to just implement your marketing ideas quickly and affordably <u>as quickly as possible.</u>

DEATH OF AN ENTREPRENEUR

One night while I was designing the merchandise branding, I received a text from my father. He told me he was preparing for a routine cardiac procedure for some heart issues he had been having for a long time. I replied that all will be ok, then I called him. We had a short talk, I told him about my event plan, he wished me well, I could sense the pride in his voice. He told me to rest for the night and will call me after the procedure. I told him good night.

I did not want to write this chapter. Usually I manage to complete a few chapters every few days. When it was time to right about this crucial event in my life story, I took almost 3 months. Even now my eyes are filling with tears and my hands are shaking, some tears are falling on the keyboard right now. Most days when I feel like writing up chapters in this book, I would skip this one as it brings back these painful emotions, and I cannot control myself. But I know I must write these words, I must tell the world about the life of this great man and his effect on my journey. If I cannot tell you every single amazing detail and hardwork of my father, atleast I will begin my healing process by telling you that my father, Dr. Mohammad Abu Sayeed Miah was the first physician entrepreneur of Bangladesh.

I grew up in humble beginnings, my parents met under even more harsh conditions too. Two young freshly graduated medical doctors in a broken health system of a broken country, fresh out of a genocide. They worked extremely hard to manage as many sick and dying people as possible; my father was an ambitious pediatric resident, and my mother an even more ambitious obgyn resident. Wherever they were posted as public sector doctors, they saw death and despair. Due to intergenerational poverty, chronic nutrition and widespread female illiteracy and ofcourse cultural ignorance; premature babies and growth restricted babies had the same fate - a painful pathetic early death. The pediatrician had no tools or skills, and could do nothing, while the gynaecologist gave the sad news. These were terrible times back in the 80's. Through great perseverance and hardwork, my father, along with his mentor, the Late Professor Dr. M. R. Khan (Father of Pediatrics in Bangladesh), instituted mechanical ventilation and other forms of artificial ventilatory support for preterm sick infants. I do not recall the exact details such as the sources, the donors and even the state of the NICU back then, what I can tell you is that I was the first premature baby to receive and survive due to this intervention.

Dr. Abu Sayeed Miah did not invent the ventilator, but he figured out a process to bring such high value medical intervention into a struggling public health institution in a developing country to help the most vulnerable of human populations. He did not get any royalties or awards, he was not that kind of doctor. His whole existence was about serving the community, any community. As such he was a man of great nobility and patience. He was extremely tech-savvy as well, which is a strange thing considered most people a third of his age did not know how to write an email even.

My whole reason for trying and trying was based on his constant belief that I could do something and be something. An entrepreneur needs a strong rock to anchor their emotions too, especially when surrounded by negative dysfunctional individuals, especially naysayers from their own family. The poison spread from one's own blood relatives destroys more than any other source, it is no wonder that most people are filled with hate and disgust due to the ignorance from their own kin. As long as my father was there I had the strength to ignore these animals. But that was about to change drastically.

I received a call from a friend of my father late one night, apparently something had happened on the operating table, and he was rushed to the ICU, my mother was there with him. He is critical but stable.

The bile and vomit rushed to my throat, my heart sank. I called his phone, it just rang. I called my mother but no one answered. In the morning I had a long talk and I realised what had happened. I do not want to overwhelm you with the surgical details, but the simple explanation is that he had a cardiac tamponade - which is basically blood from his heart chambers filled up around his heart walls. It has more than 90% mortality rate in the first 2 min. It seems that during his procedure, they identified an area of abnormal heart tissue which is creating its own electrical activity hence the difficulty in his pacemaker from working properly. They tried to remove that area, but the wall was mostly scar tissue and it ruptured, spilling the blood into the area around the heart, therefore preventing proper pumping action. Through the heroic action of the cardiac surgery team, they stabilised him and sent him to the ICU.

Being a doctor we are cursed with knowledge. We know too much. Non-medical people can worship all day, but when a medical person hears the term cardiac tamponade, we know the gravity of the situation. Over the course of the next few days I tried in vain to get an emergency Kuwait visa to see him. I was rejected many times. I was brown-skinned Bangladeshi living in a country which was on a blacklist by most of the Arab countries. My brother, who was doing his PhD in Liverpool that time managed to secure a visa to see him since he applied from the UK. I was stuck here staring at the last text message he sent me.

It was a horrible time, so many depressing thoughts ran through everyone's mind. The whole extended family was in turmoil. A few of my US-citizen family members managed to go see him, an uncle who is an interventional radiologist in Michigan came to Dhaka after seeing him. He did not have to say anything. I know that look. I used to have that look when I informed my seniors that a baby has certain congenital anomalies, or the blood tests came back with a certain report. It was the look of professional despair. The end is near.

I prayed, I bargained. I thought of emptying my bank account so I could reach their illegally if I had to. I did not care about HHS or the expo or whatever. I just needed to hold my father's hand. I was confident that if I burst into the ICU only I could save him, I saved him a few years ago when he had a stroke right in front of my eyes, I saved my cousin's son when he was in the PICU. I knew I could save him. I just need to hold his hand.

Life is not fair. Life does not care about the wellbeing of good people. In much the same was the Market does not care how hard you worked. It is all chaos. It is all unfair. The weeks went by like a bad dream. I would occasionally get updates - sometimes some good responses, some bad but mostly more of the same. I remember one day the ICU wanted to insert a tracheostomy tube to better manage his vitals, my father was so scared and refused. My mother and brother called me to ask my opinion, to convince him to do it. I told them that as long as he his conscious, he is still Dr. Sayeed - father, husband and individual, you cannot force anything, he will decide his choices as best as he sees fit. As painful as it was to write this text to my brother so that he could read it out to him, it was the last best thing I could do for him - respect his wishes as a human being.

After a few days he did get the tube through his throat. He spent the last few days in silent prayers, holding my mother's and brother's hands, asking where I was. If a doctor tells him that he will be ok, he would know they are lying. If someone tells him that I managed to get the visa and I am on my way, he will believe them. That was the last lie he probably heard.

Every week I applied through the embassy, every week I would get rejected. I paid a few thousand dollars to an *agent* to get me a worker visa, I will clean toilets in Kuwait just to get into the ICU. Even that was rejected. I spent the next few weeks just aimlessly writing emails that I would never send, business plans I would never execute, poster designs I will never print. Hours were spent in my coworking space just to avoid spending a single moment in my empty home. The event day was drawing close, I made a few wall posters and designed that lead generation game I mentioned in the last chapter. My mind was kept busy with this project, but my heart was as broken as my father's. These were terrible times.

Towards the end of August 2018, nothing was happening. I resigned my fate that I would not get the Kuwait visa. I was just hoping and praying that somehow my father could return to his ancestral village, even in a wheelchair with an attached oxygen tank. It was a hopeless dream, but most entrepreneurs start with hopeless dreams anyway. In total honesty I will confess to you that I was seriously contemplating a very drastic solution to my ordeal. With great difficulty I would avoid going to the roof of my 12-storey apartment complex, which I used to go to clear my head and walk around. I knew that in my weakness I will stand by the ledge, and do something that will hurt more people than it hurts me. This incident had to have some kind of lesson, I thought about it at every waking moment, there has to be a reason why I am made to suffer this way.

What is the purpose of this inhuman torture?

In the last week of August, I received a few messages from Kuwait that my father was doing better, better in the sense that he was not getting any worse. Stable but critical. I realised the joke in that description, I understood the humor in it as that was exactly the terms I used to tell parents after they finished crying when they hear that their newborn is still in the NICU.

I had a strange dream one night. It was like a memory playback, almost like a flicker of images you see just before going to sleep. I knew it was set a long time ago when we were living in Riyadh, I vaguely saw my younger brother trying to walk as a toddler in the corner, our maid was in the kitchen frying something, my mother was walking up the stairs in her lab coat as if she finished her afternoon shift, and I was helping my father set the table for iftar. It was not very epic, not even lavish by any standards, but there was a sense of calm and completeness about this scene. I do not believe in the supernatural, but I do not think this was not *my* memory, in some strange way my father probably realised my despair and had sent me a moment in time where there was no worry, no suffering. Even on his deathbed he was still looking out for me.

In the morning I understood everything. I was being selfish. We were all being selfish. All of us were praying for his 'safe' return, but nobody wanted him to be at peace. That day I did not pray for a miracle anymore, I prayed that his pain will be over, I wanted him to be at peace. I wanted him to pass on. All my life I had waited on him, waited for his approval, waited for his return but I never thought about what was good for him. I wanted him to be at peace, whatever form that was. It was not his approval that kept me going, it was the fact that I was finally doing something worth doing as an entrepreneur, instead of another payroll employee in a faceless corporation. Being all that I could be, kept me going.

The next day I woke up early without an alarm. Just as I was getting up from bed, I received a call from an uncle,

He was gone. My father is dead. He is no more.

The rest of the phone conversation was all static to me. I was numb but I knew I had work to do. I rushed to my grandmother before she heard the news from someone else, then I rushed to another city to hold on to my father's youngest brother. I was numb but I had to be the rock to absorb the grief. It was over. He was gone. Time to bring him home.

My father was returning in a casket in a few days. No sleep for 2-3 days. Arranging for his return was aided by family members, while I stoically managed and hosted the medical expo, the first public unveiling of a father-son health company, except without the father part. I was mostly on autopilot mode. It did not matter, I had work to do.

My mother and brother arrived late on a rainy night, I met them at the arrival lounge. For a few seconds I looked over their shoulders, just in case someone else I missed so badly would be behind them. He was not there, he arrived in a different terminal. We got him out of the airport and reached back home, his home. Waited for family members to arrive one-by-one. Prayed the morning prayer, and then the funeral prayer. A short ride later his resting place was ready for him. The ground was clean and empty, nobody was buried in our family plot for a long time.

As per tradition, I climbed down 6ft into the ground. I held out my arms to carry him down, wrapped in white linen cloth. My father was a heavy set man, but this time he did not weigh anything. I laid him down, kissed his forehead through the cloth. Gave him a last hug. Climbed out and covered him up with the dirt that contained his parents, his elder brother, his elder sister and other generations. It was only when holding the last handful of grave dirt, that I realised that my father was also someone else's brother or son. Life is strange.

I wanted to grieve in the corner, but I had work to do. After my grandmother, uncle, then my aunt passed away, I remember my father still got ready and went to complete his shift in the clinic. I got that strength that day too; I took a shower to clean the cemetery remains from my fingers, wore my new suit and headed back to the expo. I had work to do.

The pain was intense. The sadness was like a scar in my eyes. But the work must go on. I completed the 3-day expo, advertised what HHS services had to offer, gathered a lot of visitors to the stall since the gaming part was a big hit. For most it was another corporate event, for me it was what it was. My new life must go on.

A few years ago I watched a video of a famous clinical psychologist, in the seminar he was asked by a student, '*What kind of man is needed in a world of so much hypocrisy and double-standards?*', Dr. Jordan Peterson replied, '*Be the kind of man who people can look for sincerity and integrity, after he buries his own father.*'

KEEPING BUSY TO LOOK BUSY

It has been a few weeks since I buried my father, completed the Medical Expo and was more or less done with the inheritance procedures. Life has been completely turned upside down. The months after such a tragedy, a person should and *must* grieve. This is a delicate and necessary part of the human experience. But I could not have this luxury.

I was now the '*Man of the house*'. House Sayeed.

There is no time or space to cry. People are watching, and they need to see a calm composed demeanor at all times. My brother went back to the UK to continue his education, my mother returned to Kuwait to complete the necessary paperwork to complete and initiate the next steps in the inheritance procedures. And I tried to keep HHS going.

Just to keep my mind busy I kept in contact with the new India-based medical tourism agencies so I could secure that referral logistics system, fixed up the website, ordered for some more business cards and brochures and ofcourse to contact the leads to see if they could be converted to patient customers. The main activity of a company is revenue generation. As much as possible and as quickly as possible.

I tried a few cold calls and cold emails. Was met with missed calls, wrong numbers, wrong target patient or just the usual awkward refusal of services. I tried to maintain my calmness, after all sales rejections are to be expected, and in large quantities before an established market trust can be gained.

A few leads did contact me in the upcoming few days. Unfortunately most were insisting on getting an appointment at well known non-profit hospitals in Vellore or Chennai headed by a celebrity-based physician. Talk about epic inter-generational branding![39]. Some inquired about the treatment for a very low level low cost procedure, and which Indian hospital would be the best for it. To be brutally honest, now that I am a private corporation, the ROI[40] to assist in low commission low value requests, is not very appealing nor cost-effective (such cases I simply had to mention that I do not specialise in such activities). A few had asked about my credentials on whether or not I am a *real* medical doctor and why I was in international medical tourism, not in a negative way but rather to ensure that I would know the exact medical procedure that they were inquiring about.

---

[39] A family member who may have heard or had some success with this physician would spread his divine-like skills. Word-of-mouth marketing spreads like wildfire in Bangladesh. If the grandfather had a procedure with him, definitely the father, son and everyone else will follow the same path, regardless of service quality. Such is the power of intensive international branding.
[40] ROI = Return of investment (time, energy, patience)

But the majority was a no-show or no-go.

Just when my hopes were going down, and ofcourse my mental health was taking a major hit from unresolved emotional issues (from lack of timely grief processing), I received a few callbacks to have a physical meeting at my office. I hurriedly gathered my materials (cards & brochures), placed my laptop in the small shared meeting room so as to show them the details of my partner hospitals and practiced my sales persona (which I trained myself from various youtube videos).

But the majority was a no-show or no-go.

Things were getting desperate. My mother had returned from Kuwait, forever. Property and assets were being processed accordingly. Many family members' deep seated issues were being exposed due to the difficult circumstances that were in now, all part of the psychosocial transitions I suppose. And worse of all still no leads, no revenue.

The business frustration was leaking into my private life as well. There were several explosive unprovoked outbursts. I was becoming even more alienated from my support structures, had it not been for my close relationship with my little nephew, who is the only rock to anchor my humanity, all this would be the perfect recipe for an upcoming violent incident. Initially the 'go-hard' mentality of entrepreneur life was the bandage that kept me sane since my fathers' passing, but now it seems it may be tearing apart from pressure. I poured my whole life force into random social media posts with fancy posters, reposting medical blogs, commenting on several facebook patient groups to drag people into my website, in the hopes of getting leads, but all it did was to get me ignored and sometimes blocked from these groups. I spent hours on end in my coworking office space, just randomly typing things like grand business ideas, watching motivational or random Youtube videos, reading amateur business hacks blogs and other so-called 'busy' office activities. Deep down the illusion of spending so many hours at the office sort of suppressed some of the frustration and confusion I was feeling. I needed help but did not know where to turn.

Except inwards, as I had always done.

I remembered during the HBS days, I had attended a free workshop organised by the EMK Center[41]. It was an amazing event that showcased key experiences and advice for aspiring entrepreneurs (like myself). Experienced startup founders aka serial entrepreneurs and some industry experts (like bankers) would have small get together to talk about specific topics related to the whole entrepreneur journey, like testing ideas, raising funds, basic web design and other essential skills.

I figured instead of going at full speed in the wrong direction. I felt that I needed to invest time and resources to fully understand this startup ecosystem, and see where healthcare entrepreneurship would take its place, and where I would fit in.

---

[41] EMK Center = Nonprofit US-based events & education platform that has an entrepreneurship program with frequent free events. *www.emkcenter.org*

Growth Mindset #7 - Working hard is hardly working. You can fool others into thinking that hours spent in work translates to dollars in the bank, but you cannot fool the Market, because the Market doesn't care about your efforts, only benefits to the users.

EVENTS-BASED LEARNING FOR
ENTREPRENEURS

There really is no certified course for entrepreneurship, there are no graduate programs on how to establish market value in an innovation, and make some profit too. Sure you can take one of millions of MBA, Finance, Accounting and other commerce-related degrees. Some academic institutions even claim to teach something called EMBA (Executive MBA) or some kind of tailor made Entrepreneurship Bootcamp of sorts. In reality such courses are superb training programs to create highly certified employees of established traditional corporations. The Startup world has no defined process nor perfectly aligned skill sets, that would guarantee success and ofcourse solvency.

There are no traditional academic systems that you could input money and essays, and receive a measurable output that you can show to prove your credibility - to investors, shareholders and ofcourse the cruel Market forces. The startup world is all about the speed and innovation of executing plans, as quickly and as cheaply as possible. This is the core concept of the MVP[42]. As I understood in my brief entrepreneurship career so far, there are three essential learning curves that one should experience in order to be less of a failure in the days ahead:

1 - Start quick, fail fast, learn faster

Whatever business idea you have, just design a prototype, implement and execute into the real world, accept that most likely it will crash and burn. And that is ok and needed, so that you can quickly learn where it all went wrong and keep trying again and again.

2 - Learn from the failure of others, absorb their teachings

A true entrepreneur has no fear of failure, only inaction. A valuable entrepreneur is one who has made mistakes, learned from them and has restarted once again. This type of '*alpha-founder*' has a wealth of realistic information that can be a source of real-life solutions to common (and uncommon) startup challenges that an amateur entrepreneur may face, or can atleast avoid.

---

[42] MVP - Minimum Viable Product, I will discuss this concept in upcoming chapters

If you think you can do it alone, you actually need 3 co-founders.

If you already have 3 people, you will need 9 very soon.

You make a business plan that guarantees profits in 1 year, when it may

take 3. A small delay in a small process might seem to affect you for 1 week,

when in fact it multiples and delays your operations by 3 weeks, or 3 months.

Main point is to expect delays, minimise their damage to your overall

operations by being flexible, adaptive and have options available. (agile)

So where can I find these 'alpha-founders' and knowledgeable industry experts? The best place is in their new company's headquarters (good luck trying to get them to waste their valuable time trying to teach amateurs, for free), one lesson that is highly respected in the entrepreneur community, is the dollar-value of their working time. The notion that time is money, is very important; an alpha-founder knows that each moment wasted is basically a dollar unearned. So somehow stalking them in person or on social media is a total waste of your time and credibility.

Everybody wants win-win situations. You want some hard-earned advice from experts, and they want their time to be respected; if not spent on marketing, atleast they can utilise that time for self-branding. Therefore the concept of entrepreneur/startup events came about. Professional meeting events where such experts get to talk about their startup experiences, give some value-based advice to young startups and also get some future customers or followers at the same time.

Halfway through 2018 I had attended multiple events, almost 1 event per week, sometimes more often. Most were free and some were ticketed events. Ofcourse attending so many events was not cheap, even if the event was free, I still had to spend money going back and forth. But in a true open-minded spirit I considered them as on-the-go on-the-job training, plus an opportunity to hand out some cards and maybe get some customers. Most of the events were fairly well organised (10times better than the HBS event) with prominent industry professionals and surprisingly very young and successful alpha-founders.

In many international business articles like the Global Innovation Index, Bangladesh is embarrassingly the least innovative nation in the whole world. With such depressing statistics I was under the impression that there are not that many innovators and entrepreneurs in Dhaka. I would probably end up meeting shady businessmen, spoilt brats who maintain an obscure web presence for their father's business and other miscellaneous *pretend* entrepreneurs. Yes there are many characters like that, but not in these events I have been to, and continue to attend till date. I have met university students (some even younger) who are building online businesses, housewives who cater to offices, corporate office workers who grow and sell organic produce on the side, and dozens of tech startups with amazing ideas and products. Whoever measures that index needs to update their knowledge. Being surrounded by such value-driven professionals has greatly enriched my social structures and ofcourse my own mindset towards self development.

I invested at least half of 2018 just on self development and education. Like a sponge; I listened, absorbed and actively participated in a dozen or so workshops, seminars, meetups and other public events. I started listening to business podcasts from entrepreneur celebrities every now and again, including many of their books. I started using thought process exercises to think up more innovative ways to increase the HHS brand value and reach out to specific customers instead of just reaching in the dark.

But still no customers. No patients. No revenue.

But I did not give up. Holding on and moving on was a common advice from many of the successful serial entrepreneurs. I just had to hold on and keep on trying. I just had to utilise my learning.

Just when I was thinking that I should shut down HHS, I started getting calls from interested patients and their caregivers. The usual calls were there ofcourse, regarding how to get an appointment with that celebrity doctor, how much would it be, what are your rates, what papers I needed and so on. But as I tweaked and edited my ad strategy, by improving my digital marketing skills (thanks to these workshops) I started to get into the mindspace of the specific type of customer that would be value-oriented - this process is known as customer segregation, or customer avatar/persona creation. I will explain in the next few chapters.

After dozens of no-shows and outright rejections, I am happy to say I managed to send 4 *high value high revenue* patient customers to some of the partner hospitals in India. Due to patient-doctor confidentiality, obviously I cannot give you their identity nor the context of their illness, but I can say that they needed high end medical and surgical interventions. Those procedures may have been possible here in Dhaka, but as you may know about the basics of sales - give the customer exactly what they want.

The revenue structure of medical tourism is quite complex, on paper it is a lot like multi-level marketing (MLM) but the reality is that after a patient goes to that partner hospital, makes the full payment, the hospital has to provide kickbacks to the Indian-based medical travel agent and then finally I would receive my cut via bank transfer. There are many significant obstacles and delays in this financial framework. There is a risk of patients being diverted to some other hospital beyond my network, many hospitals overcharge and alter their income so they make smaller payouts to the local agent, and thus I would get pennies to the dollar. The worst part is actually the long waiting period to receive my referral commission for each successful patient transfer, sometimes atleast 2 months go by before I receive a deposit notification.

Although each individual payout is quite significant[43], there has to be a way to speed up the sales and commission process - or else I cannot scale up nor survive practically in this crowded market. I kept going on in some form or another - given that I was preoccupied with the difficult life transition since my father's passing. From an emotional standpoint I kept HHS going since it was a pet project that both of us took a part in shaping, so letting go and doing something else was an uncomfortable reality. But I knew back then that I too had to transition to something more financially feasible, now that a significant obligation is thrust upon me.

---

[43] Although I nearly broke even from whatever amount I had invested in starting HHS, the event preparations, marketing costs and shared office rent, That entire income so far did not really match the ROI of the effort that was out in.

If an employee is upset with their present situation, they can always take a chance and try the job market for a vacancy at another established corporation. This type of security is not possible in the startup world, it is not possible nor recommended to keep jumping from one idea to another so quickly[44]. The saying of *jumping out of the frying pan and into the fire* is very relevant here. In moments of doubt, the mind goes in strange directions too. Sometime ago I received occasional calls from 'G' regarding what I had been upto, whether I am interested to start some venture with him & his *new* partners.

Ofcourse I replied no. I may be desperate but I am not an amateur anymore. I knew that I would have to alter the business process and vision of HHS into something more profitable, I would have to pivot[45] my strategies, *strategically*. But before I change the company, I had to change myself. So I attended a few more events, a few more workshops until I started to reposition myself as a serial entrepreneur.

The following section highlights my key learning over a period of 4-5 months of 2018.

---

[44] This phenomenon is known as 'Shiny Object Syndrome'

[45] Pivot - A process of changing the business plan, process, direction or even the company vision in a different direction

Growth Mindset Tip #8 - Start something, anything and keep going. The best way to learn about a business is to actually start. When you are committed to succeed you will be committed to expand your practical knowledge. The best source of knowledge is meeting serial entrepreneurs in startup events. Attend as many as possible in your first few months; take notes and implement them the next day.

KEY LESSONS FROM STARTUP EVENTS

Once you accept that you know nothing, the entrepreneur brain becomes an addict searching for a fix. Throughout my life I had defined my intellect by materialistic third party measurements - such as number of degrees, medals, likes, salary, social status and other bullshit metrics. The Market does not care about you, your dreams, your degrees, it is all about the *outcome*.

The realisation that my ego was in the driving seat my whole life or rather I was simply on auto-pilot, allowed me to regain control of reality. Reality that I actually had no marketable skills, no high income skills, no startup skills. Much like an alcoholic who comes to accept the negative influences that surround them and desperately wants to become a better version of themselves; I took the initiative to attend events for the sole purpose of learning, not selling, not handing out cards, just learning. This level of humility is essential in order to fully absorb the complex but honest core concepts of starting a startup. I will try to briefly list out the essential core topics that I had learned, which were a common theme amongst all startup events and consistently mentioned by serial entrepreneurs.

SOLVE A PROBLEM

Many aspiring entrepreneurs create magnificent palaces, when all that their customers wanted was an umbrella. Just go out into the real world and look at how people lead their lives, in response to a commonly shared daily obstacle; such as heavy traffic, high prices for commodities, lack of connectivity, safe clean food, access to banking and so on. Many people create a product and waste resources to look for a buying customer, that is working backwards. Solve a specific problem that a specific demographic is facing constantly. In my perspective I saw that healthcare access is a constant significant public/global health issue. People want access to qualified healthcare professionals in a timely affordable manner.

DECREASE A PAIN OR INCREASE A PLEASURE

In reference to solving a problem, people buy anything for only two reasons; to decrease a current or recurring pain or to experience pleasure. Buy new shoes because the old ones are hurting your heels and/or makes you look classy is an example. Buy medicine to decrease migraine headaches, consult a psychiatrist, wear a plaster cast, join a gym, remove gallstones, plastic surgery, hair transplants and on and on. From this example it is quite obvious that healthcare is the perfect industry to be an entrepreneur.

DO NOT REINVENT THE WHEEL

Another ride-sharing app, another food delivery app, another boutique store, another pharmacy, these are all examples of copy-paste industries by unimaginative wannabe entrepreneurs - or *wantrepreneurs*. Once an existing effective solution exists which is rapidly scalable and massively used there really is no point to jump into that market. This is a Red Ocean[46].

NEW IS NOT ALWAYS BETTER

Not everything needs an app, or a redesign, or a 'disruption'. The essence of startup's vision is to provide a marketable solution that is better than the existing. What is meant by better? Something is cheaper, faster, portable, holdable, mobile, stationary, transparent, edible, biodegradable, eco-friendly, customisable and the list goes on. Basically anything that a customer perceives as a reasonable alternative to an existing solution. The product may already exist elsewhere, and you found a way to profitably sell locally is the best business approach.

MINIMUM VIABLE PRODUCT (MVP)

This is not the actual solution. It is merely a mockup or prototype of what a solution might look like. This early phase product (even software) tries to solve a specific problem for a specific type of

---

[46]Red Ocean VS Blue Ocean - Two revolutionary business perspectives which I will discuss later

customer, for a specific reason - to assess Product-Market Fit (I will describe in the next paragraph) i.e. is it providing the type of value that your customer would pay money for and you can be on the path to sustainability? Your early customer feedback, though harsh, is essential for your development and marketing team to edit further to release the better version. When you reach this phase, you have your company product.

PRODUCT-MARKET FIT

This concept is the golden ticket to define actual success. This stage takes a variable amount of time for various reasons. This is the true goal of a startup, the ability to perfectly solve a problem or need for a defined population, at an affordable scalable price, with majority acceptance of the population and finally the Market has accepted and repaid your efforts.

LEARN FROM LOSING CUSTOMERS (CHURN RATE)

The warm fuzzy feeling from seeing your user numbers and revenue intake growing is false. The true measure of your initial effectiveness depends on the churn rate. How many people download or used your product, became dissatisfied and never continue again. Learning about the number of people who erase an ap or n longer transact through you will tell you all the underlying defects that will eventually destroy your company survival chances. Much like the Pareto Principle, 80% of your churn rate is due to the 20% of errors still in your product or your company system (eg. after sales support, customer engagement, payment process).

GET YOUR A-TEAM

No man is an island. Anyone who claims to be able to do everything, ends up doing nothing. A group of nerds do not make a worthy startup team. Or as I had learned a group of amateur doctors do not make a healthy health company. You need 3-5 people in your team with complementary skills that are essential to market the product - someone skillful in sales, someone with excellent financial managerial skills, someone with the technical knowhow, someone with great interpersonal communication skills (soft skills) to handle customers, someone with '*street-smarts*' to get things done when needed and ofcourse the founder who may have designed the solution, but now must remove himself from the product completely and concentrate on strategy, implementation, vision and keep an eye on the *bigger picture*. If you are creating a health solution, obviously you must have a doctor on board.

BE DUMB

If you enter a room and you think you are the smartest person there, you are in the wrong room. The growth mindset is all about continuous learning and self development, you may be a specialist in a field from years of academic training but to be a leader you must get your mind into many practical aspects of real life such as finances, legal knowledge, effective communication, supply chain and many other facets involved from your point of sale until the moment a customer makes a purchase, and beyond. Business is actually quite boring, 99% of the work is extremely tedious but necessary. The right skills learned through active purposeful learning, ensures that you are constantly one step above bankruptcy.

EQUITY

Dividing ownership of a company is a delicate decision. Shares should be given according to the value and effort given by the team, with vested equity which means there is an option to redistribute if a team member is toxic or simply leaves. Shares should be large enough to promote some level of incentive; to sacrifice potential earnings from employment, time spent, personal resources and the massive risks. Much like bonds, the ultimate goal is to cash out in the future, as long as the company has achieved some level of profitability in the eyes of investors and/or stock traders.

DIGITAL MARKETING IS THE PRESENT & FUTURE

The world is fixated on 5-6 inches of glass on their hands. The days of print media are not for young starting companies. The ad campaign must utilise social media campaigns to get in front of the customer, provide immediate value, education, entertainment and have a clear call-to-action (CTA - click to subscribe, download, signup, purchase etc). The other benefits of digital marketing is the ability to measure the ROI of the marketing budget - meaning you can see in real time the cost-effectiveness of your marketing strategy on user growth and revenue. This is something you cannot do with a bloated press release, poster, billboard, newspaper, tv ad or even the street flyer campaign.

Branding is the psycho-sensory response of your target customer to interacting with your company's physical presence, such as the emotions upon seeing your logo, website design, your spokespersons's public appearance, digital ads, the overall outcome of utilising your product and other deep sensory responses. Your branding strategy main goal is to inspire a sense of curiosity, wonder, trust, quality and above all else, an undefinable human content. In healthcare industries, quality branding is very important - to show that patients' livelihoods are at the centre of their overall design. The concept of 'social proof' is essential, the potential customer should have tangible resources to prove your worth to them eg. online presence, newspaper articles, research papers/white papers, professional testimonials by industry experts and other means of telling them that your social value is well established - or atleast the perception of it.

CONTENT IS KING

Content data is the accumulated information that your company is trying to show the public in easily understandable bite-sized packets, to prove that you have their best interest in mind. Simply put, the Market only cares about the *benefits*, not the features. A common mistake for early entrepreneurs and novice marketeers. Original content can take the form of short blog articles, social media posts, webinars, events and seminars and basically any form of data that enhances your credibility as a trusted provider of that particular solution. Health-related content which educates the public adds a lot of value and trust, so that they are more likely to engage with your healthcare solutions.

LEGALISE EVERYTHING

For any act of commerce, you must have a trade license. Other documentations are essential for VAT registration too. An essential topic is whether or not your company is allowed to sell the product in the first place, what rights and obligations do you have. You cannot forget regulations either. So close communication and liaison with a commercial lawyer (with experience working with startups is an added bonus) from day one is essential. As long as papers are in order, you have one less headache to worry about. And pay your taxes!

IP OR NOT TO IP

Original concepts should be considered for Intellectual Property (IP) registration and copyright protection. It is extremely frustrating to find out that a similar solution has come out in the market from your direct competitor, even worse if it was stolen from you. IP licensing adds some credibility to your product in the eyes of investors, the Market does not care of course. Enforcing legal measures for infringement is a difficult topic to discuss in our region, but some protection is better than none.

FAIL FAST, LEARN FASTER

I had mentioned this part before. This is related to the idea of releasing your MVP to the Market. Often as corporate professionals or overqualified academics, we are hardwired to plan every small step to achieve absolute perfect execution - life is not perfect and your first attempt will be an astronomical failure. When you obsess over a perfect product, perfect business plan, perfect marketing strategy, all you have done is a perfect waste of time. You have to realise that whichever moment you choose to implement your dreams, you are already too late. You just have to catch up to the market momentum as fast as possible. Just build and release to a select population, get their negative feedback, remake and release once again and again until you get it right (Product-Market Fit as above).

CUSTOMER AVATAR

This is the mental image of your perfect customer. One who will whole-heartedly purchase your product with no question and at full price. This person has the problem that you are fixing, and your solution perfectly solves it. This character must be well defined down to the minute behavioural pattern - such as spending ability, clothes, social structures, common health issues, educational achievements, typical job life and so on. Your branding, marketing, pricing and all other business strategies revolve around solving this character's issues. His/her population becomes your defined demographic, any deviation will simply be an outlier. This avatar defines the source of the majority of your projected revenue. Most private hospitals create the ideal patient demographic to be a middle aged corporate male, with 3-4 chronic illnesses and fully insured.

GROWTH HACKING

The main difference between a typical business (shop, garage, dealership) and a startup, is the speed of growth. What growth you may ask - users, revenue, geographic expansion, social media presence, staffing, share value and so on. WIthout a *cancerous* growth strategy, a small startup will either remain small or will simply be outlasted by a real high speed startup. This is all about market capture. Investments are immediately diverted to marketing, mass production, staffing and ofcourse office space.

AUTOMATION

Due to high staff turnover in startup compared to established businesses, founding teams are very careful with hiring and quick firing. For this reason the better option is to use technology hacks to automate the customer engagement, payroll, subscription renewals and operations related activities using apps and software.

OUTSOURCING

With the age of freelancer ecosystems around the world, remote teams are a good source of price negotiable skills with measurable outputs eg. social media management, website development, app development and other specific tasks which can be outsourced and produced without a salaried employee. However the more diversified your founding team, it is more likely that you can build these systems in-house and save costs.

VALIDATION

Ideas are actually worthless. Everyone has ideas, but an entrepreneur implements them into the real world. Validation is not just asking for opinions and likes from close social circles, it is a deep focus group discussion with people who have the specific problem which your solution *may* help, and they would potentially pay for it.

FUNDING

It is strange that I mentioned financing at the end. The truth is, money is the least of your requirements, and the least of your problems (usually). Without the above foundations (and some other structures and systems) money will just accelerate your failures and magnify your incompetence as a leader/founder. Most common association with startup failure is poor financial management - not the lack of it. That is why it is recommended to produce a low-end MVP with raised funding (savings, friends & family) and bootstrap the early phase. With the early information on user growth and some revenue, you can make a clear decision on whether to continue this natural sustained growth or to apply for investment. With good data there is better probability of sustainable investment.

EXIT STRATEGY

Some people become so obsessed with executing their dreams, that they become exhausted and lose momentum. Before the founder burns out, or the company finally crashes[47], it is important to figure out a way to evolve beyond the caretaker role. Startup success is not about popularity or even about revenue. Success is being able to pay salaries and overhead costs on time. Every month. Best case scenario is to be bought out or acquired by a massive major global corporation, and cash out

---

[47] Startups have an extremely low half life. One way or another failure is certain due to the rapid changes in the Market. Cash out quickly and move on to the next project.

your shares quickly. Entrepreneurship means freedom to make the right life choices, if all I do is keep putting out fires, then I just created a job to keep busy - this is a lose-lose situation. Everything has an end, everything has an expiry. Plan accordingly.

The above topics are a tiny fragment to the subtle tips and tricks that I had learned from serial entrepreneurs and business experts. There is still a lot more at stake, but there is a limit to how much one should learn. Implementing knowledge is more important than blindly acquiring it.

Now it is time for the practical exams.

Growth Mindset Tip #8 Learn from those who have failed.
Theories and plans have no market value. All that is important
is massive immediate action.

HHS VERSION 2.0

From the accumulated knowledge over the past few months, I knew I had to make some changes, fast. But where should I start was the burning question. Overhead costs were minimal, I had no staff, I was spending the bare minimum on social media ads but I was stuck.

No growth no revenue.

Perhaps my target customer was not defined the right way, maybe my customer avatar was so high end that they can either manage their medical tourism trip themselves or they would go directly to Singapore. I was definitely attracting the lower end clients who just could not pay or did not want to pay the medical fees of my partner hospitals (they too wanted those specific non-profit hospital or that celebrity doctor) and were constantly arguing with me to lower these costs as if I was in charge of the doctors salaries.

I considered that maybe I need to be more specific in my services. I should cut away from low revenue low value healthcare services, which have very low commissions for referrals anyway. That means I need to provide effective end-to-end facilitation for commonly occurring and also high demand procedures (foreign doctor consultations will not be enough).

I focused my branding on cardiac interventions, cancer treatments, IVF and major orthopaedic surgeries. Their clinical management require highly skilled foreign trained specialists with many years of successful outcomes, from a dedicated team. And as market demand dictates, everybody has an established perception that Indian hospitals provide them with better quality than here in Dhaka.

I edited my company website, changed the facebook page a little. After viewing the graphic designs of other medical tourism agencies, I created my ads with somewhat minimalist designs and persuasive content to bring attention to my more specialised and streamlined services. I did not bother with blogs or whatever because I felt those were too tedious for me and maybe most people do not take the time to make a decision based on a health blog, or so I assumed.

I also learned some tips and tricks to targeted Facebook ads as well, a client friend of mine who has some knowledge about digital marketing told me how to edit the ad campaign so that I can increase the probability that a more high end customer (not too high of course) would see my beautifully designed Facebook ads, then click to see my equally beautiful website, then call my separate company mobile number anthem I could convince them to email me their scanned medical reports for a price quote and then they will be so pleased that I do not barge a consultation fee, and will agree to go to the hospitals that I had chosen for them.

Ironically I got even less lead conversion than before. Sure I received a lot of likes for the artwork, but the number of calls actually dropped. Is it because of the faulty Facebook algorithm or maybe the ads were not eye-catching enough. Deep down it was because of my amateurish strategy, but my founder ego (founder syndrome) would not let me realise that the fault is with me actually (as I write his chapter, I realise what "*N*" goes through continuously).

I attended a few more events, this time not so much for learning as the topics were being repeated and quite frankly was getting monotonous; but rather for networking and of course to hunt for customers. As you guessed correctly, I was in crisis mode. I wore expensive suits, gave out many business cards, posted more frequently in various Facebook groups (this is known as *trolling*). I was desperate for some validation, not just for my amazing business plans but also for my own competence in the eyes of strangers (also called imposter syndrome).

Almost 2 months went by without a commission cheque, personal life was tearing up. Maybe being a *solo*-preneur was not the right move. Taking on so many roles (MD, CFO, CMO, CRM etc) and wearing so many hats (or masks) was making the entire entreprise inefficient, and honestly, quite boring now.

Maybe I needed a fresh pair of eyes. Maybe I needed a business partner who could have the same goals but complementary (and streetwise) skill sets.

Growth Mindset Tip #9 -Every entrepreneur is a terrible boss. Egotistic, confused, desperate, cheap, and only agrees with his own ideas. Always look for someone who has a similar growth mindset, not necessary the same vision, but who will openly challenge you with every decision.

HUNTING FOR A COFOUNDER

The startup community in Bangladesh is extremely small, which means the number of active or aspiring entrepreneurs would be like an ethnic minority. In an unstable ecosystem, people look for illusions of temporary safety instead of adventure. Job insecurity and the high costs of living in the most expensive and unlivable city in the world does not offer enough hope for self development.

Again I tried networking in startup events, to give hints at interested professionals to jump into the world of entrepreneurship. But there were no takers. Corporate life was too nice. At this stage I was not certain on what key qualities I was looking for in a cofounder, of course they had to have complementary skills, but the main question was, what kind of value did I have to offer in the first place?

Since Bangladesh has an epidemic of semi-skilled youth unemployment (of course there are thousands of high skilled unemployed as well) I was only exposed to the younger and commercially naive crowd. I understood then that I needed a professional entrepreneur cofounder - preferably one who has some business experience i.e. Fellow serial entrepreneur.

A known legal associate introduced me to his friend; a medical doctor who also co-owns a rooftop restaurant directly opposite my coworking space. Perfect match indeed. We got acquainted, we exchanged our frustrations with the existing medical career, future aspirations and the business scope for international medical tourism with HHS. He was quite interested. We did not discuss equity or responsibilities per se, since it was our initial meeting, it was best to slowly ease into that conversation at a later date.

Now that I sort of have a potential cofounder, with a similar professional background in the health sector, has good business sense and apparently some influence in the pharmaceutical industry; now is a good time to edit the overall business operations to get some leads, effectively.

Most days I waste many hours on YouTube, watching business videos, motivation tapes and *growth hacks*. One day I watched a course on 'Multi-Level Marketing' (MLM). Basically I would recruit freelance field-level marketers to get in contact with private practice doctors, to convince them to send their patients to me. They would know which type of patients were in need of high value interventions *and* could afford to pay the high prices. I would share a portion of the commissions when a few patients would finally reach my partner hospitals. Greater my coverage, greater the upstream referrals to HHS and as this spider web network, grows, I can really cash in. MLM was an amazing business model.

In theory.

As I had no sales experience in the Dhaka context (or any context actually), it was difficult to conceptualise what kind of sales team I would need to build, what would be their qualifications and most importantly, what kind of value incentive would be needed. I made a job vacancy post and placed in some facebook groups; mostly generic qualifications often seen in pharmaceutical marketing jobs. As money is a major issue given that I have not gotten any revenue for the past few months, I decided to reimburse by a sales commission structure, where for every doctor lead they would bring me, and would actually send their patients to HHS, then send to India and complete the transaction, everyone would get a cut.

This MLM concept was thought up by one of my partner agents based in India, he used to be in IT but shifted to international medical tourism[48]. We often have long discussions about the whole medical tourism industry between our two countries. He has atleast 5-6 years experience, travelling back and forth, arranging free medical camps, making new liaisons and he told me the issues with this crowded market. Us two would talk a lot about innovative strategies to get more converting leads - such as trying to organise free medical camps, free consultations with Indian specialists,

As with most plans, it all looks nice when you see it on a screen. I received a few inquiries about the vacancy, two sad realities were apparent. Majority of Bangladeshi job-seekers have either poor grasp of simple English, or do not read the instructions properly (hence the unemployment status possible) as most of the queries were about the payment structure - even though the term freelancer was mentioned atleast three times.

I managed to get 3 people who seemed more curious than interested, but it's a start nonetheless. The doctor-restaurateur came by with his friend to oversee the presentation. I booked the small

---

[48]Interestingly many of the freelancer medical tourism agents in India have a tech background who are now into medical tourism, each of them have grand designs for cool website, with AI capabilities and direct teleconferencing with Indian specialists. There are many assumptions that can be made, but the theme of this book will be deviated if we over analyze this common scenario.

meeting room in my coworking space, I wore a nice suit, provided some light refreshments and made some nice slides to show them the overall process, what will be the responsibilities and potential income from each doctor lead and eventual patient referral. It all seemed good while I was rehearsing the presentation.

In reality it did not turn out fruitful in any way. The attendees were visibly confused by the process, and since I did not specifically highlight their own intrinsic gain, there was no real value to the whole exercise. Thinking back I realised I was only talking about HHS, me, my dreams, my vision and I was expecting a random stranger to go out in traffic and the heat to chase doctors - like medical/pharma reps in the hopes of me convincing that doctor to join HHS network and etc etc etc. I did not communicate the individual value to these guys, and my curious doctor entrepreneur friend, and therefore it crashed and burned even before starting.

I should have realised back then that before talking about the impact and benefits to the stakeholders; I should have spent some time investing in self development. Developing my own communication strategies to talk about values and outcome; would have been more effective than a hundred Facebook ads (literally). But the absence of this important skill set was obvious - none of the attendees called back, and my new friend simply avoided contact - as courteous as possible. Why waste time with a medical tourism agency when his own restaurant business and small clinic is paying the bills.

Growth Mindset Tip #10 - Develop your understanding of exactly how your vision will give value to everyone directly impacted by your activities, not just potential customers. You should be clear on the responsibilities of team members - but you should be even more specific on what kind of value your cofounder/shareholder will gain by working *with* you (not for you!)

HHS VERSION 3.0

- Events based concept

For a short time I consulted for an independant university advisor, who was a close friend of my father. He was a renowned education consultant and advisor for many top private universities in Dhaka. That year he was busy designing the curriculum and overall infrastructure for an upcoming medical university and teaching hospital. He brought me in to help him raise awareness to this project by organising a fundraising campaign of sorts. Since I had some idea about how *not* to set up a medical event, I could atleast tell him the right way to do it. It was a good project, not entirely sure what I would gain from it, financially or otherwise, but I helped out as best I could.

During my time with him, I had an idea which I shared with some of my partner medical tourism agents, about the concept of organising an international OPD campaign in local private hospitals, whereby experienced medical specialists would come down over a weekend to consult patients here. A few would be referred for investigations at the facilities of the host OPD clinic, and the few who wanted or needed more intensive care can be referred to the partner hospital - who would be sponsoring theseOPD campaigns. Through this collaboration we would all get the necessary coverage, media presence, local community marketing and just converting less than 3-5% of the patients who would come down just to see the high skilled Indian specialists, would more than likely cover up the costs for the next batch of OPD campaigns.

I wrote up every tiny detail of this campaign, down to where I would get the merchandise, print out flyers, digital marketing strategy, which nearby hotel they would be staying in, the criteria and address of these mid-range hospitals, trust me even as far as where I could get vegetarian catering if required. It was a nice plan. It had very nice fonts and beautiful designs and timelines. There was even the entire schedule where local doctors could come down for the seminar sessions.

It was a nice plan.

I still have that plan in my laptop, in some obscure file.

That is the problem with plans, without execution they are just idle words sitting around. You can share it with as many people as you want, but if the first step is not taken while the mental momentum is there then it just crashes and burns, or worse remains unopened in an obscure digital file in the corner of your computer hard drive.

What happened this time you may ask, why did you not hear of any such OPD campaign in Banani or Dhanmondi like I had planned in my proposals?

Answer: *Inertia* (inability or unwillingness to take action)

None of the indian agents wanted to spend money to make money, that is nobody returned the calls or reach any consensus as to how it should take place. There was some discussion about me taking the first step in raising the funds to acquire the license for foreign doctors to practice temporarily (plus bribes), booking the OPD suites in some hospital, start printing the materials etc. and they would set up the visa applications and doctors for the latter half, and then reimburse me when they come down to Dhaka. I spent most of my life around Indians, Arabs, Chinese, Pakistanis etc. I think I do not need to remind you about the expected outcome when it comes to dealing with certain ethnicities who are globally known for unprofessional and *un-entrepreneurial* behaviour (even Bangladeshis).

This events proposal will not move until I stretch my neck out for the sword. Partnerships, especially so-called international ones are extremely high risk as nobody wants to take the risk. As long either party is at comfort in their own geography, nothing will move, nothing will change.

Growth Mindset Tip #11 - Plans are dreams written down to make you feel comfortable and warm, knowing that you must be some kind of genius. If you do not act on it by clear goals, then the genius becomes the coward. Don't overthink and don't overplan. You have a tiny window of opportunity in life; do first, learn and then plan.

HHS VERSION 4.0

- Pioneer Stem Cell Therapy Advisor

So generic medical tourism facilitator/agent nor medical events management is not working out, or rather I am not the person who can bring that level of value to the target customer. I have come to realise that there really is a need for both of these concepts; obviously Bangladesh has a large public health issue with chronic diseases and there are thousands who travel abroad for expensive but essential medical interventions. But in this hyper-saturated market, I would need to invest a great deal of infrastructure and branding to be visible enough to compete with established agents.

I remember my conversation with '*B*' (my Indian medical facilitator contact) who had atleast 5 years experience with only the Bangladesh medical tourism market. He knows all the areas around Dhaka, most of the medical system players, some Bangla but most importantly he had a keen knowledge about market trends (and patient perceptions). All of his feedback was true in one form or another - the frustration in dealing with local doctors, the industry politics, bureaucratic corruption, ignorance of the masses, market saturation by amateurs (like myself) and like a prophecy; the impending closure of another Dhaka-based medical tourism facilitator.

The first-time entrepreneur is defined by his conviction to his dream, his patience to execute a plan no matter what and the absolute belief that the market must adopt to his product. These are the signs of a mental illness patient, or an amateur with a dream - the difference is at the response by the Market. In my case I tried to hold on and adapt as passionately as possible.

I went through some of the notes I had taken from the many events over the past few months. I came across the concept of the 'niche'[49]. I did initially plan to only target a specific group of Dhaka citizens - upper middle class, corporate occupation, with a valid passport, exposure to local health system quality, afford to pay for premium interventions etc. But it seems that was not enough, next I had to magnify down to the level of actual high revenue medical intervention (cancer treatment, orthopedics etc), the next step would be to include innovative and revolutionary treatments that are still not mainstream, but has an established treatment and referral infrastructure abroad.

After some careful consideration, I started researching on the economic and health outcomes of stem cell therapy. Truly amazing advances since I last read about it back in my residency in the USA. I remembered it was the talk of science fiction to even mention stem cell treatments, the idea of extracting foreign cells from aborted fetuses or whatever, raised a lot of controversies around the

---

[49] Niche - A highly defined segment of a population who is the main target of a business plan, for a specific solution, at a value-added price with a clear branding strategy only for them.

world. But what I had read and seen, and even talked with some patients (via skype), it was as simple as a liposuction.

The basic process is to first identify specific patients with specific diseases which were statistically more likely to gain the benefit of introducing naive pluripotent stem cells, into the damaged areas, mature it with hormones and nutrients and then slowly see them adapt to the functional behaviour of native cells. So far it has shown great promise in select cases of strokes, heart failure, joint damage, some neurological conditions, hematological cancers and a few others conditions. The best part, which is also why it is becoming more popular, is that the origin of the stem cells come from the patients' *own* fat cells around their abdomen. No controversy, no tissue rejection, no need for high end procedures (sometimes).

I felt that I finally found my niche product, niche patient customer and now I needed to rebrand myself accordingly. I started reaching out to stem cell centres in India, Thailand and Malaysia. I received some callbacks here and there, and with no surprise the ones based around Bangalore and Mumbai were very eager to capture the Bangladesh market. I even told my friend '*B*' about this strategy, he did not know much about the procedure but was happy to help out as long as I could secure some leads.

I fixed up the website, made some eye-catching ads and started another Facebook campaign by myself. To utilise my academic skills I wrote some short articles about stem cell therapy on

LinkedIn, Quora and various patient support pages on Facebook. The response was lukewarm, sure there were many '*likes*' but no actual leads, not even shares or comments.

Not willing to accept defeat I increased the marketing budget slightly, and the response increased slightly as well - more likes but no leads. Perhaps people were appreciating the 'aesthetic' value of the ad rather than the actual content. I received a handful of curious patients who were fed up with the present health situation, and wanted a more affordable clinical management.

Out of the few, even fewer finally agreed to come down to my office for a consult. Many had done their own research on the science, and were interested in one form or another. But when prices were discussed (which were atleast half of what a standard surgery would cost anyway) I received the all too familiar hesitation and resistance. This was reaching into a brick wall. Even with affordable innovation, I was still not capturing the right customer. The product is safe, the institutions are reputable but the treatment costs remain a major decision blocker for this segment.

Growth Mindset Tip #12 An innovation can be revolutionary. But if nobody buys, you have no business in it. Either you have to spend resources to drive up demand, or improve your sales skills to improve your expertise in that product. Either way if you did not invent the concept, don't waste time trying to sell it. Even you might not appreciate its true value.

HHS Version 5.0

- International Solid Tissue Procurement & Graft Specialist

(AKA *Black Market Organ Smuggler*)

You can read the chapter title again if you want.

I am not proud that my years of medical training and life experiences had lead me down this path. I did not plan on having my very own network and database of so many 'charitable donors' who were so motivated to help a fellow human being, *with a price tag*. Before you judge me or even contact me to get access to these 'voluntary but poor donors' to help a family member; let me say that I am honestly glad that this segment of my entrepreneurship journey did NOT work out. This network is disbanded, my affiliations with certain characters is long over.

Let me start at the beginning and lead you to its very quick end. Whether you consciously decided to go down a path or not, is mostly irrelevant and beyond your control in most cases. An entrepreneur adapts to the market, but this part of the journey was unconscious - I was responding to a market need, *a black market need*.

When I first started getting inquiries from end stage renal failure patients (dialysis failure) regarding kidney transplant services, I had no way of helping them out in anyway. All that trouble to gather leads but I did not have the resources to convert them into HHS customers. It was really frustrating.

In a weird twist of fate, I was contacted by another Indian medical tourism agent who works in the accounts department of a major tertiary hospital chain. He told me he saw one of my facebook posts in a medical tourism group, and was asking if we could form a referral partnership - sure, why not, I form a dozen partnerships every month. After a brief chat, he told me he specialises in *arranging* organ transplant procedures for international clients. He has a Dhaka-based partner who handles the *procurement, processing, remuneration* and *transfer* of certain *biological assets* that certain clients would pay a high price. You think I am exaggerating these terms, sadly I must inform you the scale of commercialisation that the global healthcare industry has gone towards. The corporate property rights for original genetic material will occur soon, but for now you are already aware of the supply chain behaviour of the global trade in 'Grey Market' organ transplants. It is not just rich Europeans or Arabs who prey on the poor for their 'pound of flesh'[50], nowadays it is globalised and democratised, with rising cases of end stage organ failure, you will do anything and pay anything to keep your loved one alive.

No matter who is giving the pound of flesh.

---

[50] In Shakespeare's *Merchant of Venice*, Shylock had to pay up a portion of his own body tissue as a loan default. In reality it is common and digitised.

I mentioned the Grey Market because although it is illegal in Bangladesh people still need a way to replace their damaged and decaying kidney, liver, bone marrow, lungs, heart etc. And there are people who have no value in life than to sell off parts of their bodies (selective but permanent prostitution if you like to call it) due to massive intergenerational debts or whatever. There is an ineffective infrastructure that does organ transplantation procedures in Dhaka, extensive bribery, long processing times, unknown quality and usually mistrust in local health system capacity. So it is obvious which way people want to go.

From some of the information given by my Indian contacts (who have long destroyed their SIM cards before I wrote this book) there are hundreds of surgical teams, who work in major hospitals in the day, in one city, then travel to a mid-range hospital in another Indian state - which has somewhat lenient bureaucratic oversight (translation: affordable bribery range), who will cut out and transplant anything to anyone at the right price, and they are very skilled at what they do. Thousands of Bangladeshi patients go through these channels, better outcomes need better payments.

Simple as that.

I was at an entrepreneurial dilemma. If I refuse, I would miss out on a lucrative opportunity, allow a patient to eventually die a horrible death and the poor person who badly needed that money would continue to suffer in poverty. If I rebranded the rest of my life in that way, I would be a member of a small but wealthy group of former doctors who made their fortunes from arranging for the surgical manipulation of an impoverished group of people, for the benefit of people who could afford to buy a few more years into their lives.

I would become a Nazi Doctor.

I was blinded by the potential revenue.

I was frustrated by the lack of traction of HHS.

I was becoming greedy.

I agreed.

I tried to rationalise my decision by imagining how all parties would gain somehow; the donor would have shorter lifespans but would get some money to solve some of their financial pain, and the recipient can get some extra time in their already shortened life spans after selling off their properties. But only my contacts and myself would gain, and gain, with no actual bodily risks.

I knew I had to be careful in the way I marketed my new 'health services', so I rephrased my ads as 'organ care specialist', 'organ health management' and 'kidney/liver health provider'. I made fancy disclaimer forms for all parties to sign, in this Grey Market they have no value as there is no scope for jurisdiction anyway. My local contact agreed for the sake of appeasing me, I think I made these forms just to convince myself I was doing the *right* thing.

So I made the Facebook ads, I posted in the patient groups, and I waited. I received more calls in one week than the entire few months of starting HHS. Most could not afford the fees. Few begged. Few considered but did not call back. But there a few who did come to my office directly as I had made a special arrangement with some local specialists (which happens more often with other agents than you can ever imagine). We talked, we discussed payment structures, we looked through albums and whatsapp groups of potential donors, their health statuses and operation theatre vacancies in India.

For every lead I was secretly thankful that they did not go through with it, or atleast not through me. I remember 2-3 who found some other arrangement to get the transplant done, and the remaining simply could not afford to do so anyway. I knew my 'special partners' were disappointed that I could not get them anymore leads. Slowly we lost contact with each other. When I did not hear anything from them or the whatsapp groups, I destroyed the HHS company SIM as well. Burn everything.

I was glad this is as far as I got in this strange point in my entrepreneurial journey. Sure I know a lot of the characters and structures that play a part in this trade. But I am just a small fish, there are sharks who have long embraced their dark entrepreneurial mindset.

Do anything for the gold. Sell anything for the gold.

A pound of gold for a pound of flesh.

This price is too high to pay for me.

Growth Mindset #13 - In any venture, when you are the
only one who is benefitting. Something is very wrong.
One day you will pay a heavy painful price. Businessmen
chase profits. Entrepreneurs create value before the price
tag. Know the difference.

HHS Version 6.0

The Clinic of the Future

It was high time for a clean start.

Time for a complete rewrite of my journey. I had gone through so many versions, the past few were just a few examples of ideas I could atleast take a personal credit for. In a short span of time (last few months of 2018) I had an abundance of fancy ideas that would revolutionise the health industry of the world, I had plans to be a Nobel Prize winner for something something, but the crushing reality of a total mind blockage was holding me down.

-Skills institute

-Medical IoT device importer

-Ayurvedic bulk product distributor

-and many more...

I remember a saying about not to *reinvent the wheel*, or *build a better mousetrap*. Basically its meaning is related to not obsess about restructuring an entire industry alone and overnight. Just solve a problem that you know well enough. That is it.

To take a break from all this useless planning, designing and imagining; I knew I had to reconnect with society - more specifically the professional community of doctors that I knew well.

On Facebook, I reached out to some of my old school friends, whom I had lost contact over the years. We had long talks about how our lives had turned out, our hopes, dreams, aspirations and each of their obstacles. So much advice but nothing practical that we could really talk about. The same audio file was replaying in our heads; write more international exams, leave the profession, leave the country etc. The core issue seemed to be the mass public distrust towards the health system. Everybody wants the very top consultants in the city, before heading to India anyway. This leaves young postgraduates in dire economic frustrations. Some doctors do not know how to talk to patients, patients vent their anger on social media, journalists enjoy the violent narratives and good doctors bear the brunt - either through harsh interactions or worse, absence of patients altogether.

Although it is not something original, but I had this idea that most of my concepts were lacking a physical infrastructure - meaning if people could somehow see that HHS (and myself) were real then that in itself would allow for some effective market traction. This led me to designing the blueprint and planning for my very own state-of-the-art futuristic polyclinic.

I must confess that this idea, which was copy-pasted by hundreds of health entrepreneurs, was motivated by a deep urge to be a business owner (instead of a business maker). Quite simply I was jealous that I had met so many clinic owners who had no real connection or training from the health industry, are now multimillionaires from their hospital projects. So in my mind, I figured that I should also run my own clinic.

Fancy building plans were drawn out, business plans drafted and superficial market research was done. I knew it would be a crowded market - there are hundreds of polyclinics scattered around the city. How would I stand out from the others?

This state-of-the-art clinic would provide the latest in stem cell treatments, have OPD sessions with various medical specialists, hold CME[51] events by International specialists and in simple terms - be the beacon for healthcare innovation.

Yes, I know one must have grand dreams to make grand impacts.

But this was too much, too quick, too risky.

If there is one thing I have learned about idea design, there really is no such thing as a bad idea - just bad execution. The magic is in raising enough demand to raise enough revenue. But before all that you have to have reasonable expertise to carry it out, and a massive capital fund source especially if going into product development and distribution i.e. the usual healthcare/medical entrepreneurship.

---

[51] Continued Medical Education

Before fully shutting down an idea, I wanted to see the look of disbelief from an honest feedback. Atleast if I could hear how ludicrous this million dollar investment in an experimental medical centre, I can atleast come to terms with reality and learn to move on. To finally destroy and burn all those loft plans - so I can properly behave like an entrepreneur.

I invited a few of my closest entrepreneur friends, some whom I had sort of mentored, to give me a deep thinking honest feedback. This violent psychosocial experience was needed to reset my neural pathways i.e. destroy ideas and plans that have no connection with the real problems in the health system.

And they did.

Hearing their feedback put me at ease at last. They helped me realise that I have to go back to my startup teachings. Relearn and apply the fundamentals of the Lean Startup methodology[52].

Back to the drawing board.

Maybe instead of hearing lectures, I needed actual business mentorship.

---

[52] Solve a problem, quickly build and implement a solution, assess the market feedback, redesign and try again. Repeat. But solve the problem.

Growth Mindset Tip #14 - Get your entrepreneur network to scrutinise your ideas. Allow them to tear it down into pieces, so you can make the decision to bury it or build it.

BUSINESS GUIDANCE BY A SERIAL ENTREPRENEUR

While scrolling through the local events section on Facebook, I came upon an announcement for a free event at the EMK Center. It was another entrepreneur workshop by some guy based in Australia. Apparently he was an expert on the entrepreneur mindset. I thought I would attend just to see what this guy is all about, maybe I can learn something new, some new tactic I can use to progress myself. Honestly when you hear one talk by some business guru, you can pretty much notice a pattern. As long as it was free I had nothing to lose.

Not many showed up that early in the morning, I was glad as I hate those big crowded venues. Those turn out to be a motivational show and all that you get is some cheap merchandise and the speakers' ego gets inflated by all the brainless clapping. Not this event. Not with this guy.

Loud techno music by a classic 90's pop band was on full volume as he burst in. He told everyone to get up and jump around, gave each other high fives and riled up the crowd like the way Tony Robbins does in his shows. Immediately we jumped right into the chaos of our lives. Unfulfilled goals, failure stories, bankruptcy, unable to make a proper decision in business, life and dreams.

This guy really knows his stuff.

'*HH*' is a globally recognised Business Coach, Speaker and Entrepreneur of the Year in Australia.

He was a Bangladeshi immigrant to Melbourne, followed the typical unimaginative South Asian

life goals, enjoyed the high-income lifestyle of the tech industry and was hospitalised with severe

life-threatening pancreatitis. Very poor prognosis. He was not an alcoholic or anything associated

with the risk factors. The doctors there thought that due to his high stress lifestyle, his body was

eventually shutting down. 'Change fast, change now' they said. 'Or else you will die in a week.'

That was many years ago. He listened, he changed, he lived. I know of a close friend in medical

school who died from acute pancreatitis. Usually not something you can survive. Usually.

Maybe '*HH*' had something valuable to teach me. He was a practitioner of Neuro-Linguistic

Programming - quite simply the words and affirmations you use on yourself, create and bend reality

to make sure you achieve your goals. I know it sounds like brain-washing or some hipster garbage.

But they actually worked.

I enjoyed his event, it was to the point, had clear personal examples that most of us could relate to

and ironically, his entrepreneur advice was so absurd it might actually work.

And they did.

The following were the main points which stuck with me and I have implemented at full force:

Beat Emotion with Motion

When you become too emotional, or you feel your current situation is overwhelming, just move. Snap your fingers and start walking around. Join a gym to vent out your feelings and get in shape.

Proximity is Power

Show me your friends and I will show you your future. Often the social circles that we have become comfortable with, are directly sabotaging our wellbeing. Be it family, friends or work colleagues - some people are designed to keep you as pathetic as they are. Surround yourself with like-minded people who want or have more than you, so you will be motivated to better yourself every time you meet them.

Early Bird

Whatever it takes, wake up early every day, every day. Even on a weekend. It takes a few weeks to form a good habit, but only a single day to break it. Wake up at dawn to pray, meditate, work out or anything physical just to get the creative juices flowing.

Diet

Eat well, eat clean. None of that typical disgusting pig food that you eat from the streets out of convenience. If you do not maintain some kind of high standard to your wellbeing, your dreams will break before your body.

MIA (*Massive Immediate Action*)

Simply wishing for change is Bullshit. Promising to take action is Bullshit. You must take a true life changing action right now, all the way before your default self-limiting beliefs put you back in the zero state.

Working with Obligations

If you do anything for yourself, eventually you will just bore yourself. When you are convinced that your success is vital to keep your family alive and safe, you will move the mountains.

Trust the Process

The Entrepreneur Journey is a Life Journey. Employee life is over, nothing is planned for short term gains. It will take a long time to see the results that will surprise you, and your social circles. Just stay the course and see it to the end.

Don't Plan. First Do It, then plan for the improvements (Lean Startup)

This was definitely a personal recommendation towards me. I have vast gigabytes of beautifully designed and idle business plans in my computer. Obsessing over perfect planning will (in '*HH*' words) make me older and fatter. Which it did. The logic behind immediate execution is that by the time you think your business plan is fool-proof, the nature of your Market has changed so that your solution has no relevance. Ideas are spread at the speed of sound, but customer decisions work faster than the speed of light i.e. speed of thought.

- Do the bare basic market research

- Gather the resources

- Define the strategy

- Implement

- Get the feedback

- Now plan for better next version

Know Your Worth

You don't need to answer every message. You don't need to attend every event. You must not waste time with *time-wasters*. Everyone has a dollar value on the time they have for people. You must decide whether you are a 'social prostitute' (always available for a chat, for free) or a busy empire-builder.

A. R. T. (Authority in the Market. Results-driven. Trust.)

Credibility is the true high income skill. People do not actually buy *things*. They buy value-based commodities from a trusted source, whom they have gradually appreciated. The entrepreneur must be recognised as an industry expert, have some tangible measurable results and above all, have a reputable source of testimonials. Whatever you do, do it so well as if you have a PhD in it.

Digitize everything

Digital marketing is the future. Everything and everyone is online. Invest in learning digital marketing strategies, or pay someone to manage your online campaigns. Print media is for corporations, not startups. The CTA (call to action button) of any digital ad will directly bring you the *right* leads.

Make a Vlog. Write a Book. Create Value. Then Sell.

Best way to practice A.R.T. is to produce original expert content. Educate and entertain your defined target customer about that specific topic, at the very end you can make a value proposition. This *soft* selling is the new proven method to success.

Master the Sales Funnel

Identify your population. Then break it down into segments (segregation) and target your sales process to the leads (people who really value your value). Take them through a process where slowly their defenses come down, they trust you then purchase from you.

Are you in the Business? Or is this an Expensive Hobby?

Clarify your vision. Unique value proposition. Business strategy. And the most important thing - actual Business Model. Quite simply you must have a clear process whereby the customer puts his money into your bank account. Shorter the steps needed, better chance at staying solvent. Non-Profit ventures are the same as being Anti-Profit, sooner or later your generous donors will stop the funds and all your grand charitable events will be erased. Business is about money, nothing more. Be serious in making money, keeping it and then multiplying the savings.

Price Up

In a crowded market, the usual response is to be in a price war. All it does is decrease quality and customer satisfaction. As you decrease prices, you decrease the calibre of your customer segment. These people cannot afford you at any price so all you have done is to shoot your own foot, and your competition together. Your prices reflect the value you want to give to a specific customer, raising prices strategically while upgrading the product/service value is the sure step to success. You will lose a few customers, those who stay will complain, but they will pay in the end. No room for *'likes'*, it is all about the profit margins.

You are the Face of your Enterprise - Use video to prove it

As mentioned, digital marketing is the right channel, and video based ads are the right tools. It is proven that videos increase lead generation and conversion thousand times over (i.e. very high ROI). You should have multiple short clear videos at each step in the value chain and the sales funnels. People want a humanised process to purchasing, your face will prove that someone *real* is trying to help them.

I think I might have shared too much too soon with you. Now you know all my million dollar tactics. The truth is I am glad to share with you. I hold no secrets, I am not interested in keeping all this knowledge to myself; as my father used to tell me, true value of knowledge is when it is shared and acted upon.

He was always a wise and generous man.

Most of these points are nothing new or revolutionary. Many are well promoted by religious prophets, gurus, mentors, teachers, parents and all the hundreds of well-meaning people in our lives. The message is clear but we are stupid. We are blind.

We are the Ego that stabs itself.

EMOTION = MOTION (Move your ass!)

Growth Mindset Tip#15 - Seek professional help. Pay for it. Do it.

EVOLVING THE MINDSET

The change was not easy. I liked sleeping late, watching Youtube videos about entrepreneurship. I liked my sleep. I liked pretending that I was doing important work. All those likes and still no revenue. Enough is enough.

WIth great difficulty I made a promise. And I kept it. I woke up at 5am everyday. I woke up before the local imam. I sat in silence to clear my head. I watched the living room illuminate with the dawn light before going to the rooftop for some power walking and listening to podcasts. I went to the gym in the morning, I was the first in so I had more time to practice my boxing. I entered my coworking space to have a second power breakfast before sitting down to *think*.

For the first few weeks I had no new ideas. I was simply watching videos on startup culture, read some downloaded books about business, did some random Facebook posts to promote HHS. Nothing much changed, but nothing got worse. In the medical field this period of nothingness is a good thing. When inflammation and toxins clear up, the battleground becomes quiet, the tissues prepare to heal.

The change was so gradual it was almost as if I never changed at all. As if I was always like this.

Every night I went to deep sleep exhausted because of waking up early that morning.

I woke up before the alarm sometimes.

I prayed, not for myself, but to give regards to my late father.

Books were in short supply as they were being read for the first time.

Mornings were defined and output related (not by the number of hours)

I returned home early to eat lunch at home instead of some fast food.

My mood quietened

My mind engine purred like a Tesla

I had nothing but I was at peace.

The neural links that were preset to quick harsh responses, some verbal, some physical. Sprouted like newborn lungs. Tasting oxygen for the first time.

The *hustler* businessman exploits.

The amateur builds something and then looks for people to buy it.

But the Entrepreneur focuses on a problem. And tries to create a sellable solution.

Growth Mindset Tip 'Alpha' - Follow this book like a Bible

SOMATECH - A product of original Physician Entrepreneurship

The fever was mild. I went to bed without dinner as I was feeling sick. Earlier, I had a chat with an old friend of mine whom I had not spoken to in many years. He was a doctor in a reputable hospital. He was in hard times. He told me the daily struggles faced by thousands of specialists - trying to make an extra living in private practice. Day in day out. No time to rest after 3 days on-call. Rushing to one private chamber at a hospital for a few hours, then to another one across the city (in our horrible traffic) just in the hopes of seeing some patients. He told me about his reality, and that of his colleagues.

Good doctors have established networks, either built up over years of peer referrals, or by dealing with third party patient touts (dalal is the local term for this type of broker). Mass prescription of unnecessary procedures and unnecessary medications. Why would they get so many private patients? What else do they know? Patients follow the herd, and the herd tells them where to go.

Desperation from shrinking bank accounts forces many to become deviants of the Hippocratic Oath and most of the modern day medical conventions on patient safety and patient rights. What else will they do? Print more cards, distribute flyers, deal with dalals. Then what? You cannot practice where you want, if you are not part of a professional affiliation - a local physician society.

The idea came to me like an epileptic fit. I was half asleep when I retraced by conversations with him. I jumped out of bed and started walking across the room, just moving just walking. Like the advice of '*HH*' I had to clamp down on my epiphany into words, instead of the rush of mental images I was having. So I got out of the house and went to the rooftop. It was before dawn. I power walked around the rooftop, in circles, in diagonal steps until my mind quieted and I could formulate the idea in words, in my mind.

Came back down. I took some paper and wrote down my idea, not in any order, just the raw concepts that came to me a few minutes ago. First in small short sentences and then basic flow diagrams. I found a large piece of paper, which was ironically a poster I made for HHS, finally put to good use.

In the centre there were two stick figures, one of them was a patient with a sad face (sick), and the other one was the doctor with a stethoscope. Both had a rectangle in their hands, signifying a mobile device. Like a spiderweb I connected the various systems, processes, speech patterns, costs, needs, risks and other random thoughts related to this idea. This was known as mind-mapping. On another piece of paper I drew a series of vertical rectangles, symbolising mobile screens. I drew boxes, wrote text, used arrows to show pathways all leading to a handful of possible real world outcomes.

I put the papers somewhere safe. Ofcourse I took a picture of them and saved them on my phone.

Then I went to sleep.

Tomorrow will be a busy day.

I know what you are thinking.

Why don't I just tell you what I was planning, why all this drama?

This is the science and art of *story-telling*.

It is an ancient human practice - that we have outsourced to amateurs (eg. Bollywood)

Before I tell you what I discovered, I have to tell you after all this time...

What I have become.

MEDICAL ENTREPRENEUR

HEALTH ENTREPRENEUR

PHYSICIAN ENTREPRENEUR

- *What is the difference?*

Entrepreneurship is a madman's game. It is a high risk high stakes business venture to market a concept to solve a deep need, for high profits, *sometimes*.

There is a global epidemic of frustrated corporate doctors and nurses, overeducated and underemployed medical graduates and let us not forget the large numbers of people in general who want something better health in their daily lives; had created a social revolution in wanting their needs met with products which are faster, bigger, smaller, cheaper, cooler, trendy and digitized above all else. I am sure you are aware of the dozens of popular ride sharing companies, ecommerce platforms, social communication apps and rapidly increasing numbers of digital health inventions. All these ideas were made real by dedicated teams of entrepreneurs who want to solve a particular *pain* that the target customer has.

The healthcare industry is a complicated set of systems; made up highly skilled teams, expensive machines, heavily researched and marketed biological products. Modern medicine relies on an even more complex supply chain; starting from medical schools, graduate medical universities, residency hospitals, top-of the line pharmaceutical laboratories, technological factories and of course the other parallel paraclinical/paramedical disciplines, leading all the way to clinics, hospitals, pharmacies and other dispensaries of healthcare products and services. The digital platform is the latest addition into this massive trillion dollar industry.

Staying alive, avoiding sickness, giving birth, replacing something, cutting something out, gaining vitality and the various life processes of humans, puts modern medicine at the very critical point in everyone's lives. And due to its complexity (and culture), it is actually quite inefficient in providing the quality care that the masses are in need of. Inefficient healthcare delivery leads to poor economies of scale[53] leading to abnormally high costs of production, education, registration, recruitment, distribution and quality assurance of everything. So with these vast systemic defects, it is obvious that many motivated and eager entrepreneurs would want to figure out a way to solve atleast some of these issues. And make some money out of it.

From my short but intensive experience in this parallel career move, I have identified three core categories of entrepreneurs who are directly or indirectly related to the health industry, these are just the broad practical definitions:

---

[53] If more users receive the same care consistently, that production line can be upgraded and costs go down for everyone

MEDICAL ENTREPRENEUR

This person is intimately aware of the day-to-day processes and issues faced in providing quality medical or biomedical services, such as portable medical devices with better battery, easier to use interface, cheaper, better diagnostic results and so on. That means there is a strong need for a measurable, repeatable and scalable product (like a device) that a personnel can use to deliver healthcare safer and more efficiently. Some form of medical qualification may be required to fully understand the customer segment, the problem and to understand the full scope of all the players involved in that particular sector.

HEALTH ENTREPRENEUR

This type can be very broadly applied to pharmaceutical providers (or any biologically-active compound like herbal products), health service facilitators (medical tourism, mental health specialists, medical skills trainer etc), consultants or even health tech innovators, that are creating methods of improving the health of a population - either by consumption of the newly marketed health product (new pharmaceutical agent or alternative therapy) or some kind of software that will aid in the process of healthcare administration (confidential file sharing, prescription tracking, fitness apps etc). The solutions are somewhat generalised and have to do with the overall quality of life (QoL) of their customers. In most cases it is not necessary to have a standard medical degree to be this type of health-related entrepreneur (it helps but not necessary), however to understand how such a product can bring value it is recommended to have atleast a medical/health specialist as an advisor.

PHYSICIAN ENTREPRENEUR

This type of 'specialist' is extremely rare. No doctor in their right mind would ever think of giving up a lucrative career in a multidisciplinary institution, an emerging reputable career, social capital given to high income earners and let us not forget the immense investment in time and money in skills development to reach that far. Unless that physician has released two things; he or she is unable to find the passion or purpose to continue in the clinical field, or that a moment of clarity had occurred when the physician notices that a solution to a core problem exists and that if they took the initiative to develop it they can be instrumental in providing the right benefit to their patients, and of course make some more revenue than their standard income. This doctor entrepreneur is more advanced in his relation to the core problem that he/she faces on a daily basis, and its effect on other parts of his profession; such as the difficulties in healthcare access, appointment tracking, patient satisfaction, information sharing, safety processes, community awareness and various areas in the medical career where there is room for innovation.

The above examples are by no means industry definitions or fixed labels, on the hard-working professionals who had risked everything to fulfill a deep calling. Whatever the label, the most important aspect is the hardwired business planning and execution that is required. Given the interconnected nature of the health system in a country, the healthcare entrepreneur usually has to fulfill all three labels.

Actually there is no real difference between this kind of entrepreneur versus any other business professional; all that matters is the strong dedication and obsession with creating meaningful value while maintaining a proactive role in generating sustainable revenue. There are ofcourse many non-profit or social businesses headed by medical professionals who want to help the community with their passion and goodwill. In real life it is always about money; someone is paying and someone needs it i.e. the social business will survive as long as the donors see a clear value output from their contributions or else funding ceases and goodwill ends. Therefore by that cold logic, sometimes the best way to impact on the health of a community, is by a profitable business that can still do good things and stay solvent, and keep on providing innovative health solutions independently from the economic whims of outsider investments.

With so much at stake, with high probability of failure and economic ruin; why would a successful medical professional risk his livelihood for a business career path? In professional life, we can devise a Venn diagram of key motivations for progressing the way we do. The three elements can be named the *3 P's of motivation* - Passion, Purpose and Profit. Most of us are lucky enough to have a job that fulfills atleast 2P's to get us through the day without losing our inner drive:

A job that gives you a lot of profit and passion only, will not fulfill your purpose in life eg. Insanely successful Wall Street Broker, who can only make money but he always wanted to do something creative.

Many social workers, NGO's, charity workers and other social ventures are skilled at helping the impoverished, and they enjoy bringing joy to them, but the capacity of their potential is limited by donor funds, and such people are at extreme risk of bankruptcy as their salaries depend on those funds as well.

A skilled physician who makes a decent living and knows the value of his higher education, will eventually burnout if he is not empowered or his passion gets tested by out of date bureaucracy and industry corruption. This had happened to me, and is happening to thousands if not millions of healthcare workers around the world.

In your mind you would say that anyone who wants all 3 P's in a single lifetime is an unrealistic dreamer, greedy even. You are correct. But you have to understand that one cannot achieve greatness and *fulfillment* without all P's. Imagine a daily job that you are very good at, are determined to better yourself at any given opportunity, have realised that all your life choices have led you to this path, and the Market has rewarded you with handsome profits and healthy share values.

This is the Path of the Entrepreneur. A rare but possible intersection between the 3 P's:

A Passion to create a valuable solution to peoples' lives

A Purpose to make sure I am successful in providing it and constantly improving myself

And a strong desire to be Profitable so I can use that revenue to build more and be more,

more than just a doctor.

Growth Mindset Tip #16 - Do what brings you as close as possible to the 3 P's

HOW IDEAS ARE BORN

I have met individuals who are 10times better, smarter and more socially connected than me. I know people who can memorise vast quantity of knowledge with minimal effort. There are experts who have consulted top multinational corporations and even governments. They are at the very top of their field. But many reach mental fatigue when it comes to producing practical and original methods in the cold uncompromising reality of the Free Market.

Much like a PhD, an industry expert is hyper-specialised in a small defined segment of a globally connected process. When it comes to *thinking out of the box*, such deep technical expertise can be a mental obstacle. Like most specialists, we only see the symptoms of a disease, its logical pathologic path, strict medical management and then the awkward conflict when years of medical training do nothing, and saves no one. This rigid thinking is in all high stress high position careers, we know the rules, we expect the outcomes.

But when this tiny world becomes ugly and soul-crushing, or worse, we are violently thrown out of it by downsizing/unemployment, we can only rely on our pieces of paper to bring us back in the game again, be part of that defined segregated society. In many cases it does work out, through industry referrals and connections many do find meaningful employment once again. But what if someone does not fit into those roles, or those roles are now obsolete due to macroeconomic pressures or technology?

Emigrate, immigrate, repatriate, retrain,relearn, reapply, replay.

Or.

Try to start a business.

Try to work on an idea to get back up again.

Try to get an idea first.

In a previous chapter I gave a brief outline of how I chanced upon a spark of intellect. A moment of blinding realisation. The birth of original thought (aka *idea*). People often ask about how an average person can come with some earth-shaking idea, a billion dollar startup, an idea that would change their lives forever. In an exclusive inner circle moderated by '*HH*' (my business mentor) we often try to inspire each other to fulfil our true potential in life. Understandably there a few who feel overwhelmed with the pressures of coming up with an original idea.

To be honest, the whole notion of coming up with high value ideas is stupid. Every Tom, Dick and Harry in the world has ideas. The rickshaw puller, the coffee barista, personal accountant, the MBA graduate, they all have ideas. There is nothing so special about coming up with an idea. If you break it down, an idea is just a mental exercise, your mind has a personal lifetime experience with an issue in reality, some kind of deep understanding of why something is happening, or not happening and the grey matter tries to form an alternative reality where an act or a product could potentially solve the problem.

This mental exercise needs to be fine tuned by accessing even higher cognitive functions. Something beyond basic bodily functions and crude automatic responses. I am talking about the empathic intelligence, the psycho-cognitive ability to imagine a point in our timeline where we *become* another person and visualise how the problem we have identified affects them. Imagine a time without Uber, a person who cannot climb the steps of a public bus, cannot afford to buy his own car, or has to go to a place with three family members comfortably, safely and should be more affordable than a taxi. This digital solution was born out of a deep understanding of the pain of this particular human being, and multiplied to an entire city population. Is it perfect? Not really, but it is a great idea with some form of financial success and it actually solves a particular problem in society.

I had brain-stormed a similar situation. Throughout my life experience in healthcare in the private, public and non-profit sector; it was a constant nagging feeling that there are so many problems faced by people of all classes to get the right healthcare services. Not much imagination was required as such difficulties are a constant reminder of the broken health system that we have, just like in many developing countries.

The pain was apparent to me:

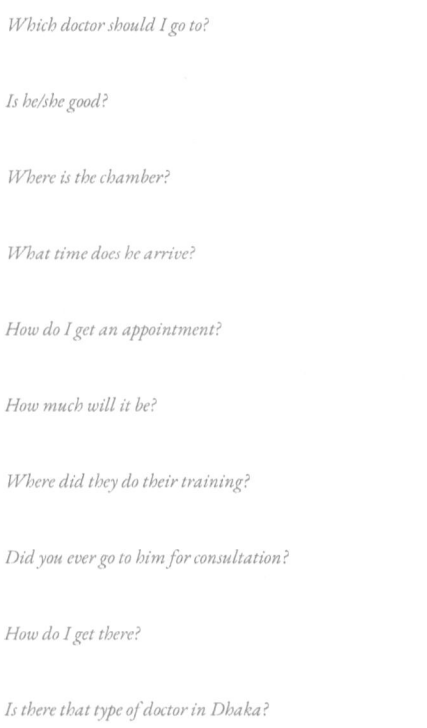

Which doctor should I go to?

Is he/she good?

Where is the chamber?

What time does he arrive?

How do I get an appointment?

How much will it be?

Where did they do their training?

Did you ever go to him for consultation?

How do I get there?

Is there that type of doctor in Dhaka?

Is the chamber nearby? Or when should I leave home to reach that place in time?

All these questions can be grouped under the heading of 'lack of knowledge'. This gap in reliable trusted information is a perfect place where an idea can be made to solve the patients' worries. There are countless Facebook groups, mobile apps, dedicated websites that deal with doctors' appointments and Google ofcourse. But still this idea has been milked to the core, hundreds of entrepreneurs and hundreds of startups have tried to bring a meaningful and profitable business idea into the real world. Still something was missing, that '*ah-ha!*' moment was not in my mind yet. True, I do indeed acknowledge that the problem exists and it is a significant one. It is simply not enough to notice a problem, one must come to terms with the question - *are you the right person to solve it?*

FOUNDER-MARKET FIT (FMF)

This is a very rare but crucial milestone in the entrepreneur journey. The 'Product-Market Fit' issue is a crucial step that founders and investors want very badly; the ultimate Market validation of the perfect solution to the problem - proven by consistent or increasing revenue. But 'Founder-Market Fit' is not openly discussed or acknowledged because in a way it sounds '*anti*-entrepreneurial', telling someone that because they do not belong to that industry (that they wish to disrupt), or is inexperienced or is simply too naive to understand the subtle nuances of that industry, can be disheartening and rude. Many first time entrepreneurs will cite examples of successful leaders who have no relation whatsoever to the billion dollar company that they now run, I know many non-medical associates who claim to have billion dollar ideas that will revolutionise the healthcare industry, even though they have only the 'front-end' experience (consumers of healthcare) and have never gone through residency.

What I am trying to explain about FMF, is that often the best place to come up with novel ideas is to really dig deep and analyse your immediate surroundings that you regularly interact with, and perform a high level empathy journey of someone who experiences the same problems that you have faced (eg. fuel efficiency of modern jet aircraft) and focus hard and long on how your special idea would impact on the problem. Because you *live* in that specific world you may have that unique insight that others would miss. As I am in the medical field, it stands to reason that I would know something real about the problems faced in providing quality healthcare, instead of commenting on an issue somewhere else.

To avoid conflict, I welcome the reader to practice their human rights at forming any number of amazing ideas. There is nothing wrong with having an amateur opinion. In many cases the actual ida itself is a collection of thoughts and opinions that gradually form a complete sentence, and with proper mind training by using something learned in an event called 'Design Thinking'. This process places the user at the centre of the whole value chain, and your solution is at the periphery, this mind exercise tries to place the solution as close to the user as possible - in IT this is known as user experience. The quality of the idea must be related to the absolute benefit to your user, the benefit to the producer comes last. This is the essence of entrepreneur empathy.

Ideas are always in abundance.

The rickshaw puller has some ideas on road safety.

A barista has a unique recipe.

The accountant wants to create a special software.

Everyone Tom, Dick and Harry has ideas.

Help yourself to as many ideas as you want.

It is free. Nobody will pay you for it thought.

You need to work on it.....

Growth Mindset Tip #17 - Don't worry about forming new ideas, just focus on the existing problem. If there is already a solution, just make it better somehow. And cooler!

VALUE OF AN IDEA

Ideas are a dime a dozen.

Ideas are as worthy as the amount of ink used to write it down on a tablecloth.

Ideas are worthless.

If everybody has some idea, then why is our world so far from perfect? Where is the utopia that

science fiction writers had promised us? Why are *you* not the next Bill Gates, Elon Musk or Jack

Ma? There must be some amazing idea that could improve the way people get access to quality

trusted healthcare, there has to be a way to improve the skills of medical personnel, there has to be a

way to upgrade a country's entire health system.

Truth is there was. Everybody has these ideas.

But often they do not go beyond their skulls.

You see the true value of innovation comes from its real life applications. The measurable benefits

that the user gets upon its use. The ever increasing revenue model from satisfied new and repeat customers. These are just a few ways an idea shows its true potential. Everybody has ideas, but the brave few take the initiative, accepts the risk to make sure it gets executed in a timely and profitable manner.

Personally I can boast of several gigabytes of *billion-dollar ideas*, I had mentioned only a few or else this small book would become an encyclopedia of failures. The only way I could really be motivated to invest in a concept was if I was the first person to act on it. The one who thinks of it, should take the responsibility to take the critical first steps. If you remember '*N*' from my previous life, the idea of a grand health summit was not his own, the idea for a country-wide patient information sharing network was definitely not his own. That could be the reason for his downfall, and that of HBS.

When someone has an idea to change the world, the sheer weight of its potential acts as its own momentum, therefore true entrepreneurs do not obsess over its originality for too long, they just want to get it out there into the Market. As I mentioned countless times, the Market will decide how cool your idea is.

As ideas are vessels of inspiration, acting on it should be done the same way a captain decides on crossing a sea, he needs to think about how the idea of crossing came about (what was the need) and what resources are required (preferably nearby). In my case, as I had contemplated a type of connectivity platform to make it easier for patients to connect with doctors, I now needed to learn as much as I could about the present status of medical doctors, the patient population, their individual behaviours, existing solutions, what form it took and most importantly; the 'how' of getting it done.

True ideas by themselves are worthless, like some kind of inedible plant. Much like plants they also have a very short shelf life, meaning without taking a *massive immediate action* to formulate it, fix it and go for it, it will be lost in my skull. Life has a funny way of distracting you, when it seems that you will just delay its execution for a later date, then you have shot yourself in the foot ie. failed without even starting anything. As my business mentor told us, there are no bad ideas, only bad execution.

Growth Mindset Tip #18 - Ideas without action are the dreams of a drunkard. You will not know its true value without the feedback from your first paying customer. Let the Market tell you its dollar value.

'SOMATECH' - A Blue Ocean Concept

For the benefit of the reader, I will now get back on track and tell you about my brainstorm moment. To recap, I had initially coined the name 'SomaTech'[54] for my very own futuristic clinic; staffed with visiting specialists, event venues with teleconferencing facilities and the first ever Stem cell clinic as well. Grand designs indeed. I pitched my idea to some of my medical friends, after the laughter stopped, they reminded me about the massive funds needed for this type of project (land lease, staff, specialised equipment, bribes, medicolegal applications etc), and then I heard the one *pain* that many have echoed time and time again, back then I was only listening to my ego, but now I heard it like there was a microphone on my face;

---

[54] It was supposed to sound like *somatic* which relates to the body. The *-Tech* suffix sounded cool.

"All these ideas are great if we can just get a big enough patient turnover"

"I am more interested in getting more patients to my clinic, what will all this technology do?"

"Sat in the chamber for 5 hours today, and didn't see a single patient"

"I need to sit in that chamber location so I can get more referrals"

"We just need more patients, or else I am not making a living........"

I heard these issues countless times from many private practice doctors, even my own mother who provides discounted consultations, but nobody knows about it. I vaguely remember reading a business article about the opinions of US doctors about the popularity of so many healthtech startups trying to disrupt the health system; they too had mentioned that all that fancy tech will be useful if they can get patients to come into their clinic in the first place.

On that night, I had the idea to form a solution that solves the pains from two interconnected populations; doctors who need more patients when they are on duty, and patients who need to see a doctor at their private chambers, at their convenience, *not the doctors'*.

I wrote down my idea in a series of diagrams and sketches, sort of like the user journey as I had studied. I also applied my knowledge of patient psychology and medical anthropology to figure out what would be the value proposition at each step as well i.e. why would they need my platform to solve their pains - the doctors and the patients. It is not enough to say that you are bringing them together, as I had noticed there were a dozen such companies all competing against each other, same value lowering prices each time. The real 'SomaTech' concept has to have something so unique and so simple that it would be a real game-changer, a *silent* disrupter.

In my self-education, I had come upon another interesting business strategy known as the *Blue Ocean Strategy*. It was a method to create a truly unique business approach that focuses on creating new market demand, not worrying about competition, a true practice in value-centred innovation. Much like Uber, Airbnb, Amazon and all the medical inventions we take for granted started out by solving a critical problem above all else. On the other hand, the *Red Ocean Business* was the classic chains of fast food restaurants all in the same location, serving the same menu, each lowering prices to outdo each other, but end up losing quality and customers.

So I had to think 'Blue'.

I concentrated hard on how to combine the market-driven behaviour of the US healthcare system, the democratic access to healthcare consultation of the UK's NHS and the global trend of on-demand, real time and location-based services that the Dhaka population is exposed to[55].

PATIENT DEMANDS

People want access to professional, trusted, qualified healthcare professionals, preferably referred by peers, whom they can approach for private consultation. With minimal hassles of the worsening

---

[55] On demand 3G connectivity, rides, food, movies, tickets, groceries etc.

traffic situation and less waiting time in the lobby. To some degree many want to promote their

positive experiences to others if needed, or provide some negative experience feedback, if needed.

DOCTOR DEMANDS

Private practice doctors can be thought of as independent healthcare contractors[56] who work in

shifts in a 3-D structure (their personal chambers) for a few hours per shift for a set number of days

in a week, then another doctor sits there later on, while they go to another location to scout for

more patients. The problem is the lack of a standard referral system, absence of business sense

(regarding effective marketing and customer communication) in most doctors, the *'dalal'* (broker)

culture that harasses and controls the doctors' prescription behaviours and the local *'brotherhood of*

doctors' actually determine who will have preference to set up a private chamber in high density

middle class neighborhoods. This lose-lose scenario propagates the brain drain and the frustration

(and eventual corruption) of dedicated medical comrades.

THE SOMATECH CONCEPT

My idea would be like the *'Airbnb'*[57] model of healthcare. Once a doctor physically enters a private

chamber that has been geo-fenced[58] and tagged to their mobile device (provided 3G is enabled),

that prior certified doctor's professional profile would be made active and visible to any person,

who is currently searching for a specialist matching that particular skill set (eg. OBGYN) within a

---

[56] No fixed salary, income is based on individual consults & referral/diagnostic commissions

[57] Airbnb - Community-based real-time room-sharing platform to help homeowners lease out spare rooms to people who need an affordable living space.

[58] Geofencing - Virtual geographic boundary that is tagged by GPS to cause a signal or process to occur in a registered mobile device.

reasonable fixed radius. The *Somatech* platform would allow direct communication and negotiation of on-demand real-time appointment between these two parties as per their discretion. Once the doctor finished his duty, or chooses to take a break, simply leaving the premises would deactivate the profile and no more potential patient connections would take place.

In effect this platform (PaaS = Platform-as-a-Service) would optimise the individual doctor's shift so as to increase the probability of getting a patient to come straight to his clinic. The doctor community will be the primary stakeholder/user of Somatech platform. This approach was taken for two crucial reasons; other health startups rely on mobilising patients to use their services, without realising that the private clinic is already a functional business model - just needs customers, and secondly as a doctor I had the industry insight to truly assess the pain points of this highly specialised population.

What about the patient population? How will they choose? After extensive design thinking and professional insight into the patient user experience - it was apparent that there are two main decision triggers when choosing a specialist; the qualification and certification of said specialist and peer recommendations (preferably a close social recommendation). The patient would search for the particular medical specialty, depending on the real-time availability of that specialist the patient could see the doctors' profile page; showing their latest qualifications and certification, and previous patient testimonials. If agreeable the patient would call to confirm the identity and chamber address, proceed at their leisure, complete the session and give a feedback rating on the patient experience.

Somatech would run on a *freemium* subscription model whereby the doctor would have access to the platform in a chamber for a free trial period, and then a pricing tier would be in effect depending on the number of chambers they would like to register. The patient would have free unlimited access to the platform since they will be paying the consult fees as normal, without external interference. Doctors will be motivated by the real-time patient turnover, which leads to increased revenue, when they keep the earnings completely. Patients do not have to submit private data to any server, and there is no prior payment to secure an appointment.

UNIQUE SELLING PROPOSITION (USP)

USP is the prime competing aspect of a product/service that places it at a higher market perception/value than other similar concepts. The Somatech USP is related to the on-demand real-time optimisation of standard health-seeking behaviour of select patients to certified doctors who are physically present and ready to see them.

VALUE PROPOSITION (VP)

Quite simply it is the '*wow*' factor of an innovation. The 'special sauce' that would attract customers to use it, and use it often. The VP in this case would be the convenience of getting patients to come to an otherwise unknown doctors' private chamber only during duty hours, and patients would have the confidence to choose a specialist based on their skills certification and ofcourse any existing patient testimonials, hopefully if a nearby physician is online in the network, the proximity of the chamber would be an additional benefit (atleast the patient party will not waste time in horrible traffic). An innovative rating system has been added to allow patients to give a binary rating (happy/sad) and a comments section; good comments are uploaded to the doctors' profile so other patients can see his excellent professionalism, leading to more patients, leading to more revenue for the doctor - a type of constructive economic incentive. Negative ratings would be dealt with by an in-house quality control committee (as far as suspension for persistent bad patient experience).

Growth Mindset Tip #19 - Know your customer better than you know yourself. Imagine their lives, imagine their pains. Your solution should improve their lives more than their payment do for you. The industry expert is an expert because of the life knowledge of interacting with that industry customer and the value it created.

MIA (Massive Immediate Action)

I was ready and willing to bring this idea to reality, like my life depended on it. I drew every single mobile screen on several pieces of paper, and on a larger paper (the size of a table) I connected each piece and pretended that if a button was pressed, what action it would cause and which screen would show it, and in reality what would happen. This was called Paper Wireframing. A simple low cost method to visualise the user journey. The next best version of this exercise was done on a free online template called Prototype Wireframing, basically it acted like a real mobile application i.e. clicking on a button icon would create an action such as activating the next page, going back to the previous slide, open camera app, open phone app and so on. Very essential piece of technology to properly see what your application would look like and *do*.

This program allowed me to add, subtract and even erase entire pathways which were considered non-essential to complete the main mission - such as showing patients where was the nearest oncologist and how to get to their private consult chamber. What was thought to be such a simple idea, turned out to be quite a strenuous mental activity. It is easy to dream because the mind is not restricted by the rules of reality like wifi signal, old laptop RAM speed and background noises. But it has to be done, it has to be started.

You may ask how would a non-tech person know anything about app development - absolutely nothing truthfully. The only way to learn is by action, as I had learned, when you decide that a task is not your responsibility or you are not smart enough then you have already blocked any chance of new neural paths to new skills development. Riding a bike is by action to assess speed, gravity, momentum and not by reading a manual. App development is a complex IT process requiring deep understanding of systems architecture, user interface, user experience and let us not forget coding language. No big deal.

The brain consumes more energy per weight than any organ, during deep thought this rate increases, during the creation of new memory (related to complex task learning) it can increase several fold. There is no physical limit to learning. The entrepreneurial mind will adapt and restructure itself to adapt to new knowledge, therefore if a former medical professional needs to learn new information to integrate himself into a new industry, so be it. But a conscious physical act must take place as well or else it is just a mental process. I know by experience now, the best way to learn about building a SaaS[59] Business Empire, is to immediately design the look of it, research about similar apps in the market, read about various aspects of app development, attend tech meetup events, talk to developers and take action.

---

[59] SaaS - Software as a service eg. apps

I do not need to get a CSE degree, there is no need to learn about code, there is no time to learn everything now. I just need to find people smarter and more talented than me, on the tasks needed to get things moving.

Growth Mindset Tip #21 - Grow your mind by accepting challenges and investing in continuous learning and execution of new skills, daily.

MARKET VALIDATION

A method to disrupt a centuries old industry sounds good to liberal newspapers journalists and in startup meetings with naive entrepreneurs. Neither of them are your customers, they will not give you the harsh criticism needed to fine-tune your idea. It is relatively easy to produce a quick consumption product like a new dessert item or fashion accessory and get feedback, as these are easy to introduce to the Market on a low cost low scale research campaign. Complex products like biomedical machines are one of the hardest as they need years of research & development, and not to mention tons of regulatory processes even before the human trial period. Health-related services are variable in difficulty. It is mostly a test of psychosocial understanding of which customer segments' pain is severe enough for them to take a leap of faith and try your services, knowing that it and the result (improved health) cannot often be measured.

The feedback from the target population, who most likely match the customer avatar[60], will help me test my innovation at this idea stage, or prototype stage atleast. As part of market research approach, I should be the silent observer as I see how a focus group interacts with every segment of the interface, what actions or assumptions are there and recommendations. This focus group should be as far from your social circle as possible to maintain impartiality. Truth is distressing to

---

[60] Imaginary profile of your ideal paying customer - age, gender, income, habits, health status, travel behaviour, social status etc

hear, especially when your concept is surgically deconstructed and many times ridiculed, but at the end of it all, I must provide the value to my customers. Their pains, or gains must be provided as close as possible while still on a future revenue potential.

Growth Mindset Tip #22- Be passionate of the process, not your product. Dedication to satisfying the Market will provide the constructive content to create something useful and valuable. Do not worry if the releasing product looks nothing like your original idea towards the end. People pay for useful products, not a stranger's dream.

DEVELOPER FEEDBACK

It is one thing to assess the attractiveness of your innovation to a potential customer base, the crucial part is can it be made by the right developer team. Any IT product needs a specialised group of professionals, much like in an operating theatre (a surgeon is only as good as the OT team). There has to be a series of developers who work on each app, specialised in the Android OS platform[61], backend servers, security features, UI/UX[62] and to bring them together, a competent team leader.

When I first entered into the business field, I had a recurring fear about where would I get the resources, who would help me, what will I sell, who would work with me; my close set of fellow serial entrepreneurs told me the same thing,

"....the best way to start a business, is to start a business. When you are in it you will automatically fill in the missing pieces as you go along. Each path is different and only you will know where to look and how to fit them together."

---

[61] Android phones are the most commonly used mobile device in Bangladesh, and its OS is relatively easier to produce and distribute compared to iOS.
[62] User interface & user experience

And so I did, when I had taken the first of many practical steps to start SomaTech, I knew I had to find a way to scout for IT teams to actually create my platform. Obviously I do not have that particular skill, and I do not need it, that is not my role. The Founder must assemble a hyper-competent team made up of people smarter than himself, and organise them to work as a functioning team. But first I had to find the global standard in market value and pricing process for IT products.

I did some YouTube deep-search learning, watching dozens of videos about how apps were made, how actionable features were integrated and number of approximate hours needed to develop them (eg. how to make an Uber-like app). With an *approximate* construction benchmark of 3000-4000 hours (~6months) I calculated the hourly rate that developers in various English-speaking countries often charge to create similar products. Obviously Silicon Valley developers start with $350+/hour, Canada a few pennies less, Eastern European tech hubs like Estonia would be almost $100/hour, Indonesia/Vietnam in double digit territory and so that leaves the most common destination for outsourced skills - Indian IT Industry. There is a heterogenous pricing structure depending on which city you ask, from my exhaustive skype calls I noticed a range of $18-$60 per hour rate. At that time I strongly considered an Indian IT firm to develop the platform, I was only concerned with the relative distance and slight time zone difference. Many online forums speak about the administrative hassle of negotiating production milestones and quality (not to mention the issue of copyrighting) in the Indian and Chinese markets.

After some thought I thought I will atleast try the local Dhaka talent and see what would be technical response as a start. I placed a Facebook ad to scout for a suitable developer, and naturally I asked my coworking coworkers for some tech recommendations. I managed to get a dozen or so interested developers, showed them the SomaTech prototype and asked point blank if they can make such a product, no need to discuss price, I just wanted a quality construct. A few looked quite young, most asked the usual technical questions regarding the interface and whatnot. Except one guy.

'R' was highly recommended by a close '*neighbor*'[63] in my office space, they had worked with various major tech projects, including government tech infrastructure projects. He has his own reputable IT firm in Mirpur DOHS, and coincidentally he had just completed a ride-sharing app project for a client in Kenya. We sat down and went through the wireframes and the users' journeys. I expected the same rhetorical question about the overall product design, surprisingly his first question was about the business model. He was inquiring about the payment process if any, onboarding of doctors, patient-side marketing and future growth strategy. Undoubtedly I was thoroughly impressed. We shook hands, exchanged emails and I waited for a development invoice from his firm.

It was a welcome experience to sit with a like-minded entrepreneur.

---

[63] I work in close proximity with many other freelancers and tech entrepreneurs. Usually every seat is taken up, used, then vacant for a few seconds before another members comes by. This is the essence of the gig economy.

Growth Mindset Tip #23 - Plan a global strategy, but first search for local talent. If you know what you are looking for, most likely you will find the desired skill sets.

VALUE FOR VALUE

A few days later I received an email with a PDF attachment. It was from 'R'. It was a Gantt chart

with the task breakdown, production milestones, team components and expected deadlines for

each task. It was very methodical, very professional and unfortunately above budget. I do not doubt

the authenticity of 'R's team, but such a price would not leave much capacity for a marketing

budget, which I desperately needed to start the demand-side marketing (hype marketing[64]).

Comparatively it was on the high-end hourly rate of many Indian firms.

I was deeply conflicted.

Over the next few days I had some more work interviews with other developers, they too had

generic tech related suggestions. Nothing wrong with that, I needed to hear those remarks too, but

'R's professionalism was still on my mind. I can always find another IT firm, the tech industry of

Bangladesh is a booming market. But I needed 'R's expertise for something else. I needed to bring

in a Chief Technical Officer (CTO), someone with complementary skills to mine i.e. has the

technical expertise with business savvy to handle the product related issues.

---

[64] Publicity-based marketing to promote future benefits of a conceptual consumer product i.e. creating market demand for a
marketable product, before the product even exists.

I knew the price was somewhat inflated as this was a service industry norm. All and any non-tangible consumer concept i.e. something the customer cannot touch, carry, weigh, see or quantify in sensory terms (just like health) could have any number of pricing strategies. Depending on the customer profile and the value proposition, the right price for the right customer, it was a standard practice to get revenue. I would know as this was going to be my pricing strategy for the platform too!

I had to dig deep into my brain to figure this out. Emotional processing is completely useless in business, after all the Market does not care about your feelings. And neither would a potential technical cofounder. There has to be a way to display my future leadership potential to negotiate for a more affordable production budget, for initial costs, and to ensure sustainable value for this A-Team.

I replied to 'R's email stating that the proposed budget was on the high side. I invited him to lunch near my office to discuss alternative methods of cooperation. I knew he liked SomaTech, I could see it in his eyes and I heard it in his voice. Old-school business is about cheating and biting your way to the high table, to get a bigger piece of the cake. I wanted to invite the baker to share a simple meal with the same bread that he bakes.

We sat down at a less-than-fancy Chinese restaurant nearby, it looked like a simple canteen, but they made amazingly fresh dumplings, fried tofu and seaweed salad. We sat, we ate, we talked.

Straight away I told him that I will not be paying that initial cost, I will instead be giving something more. More than money.

As we finished our green tea, I told 'R' I needed him as a CTO due to his entrepreneur mindset. I am ready to negotiate a suitable discount, in return for a reasonable equity to a non-existent health startup with unimaginable high risks. If not him there will be others. They will not be as talented but I will manage somehow.

Take it or leave it, either way lunch is on me and we will shake hands and carry on.

We shook hands.

He agreed for a share.

He was onboard.

He gave a price that was way below industry standard hourly rates, but with the skill set of his entire dedicated development team.

I paid the bill.

We left the restaurant.

He went back to restructure the development budget. *Same Gantt chart, new price.*

I went to get my cheque book.

Time to get to work. I needed more people on this *A-Team*.

Growth Mindset #24 - Team building is everything. The innovation may fail, the company may dissolve. But the right team for the right strategy is essential.

LEGAL BACKING

I had done frequent user testing with focus groups, I took some honest technical feedback from IT developers and from my doctor community as well. Now with something as sensitive as healthcare, especially a new concept in a developing country, there is one feedback that matters the most - legal jurisdiction.

I managed to get a meeting with the same law firm that I met when I was starting HHS and pitched them my SomaTech idea, mobile screenshots, prototypes, workflow diagrams and the business model. They were thoroughly impressed and eager to work on it. The health tort laws in Bangladesh are still developing, either due to lack of contextual legal frameworks or the powerful pharma/medical lobby that is resistant to the status quo. Regardless, I assured them that the platform promises certain regulatory oversight that is oven missed or violated by some health startups locally or regionally. SomaTech will not handle the patients' confidential health data, we will not be in charge of financial reimbursements to the doctors (FinTech is another sensitive issue) and most importantly the credibility of every doctor applicant will be assessed by way of their BMDC registration certificate and any other recognised postgraduate degree would be verified.

From a legal point of view, the main concern was if HHS had the appropriate jurisdiction to handle an IT-related product within the narrative of the memorandum and articles of association. Bearing in mind that it was originally created as an international medical tourism facilitator, they had to read through the documents to see if SomeTech could be a legitimate product of HHS.

After a few days my lawyers told me that it would not be possible. Although the name SomaTech is more or less unique and non-trademarked, HHS does not have the right description to brand itself as a software company. There were two choices; either to spend a significant amount of money to rewrite and resubmit a new HHS memorandum, or the much more cost-effective option is to simply shut HHS down and make a brand new company. The second option was more favorable, as the Bangladesh government provides some level tax exemption for software companies with the right oversight ofcourse.

The choice was clear but the emotional conflict was apparent. I had created HHS the same time my father was hospitalised, and the first public presence of HHS took place hours after I had buried him, I remember the many nights we two had discussed about HHS strategy, he was the first to 'like' the Facebook page (his profile picture can still be seen every time I visit the page). I knew emotions have no place in business, the Market does not care. Rationalising is a difficult process, but it had to be done, not for the benefit of effective execution, but maybe it would be a type of closure for me. A company actually exists only on paper, but the memory of my father and his wisdom is in my heart.

I took the decision to downgrade the HHS activities, meaning I would no longer actively promote the medical tourism or whatever services anymore, if I get a casual inquiry I would assist but I would not actively chase after customers like before. HHS had no real value, the Founder of HHS had no credibility, it was time to rebrand everything. With a swift decision I started to shut down Hybrid Health Systems. I converted the existing Facebook page to my new upcoming business, I stacked all the leftover business cards, flyers, posters and scattered merchandise into a small box (memory box) and instructed a lawyer friend to begin the legal wound up of all documents.

When I put my mind onto what the new company could accomplish, with the right framework and the right minded team; I knew HHS was not really over (legally yes) it was merely evolving into something stronger. I felt good, I felt focused.

Growth Mindset Tip #25 - It is hard to let go of an emotional investment. Try to focus on the new emotions of building something better and more meaningful. It's worth it.

REBRANDING, EVERYTHING

The platform production was contracted to 'R's IT firm, initial payments were planned out for monthly installments, a timeline of approximately 5-6 months was negotiated and now I had to think of everything beyond the product. I came up with this idea that the name sounds *too high tech*, only I knew what it meant, i.e. SomaTech sounds like somatic which means body in latin. This name would not really appeal to the target demographic, from a vocal sense, it sounded very *rough on the tongue*. I was thinking of naming it with 2-3 vowels, it should have smooth sleek sounding pronunciation and be non-geographic, meaning it should pretend to have a global origin instead of the usual startup names which have bangla words attached to the name brand. There is nothing wrong in being patriotic or romantic, but as my business mentor '*HH*' advised me, I had to have a global outreach strategy including having the right name, and the Market does not care about your '*-isms*'[65].

While I was researching and playing around with various names, I was also contemplating my own personal/professional brand. Back in HBS I looked and acted like a vagrant, a wannabe entrepreneur just because it was hip and cool. When I created HHS I was an even worse imposter, I

---

[65] Patriotism, nationalism, nepotism etc

did not have the business sense that I have now, rather I dressed and acted as if I was already hitting

a 6-figure income - I casually killed time in coffeeshops, took my laptop everywhere randomly

clicking the buttons, bought and wore expensive suits just to show off. Even my persona in my

office space was fake, even on warm days I would wear business suits (with the jacket on), I had

posters made which I would plant outside the office to make it seem as if I owned the whole floor.

HHS was fake, I was fake.

This time it is serious business. There is no win-win strategy to creating fake profiles and easy

money schemes. If this new venture is to be successful, I would have to implement my many years

of professional work experience, my adopted global culture from my many foreign travels and

associates, and above all else I must create the foundation for A.R.T. (authenticity. results. trust).

I made the decision to be true to my future customers, cofounders, shareholders and hopefully

some high value investors. Additionally, people who are in no way interested in my products

should also gain some value through *our* approach, *our* visions, *our* dedication. There has to be a

way to endorse the theme of progress as the core aim. And what better way than in a new name.

In absolute honesty I cannot recall how the name appeared in my mind. It is not an original name,

there is a computer with the same name, even car brand that name. It spoke to me, I could see it as a

distinct logo, something that can be pasted on the side of a building. I searched for its meaning

online, nothing specific unfortunately, but the abbreviations were mind-changing.

The Dutch translation of its abbreviation: *'Vooruitgang is ons Streven'* (Progress is our Aim).

V. I. O. S......VIOS...

ViOS

Growth Mindset Tip #26 Focus on creating A.R.T.

(authenticity. results. trust.)

ViOS VALUE - Building the Brand

I had another meetup with '*HH*' at a digital marketing workshop. Along with several aspiring

entrepreneurs, we had a long discussion on effective branding and marketing strategies. Especially

those done by successful global brands. One of the many reasons for their success is their

investment in the emotional connection with future customers. The value equation. The way a

person makes a decision to buy, is more than just a calculation of how much money is in the pocket

or in a bank account, it all goes down to trust, even in healthcare. That is why I noticed some

doctors who may not have that many foreign degrees, are abe to have a dedicated pool of lifelong

patients. Thinking back, I realised why many patients who could afford the fees of my senior

consultants back, when I was practicing, insisted on seeing me for their child's care. I was not that

qualified, but I had the specialist skills and the people skills to provide the right value.

Digital marketing platforms are the new tool for business success. In the workshop we talked about

the 3M's of business momentum - Mindset, Marketing and Monetization. More or less my

entrepreneur mind was in gear, now I must initiate an innovative approach, something more unique and cost-effective than usual businesses - something along the lines of a *Blue Ocean Strategy* in marketing.

Majority of new startups are mostly ego driven, fueled by the blind passions of first-time founders. Often something cool is made, a business is created to make some money out of it and then the hunt for paying customers begins. This is what most doctors do anyway, first get your overpriced medical degrees, then get a lease or some authorization for the private chamber and then wait around in the hopes of fishing for patients. It takes years of waiting, and sometimes less than honorable methods, to get a consistent customer/patient base. By then you have lost time and money, in order to earn money. This way it makes no sense.

This time I will focus on creating the brand value, set up the market demand, nurture the pool of potential paying customers from the customer avatar, and when this hype marketing campaign reaches a fever pitch - I would launch the ViOS platform. Easier said than done as every startup tries to do this. Many burn through most of their capital funds with extensive social media marketing, PR campaigns, web design, major events sponsorship, influencer partnerships, brand ambassadors, billboard leases and press releases. All the methods I have experienced in its absurdity. Everybody talks about cost-effective marketing and measuring ROI, but what does it mean? How would I measure it? How will I know how much to spend? What content should I use?

I received only one critical piece of advice in that 5-hour long workshop. Video. Convert as much of your marketing content into video format. As many expert digital marketing experts have told me, video-based content (ads, blogs, webinars, live sessions) increases customer engagement/interaction more than 10-fold compared to using standard methods. There are other industry related benefits too, such as the humanising effect on the brand. Meaning the target population can actually see a face behind the value (preferably the founder), this is the core methodology to establishing the A.R.T. foundation.

Short (<4min), crisp, clear, simple, specific, captioned video blogs (*vlogs)*, will be the sole marketing product for the ViOS brand. The crucial next step was to decide what language I would use. Language is the true rate-limiting step, or bottleneck in any sales funnel. As politically-incorrect as it may be, certain demographics in Commonwealth countries (even on a global scale) who have a firm grasp on the Englsh language can be assumed to belong to a certain income bracket. The ability to speak the global language of commerce[66] places that person at the very top end of the essential decision-making pyramid, this is very important to segregate the total attainable market demographic in any industry. The true measure of the efficacy of the campaign is not in the number of *likes*, but rather the individual profile component of vlog viewers. Basically it is not enough to make high-definition videos and flashy content, if the content is in standard English (perhaps with a slight western accent) there is a high probability of a higher value perception from the right viewer - educated, white collar occupation, brand value appreciation, forward thinking, tech savvy and many other desirable characteristics of the ideal ViOS user base.

---

[66] 1 in 4 or 1.75 billion people speak or comprehend English well enough to participate in successful commercial transactions

This funneling method is not intended to profile or segregate an entire demographic, but rather to segregate the brand. To achieve the right marketing ROI, it is not advisable to waste time and energy to entertain the non-customer masses. Their shallow responses (likes and generic one word comments) serve only to fulfill the founder's celebrity metrics i.e. to feed his ego, rather than to create a targeted brand approach. It is best to get a few of the right people to view your campaign so that over time they will view you as a symbol of A.R.T. in an otherwise crowded and nonsense social media experience.

Creating value-centered content and distributing correctly takes a lot of time. From the development perspective it is actually a good thing. A hurried product will be full of bugs and errors, and customers will not forgive you for your amateur attempts (personal experience from HBS). On the other hand, waiting too long will give chance for a competitor with a large budget to hijack the momentum, and of course the founding team will become distracted and unmotivated. The right time can be judged when your status quo within certain professional circles creates marketable persona, meaning people's hunger increases day by day as they see your value as an industry expert and are ever eager to sample your product.

There is an interesting sales concept I had come across known as *ZMOT - Zero Moment of Truth,* whereby deeply interested buyers will actively search for a brand online or offline and then immediately initiate the decision to purchase, over the years this narrow window is less than 3 seconds for a customer to decide to purchase an item. Extensive and intuitive marketing places ViOS in a position where doctors in need of a solution to bring more patients and patients in need of an easy process to find qualified healthcare services, will immediately choose to use the ViOS platform within that 3 second window. It is understandable that atleast 6 months of brand value creation is needed to secure this 3 second window of opportunity.

Therefore, this time around, I have heavily invested my time and resources into the online media portals - Facebook, LinkedIn, blog posts, certain health-related forums and of course networking in selective events. The ViOS landing page[67] was designed to increase lead generation (for early app access) by providing the absolute basic information, with video triggers to be seen by both user groups (patients and doctors) so that they know what the platform is all about. All this golden content is worthless without crosslinking and integration with each other, therefore vlog ads with originally curated content is targeted towards various populations (primarily healthcare professionals as they need to be onboarded first) with characteristics of middle to upper middle class income brackets. Interested viewers, whom I had been able to educate and share the ViOS value are led to the official app landing page, and then invited to submit their mobile numbers and emails for notifications on the app release.

Naturally the product is not ready, but this lead funnel main action is to sensitize (branding stimulation) the future user to a concept that may be a strong solution to their patient-related pains (or the doctors as well). Small scale blog posts, based on the text used for the videos have been transcribed and certain words were tagged to more reputable online post, this process is a component of SEO (search engine optimisation and Google analytics i.e. how likely people searching for data on a health-related topic would find an original editorial created or associated

---

[67] www.viosapp.com

with the ViOS platform. As tedious as it all is, hype marketing is exhaustive but essential. The Blue

Ocean Strategy of disruptive innovation is not for everyone, that is why so many ventures have

failed. If you cannot respect the customer demands, the Market will punish you.

Growth Mindset Tip #27 - Brand presence <u>is</u> Market presence.

Create such a strong demand, that customers will pay any price.

Any price.

TO FUND OR NOT FUND

Money is the fuel for any startup growth. The whole reason for the existence of business is to sell a solution for a need, or a gain, and make a handsome profit from the efforts. Like a farm you have to get the right seeds to grow your cash crops. In startups, often great ideas never go beyond the concept stage, because even a highly motivated and proactive entrepreneur team will be disbanded if there is no process to raise capital.

I had attended many startup events, the unifying issues amongst everyone is seed capital, or investment funding. To summarise this is the classic funding pathway that most companies seek, I am of course taking the example of western-based startups due to their more mature ecosystem and pro-business policies.

Step 1: BOOTSTRAPPING

Using your own savings to start off the prototype development, office rent and any other overhead costs. In this method you have saved your income over the years and have managed a wealth portfolio where your daily basic needs can be met while you work on your dream project.

Step 2: 3F's (Family, Friends, Fools)

Solvent family member who just wants to see you happy, not necessary that they believe or understand your plans but....whatever. Close set of friends, obviously more well off than you, and those who feel a mixture of pity and excitement for your dreams, and the occasional fool with money is a goldmine.

Step 3: BANKS

Only possible if the business falls under classic *brick and mortar* type ventures, if there are pending overdrafts, company assets can be quickly absorbed and liquidated, such as industrial machinery. Technology businesses have no physical asset and they are of extremely high financial risks. Services related industries have this inherent problem of non-quantifiable assets, healthcare may be an outlier due to the higher than normal market demand. The exact science behind this finding is not clear.

Step 4: GRANTS

Any social business which impacts on specific community needs; such as education, gender equality, child health, environmental protection or any other non-profit style stakeholder value is more attractive for government grants and developmental agency sponsorship, provided strict auditing oversight is maintained. For-profit ventures may have a chance, beyond the role of a tender, if part of their mission statement addresses the capacity to improve community employment in their activities. The main benefit of getting grants is that equity remains with the company, and funds may be quite significant. Early Silicon Valley startup were generously supported by the US Military.

Step 5: ANGELS

The name may suggest that they are a group of charitable philanthropists, or even like a rich uncle. But the truth is, Angels are a highly calculating walking-talking bank - they have multiple investments at ventures with a high growth velocity i.e. rapid user growth with or without some revenue as well. After all they want their money back quickly and with a return on their equity.

Step 6: VENTURE CAPITAL (VC)

This is the most widely sought after method to external funding. Often a large pool of funds has been collected, and they too behave like a collection of Angels. For some equity they will provide the negotiated funds.

There are of course many other types of funding, each specific to the type of business eg. low overhead businesses like in coaching enterprises require very little capital whereas any manufacturing venture needs significant seed funding. Perhaps the most important thing to consider is what will you do with that imaginary funding. If you need external funding to develop a product, hire a large team, rent a fancy office space, do extravagant marketing or whatever that corporations do - then quite frankly you will not get funding, and if you did manage to raise some of that capital, you will lose it.

The whole idea behind the startup culture is to implement an idea with existing resources (even non-financial resources[68]) and skills that the entrepreneur team *must* learn. To see how far you can go into the Market with your innovation, at that almost zero budget (X) in the beginning (*Day 0*), will form the benchmark to plan how far you can reach with additional support (X+1):

Sum total of research/development/production/distribution/marketing/iteration/early adopter motivation etc = X

$$X \text{ at Day } 0 = Y \text{ (Total number of users after a set time + Initial revenue)}$$

$$Z = \text{Potential growth of users + revenue + profitability}$$

$$\therefore \quad X+1 = YZ$$

Where '*+1*' is the external funding support that will *multiply* the Market capture

---

[68] *Resilience, tenacity, resolve, resourcefulness* - I strongly suggest that you check their definitions as these are the prime qualities of a successful entrepreneur

Young naive entrepreneurs want the get-rich quick/overnight success story, they will go to great lengths to hunt for the '$+1$' component of the equation without even contemplating the X. I confess my financial situation is much better than most social classes in Bangladesh, perhaps I can afford to bootstrap the 'X' component long enough to get a significant 'Y', but nonetheless I have personally met people who have fallen into the two extremes; no resources, no connections but have through sheer hard work have created their empires, and on the other hand there are many with bloated funds who have grossly mishandled the funds and are now in the so-called death spiral of a dying startup i.e. bad publicity, mass firing, low quality, decreased marketing ROI, brand image is underfunded and only a matter of time before a big fish eats them up.

I know you may have expected that this chapter would be a '*how to*' guide on securing that blank cheque from a foreign fund, but as I mentioned before, in the 3M's process of success (mindset, marketing, monetisation) without the proper leadership qualities that comes from multiple costly mistakes or the self-investment in soft skills[69], it is in my personal opinion that such ventures do not deserve a single coin. I know for a fact that without hard data, any amount of funding, regardless of its source, would be wasted in everything except business development.

Data is the new currency. In technical terms we can call it as metrics, these are specific KPIs that help founder teams make crucial decisions eg. new users per week, monthly recurring revenue from subscriptions, operations overhead costs, churn rate (number of leaving customers), burn rate (office rent, equipment hire), costs of acquiring a new customer (CAC) and many other *hard*

---

[69] Empathy, communication, negotiation, self awareness etc

metrics. These are the types of data that a serious angel, VC, bank or whoever with the right amount of cash that could take you to the right stage, want to look at.

I had approached an investor firm based in Dubai about the ViOS concept, the idea was well received but since it was still at prototype development stage back then, a cold response was given stating the absolute need for hard data, in order to properly gauge the potential value of the ViOS ecosystem, and ofcourse the probability of profitability. Founders are deeply emotional and passionate about their concept, like a pet project, often the wrong words are used during an investor pitch. Emotional value can only work on the 3F's (*family, friends & fools*), when dealing with business people you have to use their language, the language of clear numbers and clear metrics.

So it is apparent that ViOS needs to be painfully bootstrapped, atleast to get into the initial traction. Gather the cold-hearted Market feedback. '*Get the right metrics to collect the funds*' as my business mentor had told me in the beginning. The initial funding was more or less affordable to me in order to produce the early ViOS platform version. Legal and business registration costs will have to be self-funded too. My CTO has agreed to deposit the resources to upgrade the next app versions, including the iOS versions. After all if you want the bigger impact you need to solve the bigger problems, which are not cheap.

As difficult as it will be to dig into one's own savings just to get things started, it is a necessary suffering to appreciate the importance of cost-effective ROI-generating activities. When your own money is being used for ads, or merchandise, or even publishing this book, the founder will learn

the deep understanding and value of money well spent - there will be no excuse to spend money on

something without the clear path to future growth. Obviously down the line as ViOS progresses

deep into the local healthcare industry, we shall have a large deficit due to increasing operations

costs, all in the name of gathering the necessary data to approach the deep-pocketed investors.

Growth Mindset Tip #28 - You need cold hard metrics, before you get the cold hard cash.

PAID CUSTOMER ACQUISITION (Startup Suicide)

In business the first handful of people that show the slightest bit of interest to your venture, is worth more in gold than all the investor funds you think you are worth. The absolute honest feedback from these *early adopters* will guide you to how the larger Market views your efforts. There are two ways to achieve this user pool; paid vs organic. Paid advertising is obviously the easier method to rapidly enter the mind of your customer, whereas organic is good to have over time. A startup cannot afford time, a young doctor in need of a sustainable career path cannot wait that long either.

During the course of the ViOS business development plan, I was thinking of which business model I should base it on. Will ViOS be the Uber of healthcare, the Mercedes of healthcare or something else? While I was reading up on various methods at hype marketing, I came across the notion of paid customer acquisition. Many well known and successful companies *reward* their new customers for their early interest. There are cash or credit rewards when a new lead becomes an active user of their products, and also for referring a known associate to use the same product. The idea goes deeper than just incentivising user entry, rather it has to do with lowering the defenses of prospective leads. In our globalised lives, we are overwhelmed with aggressive sales techniques of all sizes, so our immediate response is to say no, especially when we may have had a negative experience with a similar product. When there is a monetary reward for simply logging in, taking a ride, sharing a file, buying groceries than the customer will naturally sign up as the mental defences have gone down, and the pain/gain pathways are addressed. And ofcourse one cannot pass up the opportunity of referring a friend if there is a bonus promo involved.

In theory, I planned to have a type of cashback offer everytime a new doctor is onboarded as a ViOS health provider, when they refer a colleague to join in the network and also the same offer to patients to use their ViOS Patient app to look for a ViOS Doctor, and for referring a family member or friend. I had assumed that as part of an active referral network I could rapidly increase the numbers of ViOS Doctors so that the possibility of a successful connection may occur, or in business terms, reach economies of scale. I was still calculating the amount of money that has to be set aside in order to provide the cashback to around 50 doctors or so, and then factored in the amount of digital advertising budget to attract the same amount. Had it not been for my close proximity to so many professional experts in my coworking space, it was highly likely that I would become personally bankrupt in the first month of operation.

The Bangladesh startup ecosystem is still in its embryo phase compared to our neighbors. As such while attending a large number of networking events, it is quite easy to form impactful professional relationships with various entrepreneurs and freelancers, from almost every industry. And by being a physician entrepreneur at my age, I would say my presence is quite noticeable at times - not to mention the disruptive concept of ViOS as the main conversation starter. It seems that my persona has become well known or atleast noticeable over time, as one day while at my shared office, I was greeted by a professional startup accountant and VAT auditor, who occasionally sits there in between meeting clients. We sat down and discussed the economics of the health system, provider payments, healthcare financing and finally towards the revenue model of ViOS. When I mentioned my idea of the multilevel referral program to attract many customers at a short time, his face became blank. In a hushed voice he had explained to me the exact economic pattern of this MLM[70] type of referral system.

It is alright to pay a very small group of early adopters to join the network, a handful of high value specialists and about a few dozen patients. However two financially explosive events may occur in a short span of time - the next larger group of customers may only be incentivised to use the platform due to the cashbacks or the product may be so good it becomes viral i.e. mass downloads and onboarding occurs. Either way I have to pay each and every sign up immediately by the second. In his *pyramid-shaped* illustration - I would spend thousands of taka in the first week, and then 10 times that much in the next week and so on. He told me in confidence that hyper-fast growth companies only look good for a very short time, as their cost of acquiring a new customer actually bankrupts them almost overnight. It seems like a strange phenomena that an unusually good product may financially ruin a young company so quickly. But the excel worksheet from an unnamed company proved his point.

---

[70] Multi-Level Marketing

His professional recommendation was very clear, just improve and upgrade the service quality of the ViOS network, to such an extent that each satisfied stakeholder - a motivated doctor who enjoys seeing the new line of patients, and patients who are pleased with the credibility and ease of access that ViOS has promised; would themselves recommend it to their peers and social circles. Super fast growth only appeals to the ego of the shareholders and potential investors, but in reality the real success lies in long term organic/natural growth - with the Market force of satisfied loyal customers.

Growth Mindset #29 - Startups should grow like muscle tissue, in response to tension and hardship. Not like a tumor, which feeds on itself and the host.

DELAYED LAUNCH VS

EXPANDED MARKETING CAMPAIGN

Ramadan was almost starting, which meant shorter office hours and a slight decrease in overall productivity, for myself and the IT team. As a business-*maker* one cannot have the employee-mindset anymore - hoping to earn a good monthly salary, purchase luxury consumables, look forward to every weekend and hope for a nice holiday bonus. As an entrepreneur any day *not* spent in business, regardless of geography, is a change for a potential global competitor to take your earnings. As extreme as it sounds, this is the dark fear that business owners face. This is known as *FOMO* - Fear of missing out.

FOMO is a type of professional anxiety disorder where you are obsessed with worse case scenarios in your industry. No other time is as stressful as the days before, during and after a major holiday (even weekends are stressful as a day off in one region may be a work day in another, and vice versa). Even in social situations you will see such people checking emails, making hurried calls, tracking shipments etc. *FOMO* is part of startup life, especially in the moments before launching.

Usually I wake up before dawn, check notifications and then get out of bed. One morning I received a text from 'R' (ViOS CTO) stating that his company's team leader has resigned after receiving his holiday bonus in order to join another firm. This poor retention is very common in the tech industry, as IT is fast becoming a lucrative and stable career, firms compete on salaries instead of perks, and most people are motivated by incremental raises instead of so-called company loyalty. In a way it is understandable, living in the world's most expensive and *unliveable* city, loyalty will not pay your rent.

The consequence of this act was that now the ViOS development project will be disorganised without a team leader. Disorganised meaning delayed production, and the launch date as per the Gantt chart will be postponed by atleast a month as a new team leader hire takes some time to get accustomed and upto speed on the project.

When I had assumed the entrepreneur founder/leader role I had to take drastic psychological reconditioning over the past few months. The daily early morning rising, regular exercises, boxing lessons, short but thoughtful prayers and the self actualisation of keeping an eye on the bigger picture. I realised early on that rushing to launch for the sake of beating an imaginary rival health startup is destructive, I risk introducing a defective consumer product to an unforgiving and judgemental Market. But this event that will lead to a month long delay is a cause for some concern. True the ViOS product that will be released will not be a *perfect* product - as that is just the illusion of amateurs and overthinkers. This version is merely the MVP - Minimum viable product, which will allow the team to get an idea on how close the solution is solving the defined problems (on demand real-time healthcare optimisation), the feedback will allow us to continually upgrade and provide better value at each cycle.

I took a mental step back to fully understand this event. There is nothing I or 'R' cold do to stop him from leaving, it is his worker rights, human rights also to seek gainful employment. There is nothing I could do to speed up the hiring and training process for his replacement. There is certainly nothing I could do increase the coding or whatever for the ViOS platform either. All I could control was my emotional response to this incident.

EMOTION = eMOTION

I went for a long walk.

Blood pumping through. Endorphins in my synapses. Alternate future realities were formed where ViOS was an ultimate success. Now I had to *retro*-imagine all the imaginary steps I would or should take to reach that success.

I had an idea.

As I mentioned, before going to the office I usually walk around the rooftop garden of our apartment complex and listen to some podcast episodes. These are a series of regular audio recordings of successful industry experts, such as Dan Lok, Dan Martell, Y Combinator, SaaS

Marketing Tips, Patrick Bet-David and many many others. I implement almost every single success

tip that they talk about, not only are they credible because of their deep knowledge, but because

they too were serial entrepreneurs who faced failure and risen. Many times before they had

mentioned a very old school technique at achieving a standard in authenticity and expert

perception in people; it is quite boring, tedious, time-consuming and honestly it seemed like the

work of old men who have nothing better to do.

Write a book.

That is all they keep talking about. Write your own non-fiction autobiography about your personal

life journey that led you to a moment in time. Write a book filled with intimate but useful

experiences you have had, that shaped you into the person that you have become, or want to

become.

I used to be skeptical whenever heard them give this advice. I thought only extremely successful

people would write a book near the end of their lives, when they made it in life, when they had

done everything. I looked at these type of books as a personal marketing act. Just another ego trip.

On any other day I would ignore such an idea. But as it seems that I might have a month or so of

absolutely no production momentum, especially during the Ramadan month; might as well try to understand what kind of book I could write, or rather what kind of author should I become is the right question.

From my quick understanding, the sole purpose of a nonfiction book was to act as an extension of the author's own life story - a sort of living memorial. Till date there are a countless number of literary works made by countless number of authors, but the vast majority never reach the kind of commercial success that could provide the financial freedom that they had hoped for. In a way an independent writer is somewhat of an entrepreneur, they are producing a work of content that they hold some value, which they hope to sell to a large number of people whom that value equates to a probable solution eg. business books for business people, practical handouts for medical exams, manual for international communication for emissaries and global policy experts and so on. Whatever the content, the author aims to be the self-proclaimed expert on that field, by virtue of their life lessons which they have considered to be a learning point for the reader.

My business mentor 'HH' also published a book a few months before I started writing my own. He had offered me a few tips, but before that he told me to keep in mind the following pointers before starting:
Focus on the purpose and theme of your book, not the book itself, meaning not to be so attached or obsessed for perfect grammar or storytelling skills. He told me that because it is so old-fashioned, certain high value people will value your efforts in writing a book and presenting it to them as a gift. After all how many tons of business cards are excessively made and idly thrown away, now imagine

if someone gave you a book instead. Perhaps you are that special person and I have considered you to be an influential professional - a fellow industry expert.

Writing a book that highlights the author's journey is a deeply personal account of their pitfalls and life struggles, especially related to embarrassing events that normal people are too ashamed to talk about. By sharing personal faults and their lessons to someone, the author wishes to entertain and educate a complete stranger so that such mistakes are never repeated in good faith. A nonfiction book holds a special value in that it also speaks about a niche topic that very few would know anything about (eg. physician-led entrepreneurship) and even fewer are too egoistic to share. The classic business mogul is more interested in hiding his success formulas, rather than teaching the next generation of change-makers. So, it is right in a way that a book acts like a living memorial, to an epic life story with clear tips on achieving greatness. Atleast one would hope so.

I spent the better part of a day just to write down the main chapters that I thought would be like the benchmarks in my life story so far, obviously starting from the very beginning would be too tedious, and frankly boring. The chapters I had chosen highlight key moments which would lead the reader through a mental movie of a character's development - my development to be exact. As you have noticed so far, as unusual and tragic as my entrepreneur journey has gone through, you must have been aware of the key learnings that I wish to share (I hope you have taken note of the tips I had written at the end of each chapter). Though I may be far from the success I had imagined, this literary journey is closely linked to the development journey of ViOS as well.

Growth Mindset Tip #30 - Write a book that would become a positive life manual to someone, long after your company or you are gone forever.

BRINGING THE VIOS VALUE TO THE PUBLIC

I had made my own website that would bring potential leads to the early adopter pool. I made a series of prerecorded and live vlogs to teach people about the healthcare career and health system. Even posted free health advice on online forums, all in the name of giving value to people. Not potential customers or leads, it was not meant to drag people to come visit my website and sign up, it was all about putting the ViOS value to the general public. This was done as part of a wider humanitarian approach to train myself to stand fast against community criticism, and to assert my own credibility when needed. And it paid off.

Few months ago a unique opportunity presented itself. A known associate who works at a major marketing firm, was organising a public event at the EMK Center, under the theme of failure stories - whereby serial entrepreneurs would share their mistakes and key learnings to the audience; at the last minute one of the keynote speakers had to cancel therefore I took the leap and applied for the vacant timeslot. With less than 2 hours to prepare some rudimentary slides and reach the venue, it was a typical sink or swim situation. Needless to say the event was a pivotal experience in public speaking and self-branding.

I managed to get a few photos of the event and some video clips. With amateur videography skills I created a short video collage of the event and used it as a marketing content. I am in a large number of Facebook groups, some for medical careers, health advice, business tips and of course entrepreneur hangouts. In one such group, a fellow entrepreneur posted an opening to come live at his podcast channel about business growth. I did not have to think twice, as I was the first person to post a reply and a DM request as well. After a week I had a very entertaining and informative radio session with 'K' from Indiana, USA; who was just starting his own podcast channel[71] featuring entrepreneurs and industry experts from around the world. I was a little bit shaky at first but I am proud to say that I had a lot of fun, and I knew 'K' learned quite a lot about the fascinating world of physician entrepreneurs and the importance of the Blue Ocean Strategy.

Locally in certain circles, word was spreading about my concept and myself. The startup community is very small and fragmented here and the entire population of active physician entrepreneurs can be counted on one hand. However major businesses, universities and the general public is slowly coming to grasp the potential of entrepreneurship as a worthy career path. There are frequent newspaper articles about the birth of a new startup almost every month. One such newspaper was researching an editorial on the popularity of coworking spaces as a viable environment to start a business - and by sheer luck I was in the office, and also invited to talk about ViOS to the reporter. It was a welcome experience to see the reporter hurriedly take notes as I was

---

[71]Go to your podcast app or simply search online with the title: *Let's Talk Business with Kenny Aronson* (my episode is the latest one)

explaining the pain points of my target community, the ViOS solution and even the future impact to the health system, in the years to come.

My vlogs were also gaining some reputation as well. The total viewership is quite low due to the very small marketing budget that I had spent for each episode, and that too for a short duration. Each one was an experimentation in content creation and the efficiency of the Facebook ad placement algorithm. I was not a digital marketing expert, but the valuable tips I had learned from my marketing freelancer associates and the workshops have really paid off. As long as the overall theme of an episode is clear (eg. future of the private practice), the duration is less than 4-5min, speech and audio quality is sufficient and the general credible appearance of the speaker (wearing a suit) was maintained, together with a continuous iteration of the target population characteristics (eg. demographic data, location, timing, social status) over time then I was able to achieve a few thousand views with only a few dollars over a week.

An important tactic to consider when choosing which channel to promote your ad is the call to action process (CTA). Basically after you promote your video, shared your value, educated/entertained the potential viewer, the main question is now what? What action do you want your target customer to do? This is why I had chosen Facebook as my primary mode of advertisement, due to their effective and user-friendly CTA options - visit site, fill form, download this, call now etc. I was able to assess an important metric during the early stages of the ViOS app development and branding campaign, that is the ROI of very ad i.e. for every dollar spent, how many viewers became potential leads who clicked on the buttone to visit the ViOS landing page and sign up for the app early release. It was an easy process to realise how to alter the content, the

targeting, the message and the budget to maximise the lead generation as cost-effectively as possible.

Growth Mindset Tip #31 - Take account of your errors, own them, learn from them.

And take every opportunity to teach others their value.

SHINY OBJECTS

It takes a certain personality to start a business, that personality is usually not well liked at first because Bangladeshi society has a perverse idea about money and wealth. Someone who has an idea is a fanciful dreamer, a strange artist, a madman. And like most people with mental health illness, they are simply ignored. The entrepreneur mind has certain characteristics of mental illness too, such as bipolar disorder, narcissism, anxiety neuroses and levels of depression. It may be due to the chicken-egg question - what came first, the illness or the intellect, maybe both. Perhaps due to the personal value attached to the innovation,and the abnormal lengths that are needed to take it into a success story often pushes founders to the edges of civilised thought processes. Either way, the sane society owes their comfort to the obstacles that the few had to endure.

I can personally vouch that I have had a pathetic existence, my life was great from a material comfort point of view, but the insight into one's life through their own eyes, is the most judgemental; until I was accidently swallowed into this startup struggle. Entrepreneurship was the vessel that carried me through the emotional turmoil of facing the realisation that I will not be able to hold my dying father's hand, the sheer horror of climbing down the family burial site to lay him down and in true psychopathic fashion, simply wash away the graveyard dirt, wear a suit and finish the company expo back in 2018. I would not wish my life experiences to any enemy of mine, but I can vouch that the emotional investment in my own creation that time kept me going, kept me sane.

The steadfast dedication to complete crucial tasks, face social anxiety, learn new skills and in general just get the startup engine rolling takes the full cerebral force of your brain. But in this pursuit for financial success, there is a symptom that often infects the hardwired brainwaves. The Shiny Object Syndrome.

Quite simply it is a disease of distraction, the founder team, or maybe just the founder' mind would latch onto another idea that sort of entered into the thinking process - much like the movie 'Inception'. There is a sudden compulsion to tryout alternative schemes at the same time as the ongoing project. Whether motivated by possible success is not always clear, if an idea suddenly seems cool it may in fact sabotage the entire company, even before getting started.

I faced this scenario about halfway through the ViOS development phase, perhaps out of boredom and curiosity I had responded to an ad by a local dropshipping[72] company who wished to collaborate with a health-based company to import high value health products via Amazon deliveries to Bangladesh. I set up a skype conference to discuss the partnership and overall operations, thanks to the strong advice of a fellow entrepreneur, I was promptly dissuaded from diverting valuable time and energy to an unknown venture - which was not my prime passion

---

[72] Small scale supply chain broker who takes leads' orders for specialised items and organizes its shipment from third party overseas sources.

anyway. After some careful thought, I realised that the dropshipping company desperately wanted

to expand horizontally due to decreasing consumer/market demand for their services. And

partnering with another venture was their version of a diversification. Risky move.

Growth Mindset Tip #32 - For every idea, always discuss it with a fellow trusted

entrepreneur and the potential user base to assess it Product-Market Fit and

Founder-Product Fit. Focus, Concentrate, Ignore the noise.

SO, WHAT EXACTLY *IS* VIOS?

People start a business to make a lot of money, very quickly. But monetary success comes much later, so in that period they will have to do it for the social status of being a business-maker or job-creator. Startups are something else. You can assume that all startups are businesses, but not all businesses are startups. Similarly, small businesses may remain small or eventually become big in their own ways. But all startups start small in the hope of becoming big by rapid growth or by being acquired by those big businesses, who recognise the value of their innovation. So you see, the main characteristics of a startup is growth and innovation.

ViOS could have been the name of a clinic, a pharmacy, a medical equipment supplier, an overseas nursing recruitment agency or another medical tourism company. But the main drive of the ViOS brand is rooted in innovation, the process to increase the economic incentive for private practitioners to provide high quality compassionate medical consultation, at their convenience; to patients who are in need of high quality compassionate medical consultation, at their convenience. The *magic* is in the power of technology to provide convenient on demand real time services. This robust network can only work if a large number of proactive and motivated practitioners realise their true skills, and be a part of something larger than themselves.

I had struggled to compare ViOS to existing types of on demand technology; should it be the Uber of healthcare, the Tinder of matching doctors, the Amazon of appointments etc? But deep down, the underlying technology is not that important, actually it is not even unique. I know the bare basics about GPS geofencing and geotagging from my time at an NGO, social ratings system used by the Chinese government and the economic potential of using appropriate soft skills in outpatient pediatric care, when I used to be a clinician. Obsessing over the technical complexity of an innovation, just to compare it to a globally known brand is not the mark of authenticity.

What is important to understand is the last part of the *3-M*'s (mindset was on point and marketing was ongoing), which was the monetisation model, or business model. There are thousands of eager entrepreneurs with ideas, that will not put a single coin in their pocket. Maybe they only care about social entrepreneurship you may say; but the donors care, the banks care and certainly their employees. A startup should produce a specific solution with value, but without the right price tag it is merely an expensive hobby i.e. starting your own business ended turning you into your own employee. Without the monetisation pathway, you cannot grow by scaling up and you cannot innovate when you have no money for R&D.

So what is ViOS?

-   In simple terms, ViOS is the Airbnb of a Health System.

I used to think that its uniqueness was that while other health startups were behind patients to use them, ViOS would be a medical solution for doctors, by doctors. It was incorrect. The concept of Airbnb is that a property owner can temporarily rent out a room or the entire house to a tourist for a few days, so when there is a vacancy, people can view the property details and make a booking and payment from their platform. If the room is not free then it will not show in the search. Airbnb solved a specific problem related to affordable temporary lodgings and it was a source of revenue for property owners. So how does this fit into healthcare?

Private practitioners in many countries require a constant, even repeated patient flow to earn a decent revenue for their duty timings. And patients want the convenience of health consultation from a certified, qualified and preferably socially referred healthcare provider. So the Airbnb model was applied to the actual chamber room itself. If you are a private doctor who is reading this, your chamber is not exactly *your* chamber. It belongs to a polyclinic, a hospital or maybe a well established consultant who is leasing it out for you to use. You may work for a few hours at a time, then leave while another physician comes in to use the premises. Dhaka doctors are extremely overworked as they cycle from one location to another, therefore it is possible for a doctors' room to be used by atleast 4-5 doctors in a day, especially if it is in the outpatient department of a polyclinic. ViOS has tagged a chamber to our service network, whenever a registered physician (maybe you) physically enters this geotagged chamber, your profile is actively promoted to a patient who may be searching for someone of your specialised skills at that time. When you finish your shift and leave, there is no need for your number to be known to others so that they do not bother you unnecessarily. Using this model, the ViOS Doctor is able to have the freedom to work at any time, from any chamber location, increase the chances of getting a patient during his duty hours, and therefore increase their income - *which they get to keep anyway*. We will simply charge an affordable monthly subscription based on the number of chambers that the doctor wishes to be registered in. Hospital directors will be more pleased as the new intake of patients can be referred for inpatient services, in-house pharmacy services and ofcourse the diagnostic/laboratory recommendations from the ViOS Doctors.

Patients (perhaps like yourself) ofcourse need an extra incentive to use ViOS. Many have a severe knowledge deficiency about what type of doctor is needed, where are they, how much are the fees, when will they go the chamber, is the doctor *actually* a doctor and will they be on time. Due to this, many have been accustomed to self-damaging behaviours, such as randomly checking online groups, waiting for hours in the reception desk after waiting through traffic in the hopes of getting a '*good*'[73] doctor, paying high fees for low satisfaction consultation, deciding to go abroad and spend 5 times the amount anyway or worse, not seeking healthcare services at all. A broken health system breaks everything.

With ViOS, it is hoped that the options of choosing a specialist becomes easier, faster and safer too. A democratic approach to health-seeking behaviour will be possible when a patient uses their patient app to search for a specialist, see who is online and available, see their registration and skills details and possible see the remarks by previous patient testimonials. Something so important as health, especially a loved on, cannot be left to chance or unnecessary delays. With ViOS, atleast you

---

[73] The concept of a doctor's goodness is not clear. Degrees, recommendations, age, accent, foreign training, training under a bigger doctor so on. Patients are unaware of the true skill of healing, and neither do most doctors unfortunately

have the honest option to see if a particular doctor is ready and waiting to see you, at your convenience. Maybe the health issues can be adequately managed in a nearby location too. SInce patients have to reimburse the doctors for their time and skills, they will have free access to the ViOS network through their app.

Obviously it is not enough to simply provide any solution. User feedback is an essential metric to find out how well we are solving these issues (Product-Market Fit and Brand loyalty). Through great consideration, I have installed a type of ratings system for both users. Patients can give a subjective icon feedback (happy/sad face) and a comment based on their doctor-patient experience, to tell the doctor and ViOS team about their session. This will inform the doctor whether to continue their great work, or improve on their bed-side manners. Doctors themselves can give a rating to ViOS, to tell us how efficient and convenient we were in providing an honest means of promoting their medical skills to the population. As unusual as it sounds, we are all in the Fourth Industrial Revolution and the ever increasing *gig* industry, and quality performance measures are very important as a source of actionable data.

The technology is not new, the idea is average compared to many existing health startups in Bangladesh and beyond. But ViOS is not about creating so many new things all at once. ViOS is about solving a deep need, or a deep pain. The need for a better way to earn a living as a doctor and the need for patients to get healthcare consultations quickly and safely - the old fashioned way; when doctors would listen to your complaints, check your pulse, tap your knee, tell you to breathe out slowly, check if you have a fever and tell you that you will be alright. Telemedicine, AI prescription, e-pharma and all others are great, but first ViOS will solve the key issues. A centuries old industry like healthcare is extremely resistant to change, especially technological change. A startup that claims to be a *disruptor* will be automatically rejected, rather the way values are communicated to improve the livelihoods of doctors and patients together, to bring them together without any middleman, is the right thing to work on.

Growth Mindset Tip #33 - Disruption is expensive, some stakeholders do not like that term. First find the quickest and cheapest way to solve a problem, and then you can call it whatever you like.

PREACHING THE VIOS VALUES

Standardising the professionalism of a group of people under your care is the pinnacle responsibility of a founding team. Leadership without a lasting impression will not take an idea to the level of quality branding, unless the various stakeholders receive an emotional connection and fulfillment after its use. So far I have described the value chain and the business model outline of the ViOS network. I have shown you the future where patients do not need to worry about finding a nearby certified healthcare provider (hopefully in under 3 clicks). A physician can have the financial freedom to go on duty, have the confidence of seeing enough patients to increase not his income but also his own personal brand, in an honorable and futuristic fashion. But the ViOS story does not end there. A lot can be done when so many people are under a unified platform.

During my entrepreneur journey, I have noticed the changes that were needed to survive in this difficult path. I had to abandon many self-limiting beliefs and toxic associations. But I am privileged to also note that my powerful persona has had a magnetic influence on like-minded individuals as well. In our daily lives we face so many social pressures, and financial obligations (bills, fares, fees, rent) that we cannot imagine a way to become fully independent and live life by design. All that is needed is for someone to slap you hard enough to break your ego, I believe I am that person. Over the course of the past year I had made it my own personal side mission to extract the hidden *intrapreneurial*[74] talent in a small group of people.

I have already told you the fascinating way I had inspired '*R*' my CTO. Before I met him, before ViOS I had a meeting with '*E*' when I was thinking of hiring some freelancer marketing staff for HHS. Back then he was about to resign from a well known food-delivery startup, due to a harsh working environment. He has experience working with pharmaceutical reps, therefore he was quite experienced with medical personnel communication. Naturally I did not hire him, as he has more superior talent with idea generation and complex relationship building. I had pitched him the concept of ViOS almost a year later, he liked the idea, not the part about healthcare optimisation, but rather the untapped potential of Big Data.

When a platform-based service is created, with the right value chain and customer engagement policies; certain positive (and profitable) outcomes occur over time. Obviously over time every founder desires consistent revenue growth as the primary gain along with increasing numbers of new users (app stickiness). In this era of digital connections as strong as social connections, there is an even more valuable asset in a tech company - user data, Big Data.

'*E*' had imagined a scenario that ViOS manages to capture a large portion of the healthcare community - such as recently graduated MBBS students, certified MD/FCPS specialists, foreign-

---

[74] A proactive forward-thinking individual in a company, who takes the lead in innovation and development. Does not have to be a cofounder or even a shareholder, but a company culture that creates the internal working environment for progressive thought, ownership and a capacity for action, will itself create a generation of inhouse intrapreneurs.

trained specialists, retired government doctors wishing to get back in the workforce, foreign citizens with medical certification from the local Health Ministry, and with strong perseverance the top consultants of the country, all of whom can be best served by registering their unique skills and their own private chamber in the ViOS network. But this is just the beginning, he said.

We had discussed the idea of creating a medical skills institute, or more precisely, *A Soft Skills Development Institute for Healthcare Professionals*. The reason behind this concept is due to an even larger issue affecting the Bangladesh Health system, and also in south asia in general. The deficiency in quality bed-side manners, poor patient communication skills and a general lack of professional soft skills. I can vouch for this finding as I had just barely passed the USMLE Step 2 Clinical Skills test back in mid-2000, many Asian doctors (especially male doctors) are incapable of adequately communicating patient empathy. There are massive online forums where some South Asian doctors discuss their failings in these types of live viva tests, they may score the best in MCQ's, but actually fail the human component, the main component of the medical career.

This social skills retardation can be due to a large number of primitive social constructs that may stereotype many ethnicities, regardless of the purpose of the institute would be to retrain healthcare professionals, including nurses, to better provide quality standard patient interactions. One purpose would be to help applicants to pass the clinical skills examinations in many Western countries, additionally this training would be another form of skills certification which can help doctors and therapists to compete for more patients (ofcourse adequately skilled doctors would get better ViOS ratings and more patients and more income).

I may sound capitalistic, but there is one thing you should realise, if you are a doctor reading this then you know about this reality. The medical profession has always been a business. If you are going to sustainably create a change, then you must analyse it from a 'gain or pain' perspective, the *pains* of being a substandard doctor due to poor skills versus the gains when adequate training allows one to compete on a global scale, and be an example of excellence for their peers.

This brings me to the next phase of the ViOS team-building phase. I needed to expand my team to fulfill more business operations tasks, which means I need to search for professionals who have entered the health industry or are deeply interested in starting some change within it, *healthcare intrapreneurship* in a way. And who better than the freshly graduated MBBS students who wish to exercise their hidden intrapreneur mindset, in a societal structure where opinions are suppressed, skills are undervalued and future is politicised - only an output-centered health startup can provide the zone to express and execute the dormant physician entrepreneur gene. By pure chance I had met two highly motivated medical graduates (both named '*I*') based in Dhaka, who were attending two separate startup-related events. When we introduced ourselves, the ViOS concept and the need for rapid personal growth, I knew I found more A-list intrapreneurs. Over the course of a few months I had been sharing my views, branding progress and business goals with them. They were both very eager and motivated to take charge of their lives (especially after seeing the obstacles that their immediate seniors were facing). With a little push and power speech[75], I shared my prized

---

[75] " Why work harder for pennies when you can work smarter to build an empire"

possession, the ViOS shares, with them in return for the blood and sweat that we all have to sacrifice for the greater good and the greater paycheck.

So far the ViOS team comprised of the dreamer/founder (me), a professional IT Entrepreneur, A sales executive with many years experience in the B2B market and 2 eager and active medical graduates. So far this is still the making of an amateur high school sports team. Business is about money, and money drives business. The sum total of our skills is slightly above zero, unless we are guided and shaped by matters of money (finances, accounting, investment portfolio). If a health company has a leader, the medical team, the HR team, the tech guy, the sales guy, then the most crucial person is the 'money guy'. In yet another networking event I had met a young banking graduate from a prestigious university, who is showing the early signs of the growth mindset as well. We discussed the phenomenon of bankrupt bankers, financiers who are wealthy but *cash-poor* and the general epidemic of mass consumerism that the banking executives are suffering from. He too was eager to be part of a startup, given the almost double-digit GDP growth potential. Without hesitation, I had introduced him to the ViOS concept, the financial goals, the need for a dedicated 'Chief Financial Officer' in the near future. Although he would be transferred to Hong Kong by the time you are reading this chapter, I was so impressed by his professionalism at a young age, I even reserved a few shares for him when ViOS enters a significant revenue trajectory in the near future (with the help of our customers ofcourse). After all, the job of the CFO is to continually assess the financial health of a health startup.

In summary of this chapter, the ViOS Values can be best described as the immediate action-oriented growth mindset, to continuously improve your skills and status, and become financially independent in the process. It may be a healthcare startup, but such values go beyond career development. It is about personal development and

team development. There are so many motivated physicians and therapists out there, I believe that the future success of ViOS depends entirely on the continuous improvement and motivation of this special group. With the mass advancement of social media technology, it is not that difficult to reach out to this target group, influence them positively and then promote the soft skills development on a global scale.

Growth Mindset Tip #34 - A company may be limited by funds, a person may be limited by the limits of his skills, but you should always have room to give more value than you take. The core principle of an entrepreneur is to always under-promise your capacity but over-deliver your values to customers and to your own team, without expecting an immediate payback.

LIFE AFTER VIOS

Grand designs require a grand ending. Not the end of the ViOS journey, because we have just begun. A startup cannot remain as such due to the extremely short lifespan, many fail in the first year of inception (I have a deep knowledge of this experience) and most disappear within 5 years. There are a long list of reasons why startups fail so often; many first time entrepreneurs would blame the customers, running out of money, team in-fighting, inadequate marketing, poor product-market fit and so many others. In reality, as a serial entrepreneur I can tell you the actual symptoms of a dying startup - inability to behave as a startup.

Startups live on continuous innovation, not just technological, but also in utilising innovative pricing, marketing, skills and general agility to adapt as the Market changes. The Blue Ocean Strategy that birthed your innovation will quickly become a crowded Red Ocean when you are surrounded by competitors, saboteurs, imposters and worse, a startup that behaves like a bloated corporation cannot quickly change as the demands of the population change[76].

---

[76] Look for the nearest Kodak, Yellow Taxi, Handset, CRT monitor and tell me about their business.

ViOS is designed to solve a healthcare problem, and make enough money to survive another day, and then the next. Until no more. Unless, ViOS finds another problem to effectively manage. Disruption, optimisation or whatever may be the description, is resource-sensitive process that requires the act of *pivoting*[77]. Another approach can be to strategically expand to other markets, that may mean expansion to other cities, and even to neighboring countries. Beyond the revenue-positive strategy of expansion, there is the potential humanitarian advantage of promoting the ViOS concept to other health systems in need.

But before all these steps, the most important deciding factor of a business strategy of a health startup, is its own financial health. Without significant cash flow to maintain the bare minimum operations, dividend payouts to shareholders, the outside CEO salary and increasing costs as a company grows, all momentum stops. Growth stops.

When the bootstrapping phase ends, revenue projection can attract the right investors to provide the 'seed capital' to scale the ViOS operations. The true motivation goes beyond just owning a fast growing company in a trillion-dollar industry - it is all about how quickly the shareholders can get the final paycheque. There are two viable options - the IPO (initial public offering) or to be acquired by a massive multinational corporation.

In all honesty I am not an expert on the stock market, what I can say is that it is the ultimate aim of any startup, to stop struggling and become a dominating figure in the Market. By raising public

---

[77] Drastically changing the company strategy

funds by public trading, a startup now becomes a standalone company and can now have a bigger portion of any Market. The true purpose of entrepreneurship is to achieve a monopoly.

Control the Market. Control the Prices. Control the Industry.

Growth Mindset Tip #35 - Get your Freedom while you still can. The best way to move on, *is to move on*. Once you become financially independent, give off the responsibilities of the company's vision to someone else; a CEO, an Investor or even the Public.

Get the Cash. Get the Life. Get on with your next Startup.

EPILOGUE

We come to an awkward position where I must leave you now. It is not that my story is finished, in fact as you have read, I have actually just begun my journey, the ViOS journey. Much has happened and I apologize if I did not share every detail. But you have read some things which even my own family does not now. In fact you know more about me now than I ever could. I wish I could finish off like some fantasy novel and tell you all the nice ways the characters led peaceful wholesome lives, however life is not that convenient. The entrepreneur journey is not about an epic movie plot where everything works out with no loose ends. The entrepreneurial story has plot holes, sad endings, lots of boring bits, no fixed theme and many times it can end on a cliffhanger. Just like this book.

This book was titled '*Volume 1*' on purpose. So far you have been reading a long prequel for a much longer upcoming series, hopefully. There are many books in the market that tells the story of how a billionaire started his empire, fell, got up and then made it big. This book is a different niche for a different reader. It is fun and inspiring to read success stories, and sometimes humorous to read failure stories. But what of the professional who followed all the social milestones but is on the verge of collapse, what about the gifted intellectual unable to pay his rent with his collection of postgraduate degrees? Who will guide the highly skilled healthcare professional in the age of global inequality? People like that always look for a manual to show them how to start their own adventure series, to break from the norm and be a creator. And what better mentor than one who has also just begun.

In all honesty, I do not have all the answers and this book offers no concrete guidance. The entrepreneur journey is an alternative to the expected, or the assumed. The red flags and tips I had mentioned were part of the insights I gained over time. They may or may not be applicable to you, now. But sooner or later they will have a meaning for you, if one day you take the leap, take the *massive immediate action* and do something real.

Growth Mindset Tip 'Omega' - Whatever you do, do it like your life depended on it.

BONUS CHAPTER:

POWER OF ACCUMULATED ADVANTAGES

You may wonder if outliers like myself always had the *entrepreneur gene* (regardless of our professional background), whether we were somehow born with a thirst for creativity, the disregard for established norms and authority, or do you just have to be a little weird to see the world differently. The *Growth Mindset*, and the strict regular behaviours you have to follow, does indeed change the mechanics of your mind, you would see things different because the negativity is out of your sight - you focus on the problem and solving it, *as a team*. The constant drive for self development itself has a pain/gain momentum - the capital/material gain from a strong business is very attractive and so is the ability to avoid the pain of poverty and leading a standardised life.

But this journey is not simple nor safe; just having the passion, learning new skills, following these tips and access to some money will not guarantee success. The journey is not shaped like a step-ladder as you expect in a normal 9-5 career (achieving an extra degree will increase your status another inch), the entrepreneur's journey is like a rolling snowball, it gathers size, momentum and speed, as long as each moment is invested in learning, executing, learning again and again. Perhaps this is why most people will not dare to follow this exhausting trip, with so many pitfalls and disappointments. Such high risks often blinds people to the possible high rewards too.

There is another concept to keep in mind, if your are the few who are adventurous to take on this responsibility. After all, those who have observed a problem in society, have the opportunity to comment on a solution - it is the brave few who take action to actually do something about it. To this brave few, I have to inform you that even with this courage, do not do it alone. You have read my story and you have seen where I fell. There were ofcourse many factors involved, but previously I was doing it all alone - ignorant of my skills deficiencies and ignorant of my hidden advantages.

Skills can be learned by professional courses or even simply by being in proximity to people who have that talent, hence the need for a diversified team with those high income skills. The advantages, or privileges, that an entrepreneur is exposed to are also ignored. In my example, my journey and intellect is the sum total of more than 30+ years of accumulated advantages gained just by being lucky enough to be alive in those circumstances. You can call it luck, or you can call it the classic nurture versus nature dogma.

I know of many successful people born in deep poverty and growing up in adverse situations (the classic rags to riches story), but the reality of so many comfortable career hunters who have also escaped that hardship, but are stuck in unrewarding circumstances is more depressing. In my context, my advantages was being born in the same era of advanced NICU technology, both parents are highly educated and motivated for empowerment, raised in small stable nuclear family in high income settings, access to top level education materials, adequate financial safety net during my formative years, exposure to diverse cultures, avoidance of addictions and many other *'lucky charms'*.

Luck is an important factor in personal growth and success too, many billionaires would confess that a large part of their own success is due to *being there at the right time at the right place.* Do not despair if you think you have bad luck, your luck has run out or you were born unlucky etc. Because in real life, luck is called 'opportunity'. Opportunity is not a character or physical being that will come to you, it is a goldmine that you have to dig for years with your own bleeding hands.

With the right insight you too will realise that specific little details or choices, like the career you are in, the people are you, your thought process etc,that were made many years ago (even by someone else) has brought you to this very moment in time and space, where you have the opportunity to read a book about business and life, in an era of prosperity and access to technology. You will realise that somehow somewhere you too have certain advantages to help solve a critical problem in your industry, you have that advantage of access to that professional insight. The people you know, and those who know you are also a significant winning advantage. As you invest in your self-development and open up to diverse skill sets and opinions of people from different backgrounds, you become humbled by the thought that there are many who might potentially share your vision. Keep these contacts close to you, you never know who you might have met in the past, that can completely alter your entire destiny.

When you choose to believe that it is ok to be privileged, it is ok to take advantage of your uniqueness, therefore it is ok to be somehow better than most people - with this collection of advantages, you will understand the powerful responsibility one must accept to be a change-maker. You never know how impactful you could be to someone's life. Even your own.

END OF VOLUME 1

RESOURCES

In certain chapters I had mentioned the many methods of self-learning and proactive processes that shaped, and continue to shape, my entrepreneurial journey. If you wish to invest in your own development of high income skills, the following resources and recommendations may assist you:

There are thousands of options available, but you do not need everything, you just need a few guidelines to get started.

BOOKS

Lean Startup *Eric Ries*
$100 Startup *Chris Guillebeau*
Zero to One *Peter Thiel*
Rich Dad, Poor Dad *Robert Kiyosaki*
Blue Ocean Strategy *Renee Renée Mauborgne*

TV SHOWS

Silicon Valley *Netflix*

PODCASTS

Let's Talk Business *Kenny Aronson*[78]
The Startup Chat *Steli Efti & Hiten Shah*
The Dan Lok Show *Dan Lok*
Build your SaaS *Transistor.fm*
Valuetainment *Patrick Bet-David*
SaaS Growth Stacking *Dan Martell*
Bootstrap MD *Mike Woo-Ming*
Startup School *Y Combinator*
Saas Marketing Insights *47 Insights*
The SaaS Podcast *Omer Khan*

---

[78] You can listen to my podcast episode (13 April 2019)

If you are based in Dhaka, I suggest you check the Facebook Events section for events hosted by Startup Dhaka, Founder Institute and events teaching soft skills development. Professional courses on accounting, marketing, sales etc are highly recommended.

CONNECTIONS

If you have enjoyed this book and it has given you some value, please complete the following tasks to show your appreciation:

- ☐ Write your favourite growth mindset tip as a Facebook post and post a picture of the cover

- ☐ Give this book as a gift to an aspiring entrepreneur

- ☐ Talk to your friends and family about what *value* or key learnings you have gained from reading these chapters

- ☐ Show your support by liking the ViOS Facebook page:
  Search - *vios healthcare* on Facebook & leave a recommendation

- ☐ Visit our website: www.viosapp.com

- ☐ Download the ViOS app and reach out to your local healthcare provider when you need to.
  If you are a healthcare professional in Dhaka, please sign up and join our network.

Google PlayStore* search: **VIOS** (*Patients*)
or
VIOS Doctor (*Doctor*)

*iOS version coming soon